P9-DVP-499

Exporting Democracy

Exporting Democracy

Fulfilling America's Destiny

Joshua Muravchik

The AEI Press

Publisher for the American Enterprise Institute
WASHINGTON, D.C.

1991

Distributed by arrangement with
National Book Network
4720 Boston Way
Lanham, Md. 20706

3 Henrietta Street
London WC2E 8LU England

Library of Congress Cataloging-in-Publication Data
Muravchik, Joshua.
  Exporting democracy: fulfilling America's destiny / Joshua Muravchik.
    p. cm. — (AEI studies; 513)
  Includes bibliographical references and index.
  ISBN 0-8447-3733-X: $21.95
  1. United States—Foreign relations—1945- 2. United States—Foreign rela-
tions—Philosophy. 3. Democracy—History—20th century. I. Title. II. Series.
E840.M87 1991
327.73'009'045—dc20   90-20840
                                                                              CIP

1 3 5 7 9 10 8 6 4 2
AEI Studies 513

Printed in the United States of America

For Manny, Mimi, and Aaron

Contents

Acknowledgments

I have benefited from the help of so many people during the course of my work on this book that I fear I will omit some here. If I do, I beg their forgiveness. Generous financial support from several benefactors made it possible for me to write the book. Among them were the Neil A. McConnell Foundation, the Lynde and Harry Bradley Foundation, and the John M. Olin Foundation. I am very grateful to them and another that prefers not to be named. I am also much in debt to the officers of the American Enterprise Institute: Chairman Bill Butcher, President Chris DeMuth, Vice President David Gerson, former Vice President Pat Ford, Director of Foreign Policy and Defense Studies Jeane Kirkpatrick.

Good things, it is said, come in twos. So they have for me. I have been blessed with two extraordinarily able research assistants, Jeffrey Gedmin, now a research associate at AEI, and Timothy Goodman, and two outstanding secretaries, Sandra Mulligan and LyneGayle Herndon. Two extremely resourceful librarians have also given me a great deal of help: Evelyn Caldwell of the AEI library and Sylvia Gear of the Montgomery County Public Library. I owe thanks, too, to Daniel Compres and Gabriele Hills of the AEI staff, who did me many helpful favors, and to several interns: Christopher Bright, Michael Stone, William Tell, Wendy Wessman, Anne-Marie Weldon, Joseph Roth, Hyong Lee, Markus Gaertner, and Tanya Osensky.

John Earl Haynes, Marc Plattner, Peter Collier, Steve Munson, Scott McConnell, Charles Horner, and Cord Meyer read parts or all of the manuscript, and their criticisms helped me to improve it. I owe a double debt to Scott, who helped me in the beginning to develop the idea for the book.

My wife Sally and daughters Stephanie, Madeline, and Valerie endured the deterioration of my disposition that seems inevitably to accompany difficult writing assignments—just a trivial addition to the long list of reasons why I love them each so much.

1
The Strength of Democratic Ideals

America has won the cold war—almost without trying. America's aim, at least since 1956 when the stark exigencies of the Hungarian uprising disabused Americans of the illusions of a Communist rollback, has been not to win this conflict but to negotiate a truce. It won nonetheless, not on the strength of its arms or the skill of its diplomats, but by virtue of the power of the democratic ideas on which the American system is based and the failure of the Communist idea.

America's founders began with the premise that man had been created in the image of God and that all were of equal worth and endowed with unalienable rights. In founding the modern world's first democracy, they set out to create a system that would follow this premise and that would suit human nature as they understood it. Their vision has been profoundly vindicated.

The system they created has proved enduring, in large measure because its flexibility enables it to repair its own flaws, even the most grievous flaws of slavery and racial discrimination. The system has also proved successful, the most successful of any in history, in providing the good life for the vast majority of its citizens, including numberless refugees who arrived empty-handed. And it has proved that it is indeed natural.

Natural does not mean that democracy is the state in which man is ordinarily found. On the contrary the founders were well aware that they were creating institutional arrangements that were quite new, bearing little resemblance even to the democracies of classical antiquity. But democracy has proved itself natural in the sense that it answers something innate in human nature: a longing to be treated with dignity and not to be subjected to the arbitrary rule of others. Its naturalness has been proved by America's polyglot history. Immigrants of every conceivable stock have melded into American life, enriched it, and died defending it. And it has been proved too by the fact that where democracy has been transplanted, even by force, to extremely distant and

1

diverse lands, such as Japan, Germany, or India, it has often sunk roots and flourished.

Communism in contrast began less with a theory of human nature than with a theory of history, one that has long ago shown itself to be erroneous. The system it spawned proved as unnatural as democracy is natural. Where communism was transplanted, it rarely outlasted the coercive force that brought it. When the Soviet Union decided to give up its empire in Eastern Europe after forty years, those polities sloughed off communism like a body rejecting a foreign organ to which it is violently immune.

The impending final collapse of communism in the Soviet Union and China will free America from the threat that has disturbed peace for forty-odd years. It will be America's greatest victory, greater even than the victory over Hitler and the Axis in the sense that the victory in World War II came at the expense of nearly a million American casualties and millions among the Allies. In contrast victory over communism has come at much smaller human cost. Like nazism, communism has devoured scores of millions of lives, including thousands of Americans in Vietnam and Korea. Until 1989 there was every reason to suppose defeating communism would require horrendous sacrifice. But this final struggle has been almost bloodless so far, save for a few thousand martyrs in Tiananmen Square, a few score in Timisoara, a few dozen in Tbilisi. It is too much to hope that these will be the last martyrs of this cause, but there is every reason to hope that their numbers will in no way approach those lost in defeating fascism. This new victory has largely been sealed in the minds of men and women.

The Potency of Ideas

There is an important lesson in this: the potency of ideas in international politics. Ironically we Americans, who possess a profound and successful idea, have rarely understood the potency of ideas, while the Communists, who possess a false and failed idea, have understood it quite thoroughly. Thus, during most of the cold war, even dealing from a weaker hand, they outdid us in the realm of political competition, merely by working at it so much harder. Their success consisted in their ability to recruit devoted cadre, to infiltrate broader popular movements and to influence them toward their own ends, and to sow division and defeatism in the non-Communist world. Even today Communist movements bid for power in El Salvador, Peru, the Philippines; when Nelson Mandela sits down to negotiate with the government of South Africa, the man closest to his side is Communist chief Joe Slovo. With communism shriveling up at its center, these forces no longer endanger American security, but they continue to exact a toll of pointless suffering their own countries and to provide a last reminder of the leverage of the Communist idea.

Understanding the relationship between ideas and power was the essence of Lenin's genius. Everywhere that communism triumphed, it did so by force of arms, but first it paved the way with political maneuvers to weaken, to disarm, and to divide its opponents. Whether in Nicaragua, Vietnam, Cuba, China, Eastern Europe, or the Soviet Union itself, Communist ideology motivated a dedicated, disciplined core of revolutionaries. In each case Communists forged alliances by seeking common ground with non-Communist leftists whom they ultimately would coopt, discard, or liquidate. And in each case they employed agitation, slander, and deception to discredit their most powerful opponents and to isolate them from outside support.

Americans conversely have understood little about ideological combat, and most of what we have learned was born of the necessity of reacting to the Communists. Our slowness in this field is the product of two factors. The first is our disinclination to think of ourselves as bearing an ideology. Our ideology, it is true, is not equivalent to totalitarian and utopian ideologies. Not only are democrats more scrupulous in the means that they are willing to employ in pursuit of their ideals, but also the tenets of their belief are more open, flexible, and limited. Democracy is not a blueprint, not a set of results; it is only a principle about how disparate or conflicting human goals should be reconciled. Other ideologies promise happiness; democracy promises only the freedom to pursue happiness. But for all the differences between our ideology and theirs, America, like the Soviet Union, was built on an idea, and we can no more separate our fate from the fate of that idea than can the Soviet Union save itself from the wreckage of the Communist idea.

The second reason why we lag in ideological combat is that we have no taste for combat. By the end of World War II we had convinced ourselves that our Soviet partner in war—that other "democracy," as we were all too willing to think of it—would remain our partner in peace. While we went happily about the business of constructing the United Nations and demobilizing our forces, Stalin erected an empire within the perimeter of his armies. Still the American response was restrained. President Harry Truman pronounced a doctrine that embodied the strategy of containment, a strictly defensive strategy. Its goal was to resist Soviet expansion, but it studiously eschewed any thought of putting the Soviet Union itself at risk, or even challenging existing Soviet conquests. The strategy worked fairly well until Americans lost their stomachs for containment in the jungles of Vietnam.

America turned next to the strategy of détente, which aimed to dissuade the Soviets from expansion by acknowledging their status as coequal superpower and by furnishing economic inducements. When this policy, as implemented by Henry Kissinger, failed, we attempted a still more conciliatory version of détente under President Jimmy Carter. But for all of Carter's efforts to show the Soviets a friendlier face, they continued to widen their empire and overstock their arsenals.

The Renewal of American Spirit

The American people's anger that the Soviets had taken advantage of our lassitude during the 1970s helped bring about the election of Ronald Reagan as president. He refurbished and strengthened American military forces, tightened the restraints on the transfer to the Soviet Union of militarily relevant technology, and launched the Strategic Defense Initiative, which holds the potential for neutralizing the enormous Soviet investment in nuclear missiles. He inaugurated the Reagan Doctrine, supporting anti-Communist insurgencies, and thereby challenging communism's claim to represent the inevitable course of history. He also challenged that claim rhetorically as no president had done before, branding the Soviet Union an "evil empire" and describing communism as a "sad, bizarre chapter in human history whose last pages are even now being written."

Nor was that the only way Reagan showed an instinct for the war of ideas uncommon among Americans. He spoke often and passionately of the virtues of America and of democracy. He made much of the growth of democratic governance around the world; when the chips were down, his administration threw its weight behind democratic transitions even in places like the Philippines, where the unhorsed dictator had been an American ally. What gave Reagan's rhetoric its deep resonance was the growth of democratic governance, perhaps more rapid than ever before, for which he could claim only some of the credit. Dictatorships had given way to elected governments in southern Europe and Latin America and began to do so in parts of Asia.

This renewal of America's spirit and of the élan of democracy provided the context for communism's terminal crisis. Ilya Zaslavsky, a leader of the democractic bloc in the Soviet Congress of People's Deputies and the Moscow municipal government, said that the originator of *perestroika* was not Mikhail Gorbachev but Ronald Reagan.[1] Whether or not this is true, the explanation that the crisis of communism arose solely from domestic economic problems is unconvincing. The spirit that informs Mikhail Gorbachev's drive for radical reform is a sense of the broad failure of the Communist system. As he himself put it, "everything pertaining to the economy, culture, democracy, foreign policy—all spheres—had to be reappraised." Moreover, he added, "we would have been able to avoid many of these difficulties if the democratic process had developed normally in our country."[2] When Gorbachev spoke of the democratic process developing normally, he surely did not have in mind the models of China or Albania or North Korea but obviously America and the West. He was confessing a sense of the inferiority of his society to that of the democracies and suggesting that the very reason is its lack of democracy.

Gorbachev has thrown in the towel for communism precisely because he has recognized the validity of the democratic idea. Perhaps I overrate the importance of Gorbachev's own thought processes to the disintegration of communism.[3] Certainly other figures are playing important roles in reshaping the Soviet Union. Within the governing elite, men such as Foreign Minister Eduard Shevardnadze and Aleksandr Yakovlev have pressed for reform, as have the editors of *Moscow News*, *Ogonyuk*, and *Argumenti I Facty*. Still more insistent pressures are coming from those who have taken on the role of the more-or-less official opposition. They constitute the Interregional Group in the Congress of People's Deputies and the majority in the Moscow and Leningrad city governments: Boris Yeltsin, Gavril Popov, Anatoly Sobchak, Yuri Afanasayev, and the like. And then there are all manner of grass-roots dissident groups and movements like Memorial, the unofficial publications *Glasnost* and *Express-Chronica*, and the national movements in the Baltics and elsewhere. In general the farther from the center of power, the stronger the democratic credentials are. To the extent that the impetus for change comes less from Gorbachev than from below, the force of democratic ideas in the metamorphosis of the Soviet Union is even stronger than I have argued.

As Communist regimes tumbled in Eastern Europe, we Americans were surprised to see the depth of yearning for democracy and the degree to which people understood at least the essential outlines of the democratic idea. When East Germans took to the streets of Leipzig, Czechs to the streets of Prague, or even Romanians to the streets of Bucharest, they were strikingly clear in their demands. They asked not for a true press but a free press, not for enlightened rulers but for free elections, not for a reformed party but a multiparty system. They homed-in on the essence of democracy despite the confusion that their rulers attempted to sow about the meaning of "democracy," an effort that seems to have borne more fruit among Western academics and publicists than among East European subjects. And now that we have seen how firmly East Europeans grasped the concept of democracy, we often hear that the Chinese students who gathered in Tiananmen Square to demand democracy did not really understand the meaning of the term.[4] Perhaps not. But it is striking that they chose to model their goddess of democracy in the shape of the Statue of Liberty.

Democracy as Foreign Policy

The lesson in all of this is that advancing the democratic cause can be America's most effective foreign policy in terms not merely of good deeds but of self-interest as well. The immediate goal of U.S. foreign policy must be to complete the dissolution of communism. This is within reach in the Soviet Union and China. Cuba, Albania, and the rest will surely follow. The end of communism in China and the USSR means the end of communism per se. This will be not only a blessed deliverance for all of its unhappy subjects but also the greatest possible boon to America's security.

This is why the policy of the Bush administration toward China has been so incomprehensible. The Chinese people demonstrated in the spring of 1989 that a vast majority want to be free. They were thwarted by a clique of octogenarian autocrats who still hold a preponderance of the levers of coercion. What possible cause can we have for succoring this clique rather than using our leverage to help crack the desiccating facade of their rule?

True, China has been a strategic ally of the United States. But this alliance at its most vital was always more essential to China than to us. We have always had the strength to deter the Soviets ourselves. Leonid Brezhnev, according to Kissinger, proposed a nuclear strike against China. To the best of our knowledge, no Soviet leader ever entertained the idea of such an attack against the United States. Even if this alliance were more important to us, to turn our backs on the Chinese people in the interest of strategic considerations is the kind of cynical calculation that is justifiable only under extreme duress, as when we allied with Stalin to stop Hitler. But with the Soviet threat receding fast, the strategic justifications for cosseting China's rulers have never been weaker. We have every practical and moral reason for casting our lot with the masses of Chinese demanding democracy.

The tactical exigencies of policy toward the Soviet Union are murkier. In contrast to Deng Xiaoping and his clique, it is hard to determine whether Gorbachev is still a force for democratization or an obstacle to it. But clearly Gorbachev has hoisted a banner of democratization and has allowed an unprecedented degree of freedom, and in response a panoply of democratic movements has sprung up at the grass roots. The goal of American policy should be to aid those movements while avoiding any weakening of Gorbachev in the face of whatever reactionary, restorationist forces may still be lurking in the KGB, the military, and the Communist party. We also must encourage the Soviet government to bite the bullet on transition to a market economy, without which the political reforms are likely to founder.

Whatever the tactical uncertainties, there can be no doubt that democratizing the Soviet Union must be by far the highest goal of U.S. foreign policy. A democratic Soviet Union or a constellation of democratic successor states would be no enemy of ours, or probably of anyone else's. We would be free from the nightmare of nuclear holocaust. And this would be only the beginning of benefits. The Soviet Union would add almost irresistible weight to the democratic camp. As partners rather than adversaries, America and the Soviet Union, backed by a democratic Europe and Japan, could foster a new global order in which peace is less broken, human rights less violated, and the environment less despoiled.

But the end of communism will not mean the end of all troubles. As many are pointing out, national and ethnic conflicts may again come to the fore in Central and Eastern Europe. These will be less threatening to us than communism has been, and in most cases they should be amenable to reasonable adjudication. Many of the local intergroup conflicts of recent decades have been exacerbated by deliberate Soviet policy. Turmoil offered more opportunities than did peace for the Kremlin to expand its influence and discomfit the West. With the abatement of Soviet imperialism, the conflicts in Central America and even southern Africa seem on their way to resolution. Without the cold war to envenom them, many local broils may prove less intractable than we expected.

These hopes may be disappointed; there may be a Tiananmen in Red Square, a brutal forced restoration of Communist orthodoxy. In this scenario Gorbachev could play the role of Deng or of Zhao Ziyang. With the enormous democratic, nationalist, and other anti-Communist energies that have been unleashed within the USSR, a successful crackdown of this type grows less likely every day. But the possibility cannot be ruled out.

That event, however, would make it no less important for the United States to continue to aim for democratization. Such a restoration would not endure long. Communist regimes have always rested on a combination of coercion and belief. A restored orthodox regime would rest on coercion alone. It could not revive the ideology now that it has been denounced from its own pulpits. But even a regime of pure coercion needs the loyalty of its apparatchiks and soldiers. And as Nicolae Ceausescu learned, that loyalty cannot be relied upon once a regime has lost its legitimacy and its people have had a glimpse of freedom.

In this scenario the democratic groups with which we sympathize would probably be crushed, and our lines of access directly into the Soviet Union would be curtailed. Nonetheless we could bring diplomatic and economic pressures, step up our radio broadcasts, and underwrite exile groups, which in turn could nourish the democratic underground that would surely spring up. We would act too, presumably in concert with NATO allies, to shore up the new non-Communist governments of Eastern Europe even if some Soviet troops remained on their territory. If we pursued such a course, we could be confident of success before long. The Soviet regime was in deep trouble, as Gorbachev has told us, when he began his radical reforms. And a new restorationist regime would be much more troubled and fragile.

If, conversely, communism soon completes its demise, U.S. policy still should make the promotion of democracy its main objective. Voices are already being raised to say that if the Communist threat disappears, America should withdraw into itself. But withdrawal would be foolhardy as well as selfish. Once before, in 1919, we withdrew to isolation as soon as we had won the war and "made the world safe for democracy." The result was the rise of forces more terrible and destructive than those that we had put to rest. In the wake of communism, we are unlikely to see forces more terrible and more destructive, but we would be foolish to assume that all troubles will cease or to risk turning our back on the world. That we cannot foresee the shape of any possible new threat does not mean that none exists; it may show only the limits of our imagination.

The Post-Communist World

We should concentrate on continuing to spread democracy in a post-Communist world for three good reasons. The first is empathy with our fellow humans. Democracy does not make everyone happy, but it does deliver on its promise to allow, in our forefathers' brilliant phrase, the pursuit of happiness. Some people will never find their own happiness no matter how free they are to pursue it, but more people find happiness through their own pursuit than when it is defined for them by others.

Second, the more democratic the world, the friendlier America's environment will be. True, some democratic governments have been nuisances for the United States. Those of Sweden, India, France, and Costa Rica have at times played that part. But none has ever been our enemy. We could live comfortably indeed in a world where our worst antagonists were an Olof Palme, a Charles de Gaulle, an Indira Gandhi, or an Oscar Arias.

Third, the more democratic the world, the more peaceful it is likely to be. Various researchers have shown that war between democracies has almost never occurred in the modern world.[5] Paul Gottfried and Patrick Buchanan, two conservatives who seem wary of the rising prestige of democracy, have each sought to rebut this evidence with a single contrary example: democratic England declared war on democratic Finland in World War II.[6] But such a forced example dramatizes the weakness of their case. Finland, which had ceded territory to the Soviet Union after its 1939 invasion, joined forces with Germany when it attacked the Soviet Union in 1941. Winston Churchill eventually acceded to Joseph Stalin's pressure to declare war on Finland after laboring to avoid it. Despite the declaration, Finnish and British forces never fought each other. Thus, giving Gottfried and Buchanan their due, we can qualify the generalization: democracies do not go to war with each other except when they are each fighting for their lives as smaller allies of two warring totalitarian giants. Some exception!

Another exception that might be cited is the attack by relatively democratic Lebanon against the nascent democracy of Israel in 1948. But Lebanon acted as a junior member of the Arab League, in whose councils it had unsuccessfully opposed the invasion. Left to its own devices, it would not have joined the war, and once it did join, its forces barely went through the motions.[7] Exceptions like these prove the rule. It may not be true that democracies never go to war with each other, but they rarely do so.

There are probably two reasons for the peaceableness of democracies. One was identified by Immanuel Kant some two hundred years ago, when there hardly were any democracies:

[When] the consent of the citizens is required to decide whether or not war should be declared, it is very natural that they will have a great hesitation in embarking on so dangerous an enterprise. For this would mean calling down on themselves all the miseries of war. . . . But under a constitution . . . which is . . . not republican, it is the simplest thing in the world to go to war. For the head of state is not a fellow citizen, but the owner of the state, and war will not force him to make the slightest sacrifice. . . .[8]

A second reason may be that the ethics of democracy conduce to peace. Democracy is at bottom an ethical system, in which the citizens discipline themselves to the principle that it is better to decide things by the right means than to get their own way. It is very like a lesson we try to teach our children. Once individuals have internalized these ethics in their behavior within the polity, they can readily see that the same principle can apply to relations between states; namely, a state should compromise some of its goals or interests rather than resort to war, especially if it is dealing with states that are willing to behave in a like manner.

A world in which the proliferation of democracies leads to a diminution of armed conflict would be a real Pax Americana. Is this vision utopian? Some would say that fostering a world of democracies and of peace is more ambitious an undertaking than the conquests that made the Pax Romana. To be sure, the evolution of other states is difficult to influence, but this truism can be overemphasized. Today roughly 40 percent of the world, measured either in numbers of countries or in population, lives under democratic government. Most of those democracies arose in large part as a result of the influence of America or of England (many were once British colonies).

Although exporting democracy is never easy, it will grow easier with the demise of communism. With the collapse of its ideological rival, democracy gains new normative force in the global Zeitgeist. Rulers and subjects alike will find it harder to escape the idea that democratic behavior is right behavior. For decades, communism blurred that recognition. It vitiated the international consensus that had been growing since the Enlightenment that popular sovereignty is the sole basis on which states can claim legitimacy. Paying lip service to that principle, communism claimed that through the vanguard party the people could somehow be sovereign even without being consulted. Now, however, the Soviet president himself has acknowledged the preposterousness of this claim: in the name of democratizing his country he called for rule of law, competitive elections, free expression, multiple parties—in short the very institutions that Communists once dismissed as bourgeois democracy. Is it too much to expect the world to resist another such egregious imposture?

The death throes of communism mark the beginning of the twenty-first century. It may be the American century. Henry Luce once said that the twentieth century would be the American century. But in fact it is better recognized as the totalitarian century. The various totalitarian systems now all seem to be ending in failure, but while they lived, they called the action. America emerged victorious over them all, but each of those victories came in defense. If, however, we can advance the spread of democracy, perhaps not everywhere but at least to the majority of mankind, then the twenty-first will be the true American century. This will come about not by the spread of American power or by the exact imitation of American institutions but by the spread of those profound and humane ideals on which America was founded.

Ironically such a triumph is bound to lead to the relative decline of America's power, the very decline that those who view the American experiment through jaundiced eyes have been yearning for or proclaiming. As other nations become democratic, they will discover the key to our success and come to rival it, as Japan and the democracies of Europe are already doing. Our preeminence will diminish. Just witness how Asian immigrants have flourished in recent decades with the opportunities they have found in a democratic America, and imagine the prowess of a democratic Asia. As more countries become democratic, America will for a time retain the advantage of our heterogeneity. The invigorating transfusion of immigrant talent that flows into our economy is matched by no other country. But even that advantage will eventually fade: as more countries become democratic, fewer of their citizens will flee, more will find their happiness at home. Deprived of that tonic, America will find that its stature will continue to sink to that of one country among countries, one democracy among democracies. It will be our greatest triumph.

2
Currents in
American Foreign Policy

A foreign policy that emphasizes America's identity with the cause of democracy finds deep roots in American history. America entered World War I, so we said, to make the world safe for democracy. In World War II, we first declared our country the arsenal of democracy and after Pearl Harbor joined directly in an alliance of democracies. After the war American policy spawned the United Nations, which declares among its goals the promotion of "universal respect for, and observance of, human rights and fundamental freedoms for all." To this end a Universal Declaration of Human Rights was composed under the leadership of an American, Eleanor Roosevelt. This solemn covenant makes democratic norms the standard by which the political arrangements of all UN member-states may be judged.

In the previous century solicitude for the growth of democratic institutions was a major motivation given for entry into war with Spain in 1898, war with Mexico in 1846, and war with the Confederacy in 1861, as well as for the Monroe Doctrine and even the despoliation of the Indians. As in the latter example, the democratic goals proclaimed were sometimes mere rationalizations masking venal or egoistic motives, but even so the choice of rationalizations illustrates the resonance of the democratic cause to American ears.

Conversely the most important arguments against such an ideological approach to foreign policy have equally deep roots. All the way back to the dispute between Alexander Hamilton and Thomas Jefferson over whether to aid France in its war with Britain, American policy has been the product of contradictory impulses. The most powerful impulses can generally be called isolationism, realism, and idealism.

The rubric "idealism," however, actually comprises two distinct themes that, though not necessarily irreconcilable, are more often in conflict than in harmony. Robert Osgood has distinguished between "militant idealists" on the one hand and "pacifist idealists, international reformers, and moral optimists" on the other.[1] The latter congeries is broad and vague, but the distinction he is aiming at is clear enough. I would prefer to call one group democratic idealists and the other pacifist idealists. While both strands of idealism agree that moral considerations should inform foreign policy, the kinship ends there. Democratic idealism has been associated frequently with America's wars, while pacifist idealism has often manifested itself in antiwar movements. Although this distinction goes unrecognized in most of the literature about idealism, it constitutes no less fundamental a divide in our foreign policy debates than the divisions between either strand of idealism and the isolationist or realist impulses.

Thus we can identify not three but four major currents in American foreign policy history: isolationism, realism, pacifist idealism, and democratic idealism. Some prominent individuals and even some organizations have clearly espoused one or another of these approaches, but in the main they are tendencies more than ideologies. American policy toward any given international problem is likely to be influenced by more than one of them, and American leaders may be moved by different tendencies in addressing different situations. Many of the most prominent isolationists of the interwar years, for example, were isolationist only in their attitudes toward Europe, not at all toward Latin America. Today by ironic contrast Europe is the one area of the world (except perhaps Canada) that is least likely to be the focus of isolationist sentiment.

A major purpose of this book is to advance the case that democratic idealism rather than any of the other three approaches should guide U.S. foreign policy. In the balance of this chapter I make my case against isolationism and pacifist idealism. The argument against realism is reserved for chapters 3 and 4.

Isolationism

The classic statement of the isolationist impulse can be found in President George Washington's Farewell Address: "The great rule of conduct for us in regard to foreign nations is, in extending our commercial relations to have as little political connection as possible." Underlying it are both a moral idea and a pragmatic one. The pragmatic idea is to reap the benefits of America's geographic isolation to keep the country safe and free from Europe's broils. "Our detached and distant situation invites and enables us to pursue a different course," said Washington. "Why forgo the advantages of so peculiar a situation?"

By isolating itself from European quarrels, America could avoid being victimized, but it also would forgo any concomitant chance to aggrandize itself. This was the idealistic side of Washington's argument:

> It will be worthy of a free, enlightened, and at no distant
> period a great nation to give to mankind the magnanimous
> and too novel example of a people always guided by an
> exalted justice and benevolence. Who can doubt that in the
> course of time and things the fruits of such a plan would
> richly repay any temporary advantages which might be lost
> by a steady adherence to it? Can it be that Providence has not
> connected the permanent felicity of a nation with its virtue?
> The experiment, at least, is recommended by every sentiment
> which ennobles human nature.

From Washington on, isolation remained one of the main currents of American foreign policy, even when it was not dominant. Although the term "isolationism" is today most commonly associated with the interwar years, Osgood has pointed out that "the isolationism of the thirties was distinguished from the isolationism of other periods not by the number of its adherents but by the number of its opponents."[2] The number of its opponents leapt to near unanimity once America was attacked at Pearl Harbor, and isolationism has been in disrepute ever since. After the war, a consensus accepted the judgment that the sway of isolationist sentiment in America in the decades following the first world war had contributed to bringing on the second.

But while few today will accept the label "isolationist," popular reaction against the war in Vietnam inspired a sentiment, branded neo-isolationist by its critics, whose main thrust was a reduction of American involvement abroad.[3] "America cannot be the world's policeman" and "No more Vietnams" suggest an isolationist sensibility that was made most explicit in the peroration of George McGovern's speech accepting the 1972 Democratic presidential nomination: "Come home, America." Although McGovern's poor showing in the general election made McGovernism something of a term of opprobrium among Democrats, faint echoes of his theme could be heard in speeches of Democratic presidential candidates as recently as 1988, when Michael Dukakis in his acceptance speech said, "This election isn't ... about overthrowing governments in Central America; it's about creating jobs in middle America." Rather than spell out his differences with Vice President Bush over the substance of U.S. policy toward Central America, Dukakis's message was that America ought to concern itself more with domestic issues and less with foreign affairs.

Modern isolationism is not, however, reserved to the Democrats. Indeed the one organized center of opinion that comes closest to articulating an unabashed isolationist position is the libertarian movement. Although a few of its figures make their home on the left side of the political spectrum (notably foreign policy scholar Earl Ravenal, long affiliated with the far-left Institute for Policy Studies), the roots of the libertarian movement are on the Right. When the Libertarian party is not running candidates of its own, most libertarians are likely to prefer the Republicans.

As isolationism may be found on various points of the political spectrum, so the isolationist impulse also expresses itself in different, sometimes contradictory themes. Historian Jerald Combs summarized these in describing the isolationists of the first decades of this century:

> Conservative isolationists assumed that American rule was probably beneficial to all who fell under its sway but were afraid that imperialism overextended American power and risked foreign entanglements that might lead to further major wars. Liberal and radical isolationists were inclined to think that American imperialism was harmful to the colonized peoples.[4]

These two strains of isolationism—one growing out of the fear that entanglement with the outer world will be harmful to America, the other out of the fear that America will be harmful to the world—have persisted, although they have not always corresponded so neatly to a conservative-liberal division. The isolationism of the interwar years embraced Americans both on the Left and on the Right, yet liberal and conservative isolationists alike argued in terms of the harm that would come to America from foreign involvement, not the harm America might do. More recently the neo-isolationist reaction against the Vietnam War was a sentiment rooted overwhelmingly in the liberal side of American politics, but it readily employed both variants of the isolationist argument: America was inhumanely wreaking havoc on Indochina, and involvement in Indochina on behalf of unworthy allies was tearing America apart.

Pacifist Idealism

Pacifist idealism has its earliest American roots in the religious convictions of certain groups of the original settlers in the New World, like the Quakers and the Mennonites. For these believers and other absolute pacifists, refusal to use force is a categorical imperative. Such absolute pacifism has not been a powerful stream in American life, but more attenuated forms of pacifism have been important. These have expressed themselves in movements opposed to participation in specific wars, as distinct from opposition to all war. Protests against American participation in the Spanish-American War and World War I reached significant proportions, and in the case of Vietnam the antiwar movement was instrumental in persuading the nation to withdraw from the

15

war, on terms that ultimately spelled defeat.

More important, the pacificist idealist impulse has made America the world's leader in the sometimes quixotic quest for devices to prevent war. These have usually taken the form of legal devices, such as arbitration treaties binding the signatories to peaceful adjudication of disputes. In the early years of this century the United States signed dozens of such bilateral treaties, most often with Latin American states. No doubt many Latin leaders found it the better part of valor to indulge the United States, but the president of, say, Ecuador or Paraguay must have been perplexed about why the Yanquis sought a written pledge from his country not to initiate war against the United States in the event of a disagreement.

In addition to bilateral agreements the United States has also been avid in the pursuit of multilateral legal devices to protect peace, such as the UN Charter, which outlaws aggression. The most remarkable such device was the 1928 Pact of Paris, which made war illegal. French Foreign Minister Aristide Briand was actually seeking a mutual renunciation of war between France and the United States that would have constituted an implicit alliance. But when his American interlocutors countered with their scheme to outlaw war, the Frenchman realized that the best way to court American good will would be to go along with them. Here again was something tragicomic about America's role on the world stage. In light of America's emerging might, the other nations were loath to disappoint it, even to the extent of acquiescing in pacifist schemes that they otherwise would have scorned. The Pact of Paris was signed by Germany and virtually all of the other states that were soon to participate in World War II, including Russia and China, which began skirmishing in Manchuria virtually at the moment the treaty came into force.[5]

The most ubiquitous of America's peacemaking devices have been arms control conferences and agreements. These date back as far as the Rush-Bagot Convention of 1817 limiting American and British warships on the inland waterways separating America from Canada, a rare success in the annals of arms control. The United States took an active part in the First Hague Conference on arms limitation in 1899 (an initiative of Czar Nicholas II) and was the prime mover behind the Second Hague Conference, which met in 1907 (although the czar remained in the foreground). The United States was also the initiator and leader of a series of naval disarmament conferences beginning with the Washington Naval Conference of 1921–1922 and continuing through the Coolidge Naval Conference held in Geneva in 1927 and the London conferences of 1930 and 1935. After World War II the United States formulated the Baruch Plan for the international control of atomic weapons; ever since, it has pursued nuclear and conventional arms control in bilateral and multilateral negotiations with the Soviet Union.

The pacifist idealist impulse has also made America the world's pioneer in the realm of international organizations. Both the League of Nations and the United Nations were American brainchildren. Here too it might be said that both organizations were foisted on a bemused community of nations by an American colossus, which no other nation wished to disappoint even in schemes that the others did not take seriously.

Even more than isolationism, pacifist idealism remains an active current in American debates over foreign policy, although not in the form of absolute pacifism.[6] Thus arms control remains one of the sacred cows of American politics, although it is far from clear that such agreements make nuclear war any less likely. During the twenty years before Mikhail Gorbachev's "new thinking" revolutionized Soviet foreign policy, the USSR was devoting, so Moscow now tells us, something like one-quarter of its economy to the military, and it baldly cheated, as Americans knew and Foreign Minister Shevardnadze has confessed, on the ABM treaty. Nonetheless Americans continued to treat such agreements as intrinsically desirable, rather than judging them by their effects on nuclear stability, the only logical standard.

Democratic Internationalism

The pacifist and isolationist impulses each militate against the policy of democratic internationalism that I espouse. Pacifist idealism has nothing against democracy, but its sensibility runs deeply counter to the energetic assertion of American influence. Moreover it leans toward the kind of cultural relativism that disputes any right to judge democracy superior to tyranny. Whereas democratic idealists want to pursue peace by making more governments democratic, pacifist idealists want to construct peace between governments as they are and fear that the attempt to change them is itself destabilizing.

Isolationism objects to my belief that our surest safety comes from actively working to shape an international climate congenial to us, one where democracy is on the rise. Isolationism argues that America risks becoming entangled in war by meddling abroad and can keep itself safe merely by maintaining sufficient military strength to deter any outright attack.

Yet neither pacifism nor isolationism offers a formidable challenge. The contrast between the Reagan and the Carter years in terms of U.S.-Soviet relations illustrates once again the fallacy of pacifism. America evoked a more satisfactory response by being firm than by striving "to demonstrate to the Soviet Union . . . our good will" which President Jimmy Carter had described as "the great challenge we Americans

17

confront."[7] The democratic transformation under way in the USSR, destabilizing though it may be, has reduced the risks and burdens of the cold war far more than an infinity of arms control agreements.

The isolationist argument ignores the links of culture, blood, commerce, and human compassion that bind America to the rest of the world. Its divided morality is more suited to an insular, homogeneous nation like Japan than to a nation of immigrants. The wisdom of Washington's farewell warnings against entangling alliances was a wisdom suited more to the tiny nation that we were than to a superpower, suited more to an era when weapons traveled for weeks between continents rather than for hours or minutes. Isolationism proposes to abandon the policy of internationalism by which America has kept itself and the world in a state of relative peace since 1945 in favor of a bet that we will remain invincible no matter what goes on outside. Why take such a gamble? These forty-five years of internationalism were in a sense experimental. In this time we faced the most formidable foe in our history and came away with our most remarkable victory. What greater vindication could a policy secure?

For all the perdurance of pacifist and isolationist currents, powerful historical experience has largely discredited them. Both these currents, ascendant during the interwar years, were widely blamed for having helped to bring on World War II. Few Americans today call themselves pacifist or isolationist, and few will sit still for being so labeled. Those whose views seem to embody isolationist and pacifist currents do not in most cases think of themselves as isolationists or pacifists. More often pacifism and isolationism seek to hide behind the skirts of realism, the third major current of American foreign policy other than democratic idealism, and the most potent source of opposition to the approach to foreign policy that I espouse.

3

The Folly of Realism

In contrast to isolationism and pacifist idealism, realism suffers no disrepute. It even is enjoying something of a vogue. Foreign policy advocates of many different stripes today cloak themselves in its mantle.

Realism's roots go all the way back to Alexander Hamilton's argument with Thomas Jefferson over honoring the 1778 treaty of alliance with France. Jefferson emphasized America's contractual obligation and its ideological affinity for republican France over monarchical England. Hamilton, favoring neutrality, argued that a small nation such as ours could not afford to quarrel with either major European power. That insistence on putting self-interest first is the essence of realism. Policy must be guided by interest, says the realist, and not by sentiment, ideology, or abstract principles.

Often in our history the counsel of realism has been forwarded against the democratic idealist impulse, as when democratic enthusiasts in the 1820s sought some form of American aid to the Greek patriots fighting for independence from Turkey. John Quincy Adams's response is quoted by realists to this day. America, he said, "goes not abroad, in search of monsters to destroy. She is the well-wisher to the freedom and independence of all. She is the champion and vindicator only of her own."[1]

Even when realism has not advocated a different course from democratic idealism, it has often sought a different spirit. Thus while Theodore Roosevelt did not demur from the decision to enter World War I, he did object to President Woodrow Wilson's rhetoric about fighting to make the world safe for democracy. Roosevelt's tart riposte stands as another classic expression of the realist sensibility: "First and foremost we are to make the world safe for ourselves."[2]

Since the 1930s, the term "realism" has come to signify something more than the mere principle of looking out for number one. It designates an approach to analyzing international relations and a prescription for U.S. policy that derives from that analysis. It is an approach identified with some of the most luminous names in the field: Walter Lippmann, George Kennan, Hans Morgenthau, Reinhold Niebuhr, and Henry Kissinger.

The realist current divides into two major streams. One holds that it is impossible for a country to base its policy on moral principles. Reinhold Niebuhr warns against the consequences of trying or pretending to do so:

> We may claim that we use our power in the interest of the total community with as much justice as is possible for nations, when all nations are instinctively prompted to consider their own interest, and the interests of others only as these are compatible with their own. But our moral claims ought not to go beyond this limit. We are not a sanctified nation and we must not assume that all our actions are dictated by considerations of disinterested justice. If we fall into this error the natural resentments against our power on the part of the weaker nations will be compounded with resentments against our pretensions of superior virtue.[3]

Like Niebuhr, Walter Lippmann believes that the moral principles expressed by the United States fall mostly in the category of illusion while in practice the nation's policy is dictated by strategic interest even if this is not consciously recognized. He argues that the reasons President Wilson had proclaimed for America's entry into World War I "were legalistic and moralistic and idealistic reasons, rather than the substantial and vital reason that the security of the United States demanded that no aggressively expanding imperial power, like Germany, should be allowed to gain the mastery of the Atlantic Ocean."[4] This reason, says Lippmann, was "undeclared" and "only partially realized" although "a majority of the people ... recognized [it] intuitively."[5] Lippmann believes that the United States was right in entering the war but that it suffered considerable harm because it deceived itself about its reasons for doing so:

> Because this simple and self-evident American interest was not candidly made explicit, the nation never understood clearly why it had entered the war. As time went on, the country was, therefore, open to every suggestion and insinuation that the nation had fought for no good reason at all. ...[6]

In contrast to Niebuhr and Lippmann, George Kennan embodies the second stream of realism. Its adherents do not doubt that the United States can follow a policy shaped by its moral principles, or at least by its passions, rather than by its interests. Kennan argues that the United

States and other democracies are in fact prone to do exactly that—with dire consequence. Democracies, he says, tend to act viscerally precisely where visceral action is most dangerous—on questions of war and peace:

> A democracy is peace-loving. It does not like to go to war. It is slow to rise to provocation. When it has been provoked to the point where it must grasp the sword, it does not easily forgive its adversary for having produced this situation. The fact of the provocation then becomes itself the issue. Democracy fights in anger—it fights for the very reason that it was forced to go to war. It fights to punish the power that was rash enough and hostile enough to provoke it—to teach that power a lesson it will not forget, to prevent the thing from happening again. Such a war must be carried to the bitter end.[7]

This mindless fury on the part of democracies is a consequence of their moralism, which leads them to the mistaken belief that national interest can be transcended, that conflicts between the interests of different states can readily be reconciled. Kennan found

> the most serious fault of our past policy formulation to lie in something that I might call the legalistic-moralistic approach to international problems. . . . the belief that it should be possible to suppress the chaotic and dangerous aspirations of governments in the international field by the acceptance of some system of legal rules and restraints.[8]

Hans Morgenthau is recognized as the leading theoretician of realism, and his writings endorse both of its major streams, although they are mutually contradictory. At one moment he wrote, "We have acted on the international scene, as all nations must, in power-politics terms; but we have tended to conceive of our actions in non-political moralistic terms."[9] But in the next breath he said that this was true only during the nineteenth century and that throughout the twentieth century we committed the far graver error of both thinking and acting in terms of moral principles.[10]

The Morality of States and of Individuals

The realist critique of moralism in foreign policy springs from the observation that states cannot be bound by the same moral rules that bind individuals. Kennan goes so far as to deride "the assumption that state behavior is a fit subject for moral judgment."[11] On this point too, Hamilton serves as the realists' oracle. Morgenthau offers this quote from Hamilton's "Pacificus" articles:

> The rule of morality ... is not precisely the same between
> nations as between individuals. The duty of making its own
> welfare the guide of its actions, is much stronger upon the
> former than upon the latter; in proportion to the greater
> magnitude and importance of national compared with indi-
> vidual happiness, and to the greater permanency of the ef-
> fects of national than of individual conduct. Existing millions,
> and for the most part future generations, are concerned in the
> present measures of government; while the consequences of
> the private actions of an individual ordinarily terminate with
> himself, or are circumscribed within a narrow compass.
>
> Whence it follows that an individual may, on numerous
> occasions, meritoriously indulge the emotions of generosity
> and benevolence, not only without an eye to, but even at the
> expense of, his own interest. But a government can rarely, if
> at all, be justifiable in pursuing a similar course.[12]

The essential point, as Arthur Schlesinger, Jr., another luminary
with one foot in the realist camp, puts it, is that "governments are not
individuals. They are not principals but agents. They are trustees for the
happiness and interests of others."[13] To sacrifice or put at risk something
of our own is our business. To sacrifice or put at risk something being
held for someone else is not gallantry; it is irresponsibility.

To this Schlesinger adds two other arguments. First, he says that
most foreign policy issues "do not lend themselves to categorical moral
judgments" because they concern technical matters such as trade. Second, he says the application of moral principles is impossible because
"no international moral consensus exists in sufficient depth and strength
to sustain a comprehensive and binding international morality."[14]

The latter point has been emphasized by several of the realists.
Kennan argues that "no people can be the judge of another's domestic
institutions and requirements," and he appeals to his countrymen for

> a new attitude among us toward many things outside our
> borders that are irritating and unpleasant today—an attitude
> more like that of a doctor toward those physical phenomena
> in the human body that are neither pleasing nor fortunate—
> an attitude of detachment and soberness and readiness to
> reserve judgment. It will mean that we will have the modesty
> to admit that our own national interest is all that we are really
> capable of knowing and understanding. . . .[15]

Morgenthau contends that within states individuals are subject to
"supra-individual moral principles" but that between states "relations
are not controlled by universal moral principles concrete enough to
guide the political actions of individual nations." Thus the attempt to

apply moral principles beyond the bounds of one's own nation is itself a form of "immorality" that reaches its apotheosis "in the contemporary phenomenon of the moral crusade."[16] To Morgenthau, bolshevism represented the "full bloom" of the immoral impulse to engage in moral crusades, but Woodrow Wilson's democratic idealism displayed "an inkling" of the same thing.

In emphasizing the absence of universally recognized moral standards, realists are eager to disabuse Americans of any notion that our nation stands on a higher moral plane than others. Again they take their lead from Hamilton, who urged the nation "to adopt as a practical maxim for the direction of our political conduct that we, as well as the other inhabitants of the globe, are yet remote from the happy empire of perfect wisdom and perfect virtue."[17] Echoing this, Niebuhr complains that "we are still inclined to pretend that our power is exercised by a peculiarly virtuous nation. The uniqueness of our virtue is questioned both by our friends and our enemies."[18] He is not quite so relativistic about this as Kennan, who gibes: "A nation which admits that its own capacity for assimilation is limited once you get beyond the peoples of Caucasian origin should observe a special reserve in its dealings with other peoples."[19] To Niebuhr Americans are among the "children of light," who are not evil like the agents of totalitarian systems, "the children of darkness," but neither are they as wise. The children of light "are foolish not merely because they underestimate the power of self-interest among the children of darkness. They underestimate this power among themselves."[20]

Although it sometimes speaks against moralism in foreign policy, realism embodies a morality of its own, the closest analogy to which might be the ethos of certain schools of psychotherapy. It counsels that the road to healthy international adjustment begins with recognition and acceptance of the imperfectibility common to all states—"I'm okay, you're okay." Osgood puts it:

> [The] competition for power may be mitigated by a variety of restraints upon rampant egoism . . . but it will never be abolished or even transformed into orderly procedures enforced impartially by reference to custom or law until men undergo a psychological revolution that will permit them to owe their primary allegiance to some community greater than their nation-state.[21]

Morgenthau would go further:

> If we look at all nations, our own included, as political entities pursuing their respective interests defined in terms of power, we are able to do justice to all of them. . . . in a dual sense: We

> are able to judge other nations as we judge our own and, having judged them in this fashion, we are then capable of pursuing policies that respect the interests of other nations, while protecting and promoting those of our own. Moderation in policy cannot fail to reflect the moderation of moral judgment.[22]

This thought is echoed by Schlesinger: "National interest, consistently construed, is a self-limiting motive. Any rigorous defender of the idea must accept that other nations have their legitimate interests too. The recognition of equal claims sets bounds on aggression."[23]

But fundamentally realism's claims on assent or at least respect rest not on its own moral content but on its analytic force, that is, on its ability to present an accurate picture of how the world works. The picture consists of several propositions. The first as Morgenthau puts it, perhaps somewhat starkly, is that "politics ... is governed by objective laws" whose "operation [is] impervious to our preferences."[24] The second is that "the idea of interest is indeed of the essence of politics."[25] In short the political behavior of individuals, and even more so of states, is motivated not by ideas, values, or passions but by interests. What are interests? To Morgenthau the answer is axiomatic. In politics interest is "defined in terms of power."[26] Finally, realism holds that the need to protect or expand power gives each state a relatively fixed set of objectives in relation to surrounding states. To the realist, geography is destiny. As Schlesinger put it, "Every state has a set of fairly definite strategic interests. One has only to recall the continuities of Russian foreign policy, whether directed by czars or by commissars."[27] Similarly Morgenthau pointed to an "astounding continuity in foreign policy which makes American, British, or Russian foreign policy appear as an intelligible, rational continuum, by and large consistent within itself, regardless of the different motives, preferences and intellectual and moral qualities of successive statesmen."[28]

Realism versus Democratic Idealism

It is easy to see then why a foreign policy that devotes itself in large measure to advancing the democratic cause is anathema to realists. They argue first that America cannot carry out such a foreign policy even if it wishes to do so because its foreign policy is ineluctably dictated by its interests. Second, to the extent that America attempts to freight its foreign policy with such ideological content, the realists say, it is asking for trouble because it is deviating from its concrete interests. Such moral crusades in the past have been the bane of U.S. policy, they say. Third, a foreign policy that focuses on the advancement of democracy knows no geographic limits and carries American attention far from home rather than focusing on those regions that are strategically vital to the United States. Finally, they say, such a foreign policy is morally flawed because it seeks to impose our values on cultures that are different from our own.

The realist arguments, however, do not bear scrutiny. Do states inevitably behave as the realists describe? The realists' own lack of confidence in this cardinal tenet of their faith is betrayed by the insistence with which they criticize past foreign policies of the United States (and other countries) and prescribe for the future. If states behave only as geography and human nature ordain they must, then why criticize and why prescribe? Yet this logically fatal contradiction seems to trouble the realists no more than the analogous contradiction troubles Marxists or Calvinists. (If history itself intends the triumph of the proletariat, why should Marxists labor on its behalf? If God himself has predetermined the fate of each person, then why strive to demonstrate grace?)

The Impact of Humanitarianism. Not only is the realist argument thus self-evidently flawed in its logic, it is also refuted by a mound of empirical evidence. Although many state actions aim to defend interests, many do not. Some are motivated by altruism. The United States rushes aid to the victims of flood, famine, or other catastrophe wherever these occur for no motive other than human sympathy. Several other countries do the same. Various states offer asylum to the persecuted, provide good offices for the mediation of distant disputes, and even contribute troops to international peacekeeping forces, all for reasons that are essentially humanitarian.

In addition the United States gives foreign aid each year to about one hundred countries, including some whose governments are intensely hostile to America, for example, in fiscal year 1987 Afghanistan, Ethiopia, Kampuchea, Angola, and Mozambique. Cynics invariably see self-interest lurking behind foreign aid programs, but how can they explain that a significant fraction of American economic assistance is given to multilateral development agencies established for the express purpose of preventing donor nations from using aid as a lever to influence recipients? In truth the motives underlying foreign aid are a mixture of geostrategy, domestic politics and economics, and just plain charity.

The Impact of Domestic Politics. It may be argued that such acts as disaster relief, asylum, good offices, and even foreign aid constitute an inconsequential part of foreign policy. But humanitarian sentiment is only one of the motivating forces other than self-interest that shape foreign policy. Another is domestic politics. Consider, for example, the

25

impact of ethnic groups. It may be that its close alliance with Israel serves America's interests well (indeed I believe as much).[29] But even if this is true, who would argue that American policy toward the Middle East has not also been affected to some degree by the political activity of those American Jews who feel an attachment to Israel? Much the same could be said about American policy toward South Africa. Clearly the turn from constructive engagement to the application of sanctions reflected the political potency of black America's outrage at apartheid. Similarly U.S. policy toward the Greco-Turkish quarrel over Cyprus has been influenced by the fact that Americans of Greek descent, though not a particularly large ethnic bloc, are more numerous than Turkish-Americans. In each of these examples, advocates of Realpolitik have pointed with dismay to the costs of U.S. policy. The Arabs have oil and numbers, they say, South Africa has vital minerals and command of the cape, and Turkey controls the Dardanelles. But whatever its merit, such counsel has fallen on ears deafened by the realities of domestic politics.

The role of ethnic groups is only one manifestation of the influence of domestic politics on foreign policy. Another is political competition within the government, both between the legislature and the executive and within the executive. Indeed the theory of bureaucratic politics enunciated in the 1970s by Graham Allison, Morton Halperin, and others argues that policy is largely the outcome of conflicts among government leaders motivated not by concern for national interests but for the interests of their respective government agencies.[30] These theories cannot bear the explanatory weight they were intended to carry, but they are useful in reminding us that government leaders involved in the formulation of foreign policy often have their attention turned inward rather than outward. Thus during the Reagan years Secretary of Defense Caspar Weinberger seemed entranced by the legacy of the Vietnam War, when America made the military the scapegoat for its own change of heart. Weinberger was determined that under his authority American fighting men would not go into action without firm public support. This made him a determined opponent of the use of force in several situations in which other officials were recommending it—in Lebanon and against terrorists in the Middle East and Central America. Because of the post he occupied, his views often prevailed. But sometimes he appeared more sensitive to the interests of the military than those of the country.

The Impact of Ideas and Ideals. Besides national self-interest, another force that helps to shape American foreign policy is the force of ideas and ideals. To return to an earlier example, not only Jews support a strong pro-Israel policy; not only blacks support strong action against apartheid. Other Americans embrace such causes simply because they believe them to be right. Even when they present their case in terms of American interests—who advancing a foreign policy position will acknowledge it inconsonant with the national interest?—the true motivation is often a sense of justice. Some people argue that America's interests require strong opposition to apartheid because white rule is doomed in South Africa and because the attitudes toward America of the blacks who will take power will be determined by America's record on apartheid. This may or may not be true, but the very people who put forward this argument are themselves motivated by something else: a feeling of revulsion toward apartheid.

The issue of apartheid brings moral considerations into bold relief, but it is certainly not the only issue on which a sense of right and wrong influences American policy. On Middle East issues many Americans support Israel simply because they believe that its democratic ways are more meritorious than the dictatorial practices of its Arab antagonists or because Israel has demonstrated a greater willingness to accept a peaceful solution. The fierce dispute of recent years over U.S. policy toward Central America has been argued in terms of America's interests but also in terms of right and wrong: one side says that America should not throw its weight around with small countries; the other, that it should not leave the people of Nicaragua to the mercies of Communist rule.

It is often no easy matter to separate ideas from interests as determinants of policy. Advocates of a given policy often believe that the policy is both just and good for their own country. This is usually the case when states pursue what Arnold Wolfers called "milieu goals" as distinct from "possession goals." The latter refers to rewards that the state seeks for itself; the former to "the shape of the environment in which the nation operates."[31] The United States, for example, has included the promotion of international law and world order among its foreign policy priorities. The main goal of the United States in the resolution of World War I was the creation of the League of Nations, and its main goal in World War II (beyond sheer victory) was the creation of the United Nations. In each case the United States intended that the envisioned structure of world order would serve its own security needs, but it was also strongly motivated by an idealistic sense of how the world ought to govern itself. Without such an idealistic component, American leaders could scarcely have believed that an international organization was the logical key to safeguarding America's security.

The impact of ideas and ideals, as distinct from interests, as determinants of policy can be especially vivid in the case of states that are motivated by ideology. Many commentators have pointed to the continuities between czarist and Soviet foreign policy. Some have pointed out that even the sponsorship by the Kremlin of foreign Communist parties can find analogy in sponsorship by czarist governments of Pan-Slavic and other politically motivated fifth column groups abroad. But these analogies can be stretched only so far. What Russian-oriented party ever contested for power in Italy? What czarist government ever tried to dominate Cuba? (For that matter, what Cuban government ever sought to throw its weight around in Africa?) Ideology may be used as a mere instrument of national imperial interests, but ideology can also give imperialism a scope that mere national interest never would have conceived.

What Is "Interest"? In sum a variety of factors besides interest help to shape foreign policy. But this is not the only flaw in the realist argument. For even to the extent that realists are right in asserting that interests determine policy, they only beg the question of what interest is. Each state has an interest in defending itself from attack. By obvious extension each has an interest in avoiding a preponderance of antagonistic power being amassed on its borders. And by slightly further extension, topography, economics, and history may give a state an enduring interest in certain pieces of geography. Thus Russia, whether ruled by czars or commissars, craves a warm water port and therefore covets the Dardanelles. Moreover Russia, both under czars and commissars, has been a self-aggrandizing power pushing outward to subdue or despoil others.

Such continuities, say the realists, show that states behave not as they will but as they must, driven by immutable laws. But for every continuity there is a discontinuity, and the realists cannot account for these. In the 1960s America intervened heavily in Vietnam; in the 1970s it withdrew from Vietnam. From George Washington through Franklin Roosevelt, America remained aloof from European affairs; since World War II it has maintained permanent military deployments in Europe. In the nineteenth century Britain built the world's greatest empire; in the twentieth century Britain withdrew from empire. In the 1930s Japan became a paragon of militarism and conquered much of the Pacific; since regaining its independence from the occupation in 1952, Japan has refused to rearm and remains the world's only constitutionally pacifist state.

Under the rule of Anastasio Somoza Nicaragua sought to make itself America's most loyal ally; under the Sandinistas Nicaragua made itself the bastion of anti-Americanism on the American mainland. Under Gamal Abdel Nasser Egypt sought to lead a pan-Arab revolution whose first target was the state of Israel; under Anwar Sadat Egypt turned its back on the rest of the Arab world to make peace with Israel. Under Haile Selassie Ethiopia allied with the West; under Mengistu Haile Mariam it allies with the East. In the early 1950s China allied with the Soviet Union against the United States; in the 1970s China allied with the United States against the Soviet Union. Even the USSR, whose continuities of policy are so integral to the realist catechism, withdrew from Afghanistan under Mikhail Gorbachev, after invading it under Leonid Brezhnev, and in 1989 disgorged its East European empire, the same empire whose conquest and defense had been the centerpiece of Soviet policy for the preceding forty years.

The statesmen who formulated each of the acts and policies mentioned here—and one could go on with this list ad infinitum—believed they were acting in their country's interests. To different leaders at different times, however, the national interest seems to demand different things. (Indeed this may be said of different leaders at the same time, or even of the same leader at different times.) The reason is not hard to fathom. For most states, defense against the threat of imminent attack occupies only a small part of the total energy devoted to foreign affairs. A greater share goes to enhancing security for the longer term. But the exact form and direction of future dangers can be foreseen only imperfectly.

In that sense international politics is something like chess, with statesmen constantly seeking to gauge the effect of the loss of a pawn here, the movement of a rook there. The problem is that in chess the number of permutations is virtually infinite, and so is the number of possible strategies. This is all the more true in international politics, which has more pieces than a chess game, a board that is unbounded, and no fixed rules governing how each piece may move. Each statesman has an infinite choice of moves and a vast menu of strategies for advancing a nation's interests. Therefore to discover a law of politics saying that states will behave according to their interests is to discover almost nothing about how any state will actually behave.

This indeterminate character of the national interest was inadvertently acknowledged by Morgenthau: "The relation of Asia to our national interests has never been obvious or clearly defined.... Yet [in] our Asiatic policy since McKinley, one can detect a consistency that reflects, however vaguely, the permanent interest of the United States in Asia."[32] This suggests that American interests can be discovered through study of America's behavior. But the logic seems circular. Morgenthau's main thesis is that America and other states behave according to their interests. To test this thesis, their interests must be known. And how can these be discovered? Why, by seeing how the states behave.

The Critique of Idealism

So much for the realist tenet that states behave simply as they must. What about the contrary realist argument (more along the lines of Kennan's analysis than Morgenthau's) acknowledging that states are free to choose their own behavior but holding that American policy has suffered from excesses of idealism when it ought to have grounded itself in the firm soil of interest? Plentiful evidence exists to buttress this line of argument. In the hopes it invested in the League of Nations and the United Nations and in the outlawry of war and arms control, U.S. policy has indeed exhibited naiveté. But these visionary schemes were all excesses of pacifist idealism, not of democratic idealism. They were designed to keep the world's peace, not to make the world democratic.[33] It is harder to find examples where an excess of democratic idealism led America astray.

To be sure, Americans have been naive as well about the democratic prospect, such as in the casual assumption after World War II that newly independent states of the third world would naturally evolve to democracy. But this has had no consequences for the United States more severe than disappointment. Are there instances in which democratic idealism has actually harmed us?

The prime exhibit in the realists' indictment of idealism is Woodrow Wilson's handling of peacemaking after World War I. Wilson's approach embodied both pacifist idealism and democratic idealism. The former expressed itself in his quest for a peace without victory (or at least a peace in which the victors did not aggrandize themselves and the vanquished were not subjugated) and his insistence on the creation of the League of Nations. His democratic idealism expressed itself in the principle of national self-determination, which he championed. The peace of Versailles was indeed flawed, lasting only twenty years before giving way to a conflagration still more terrible than the one it had brought to conclusion. And Wilson's performance as a peacemaker no doubt deserves criticism. But on what score? It is far from obvious that those elements of the peace that were motivated by democratic idealism were the harmful ones.

It is easy to imagine scenarios in which a different Versailles Treaty might have yielded a more secure peace and ended less tragically: had the terms given to Germany been more generous, or conversely had they been more Carthaginian; had the league not been created and more attention paid instead to ensuring a balance of power; or had Wilson not failed to secure U.S. entry into the league. But in what scenario would the peace have endured had it only been shorn of the principle of self-determination? To be sure, the story of the various republics of Central and Eastern Europe born at Versailles is a sorry one. Most soon lapsed into dictatorship of one kind or another, and their instability contributed to the instability of Europe.

But what should have been done with Poland or with the nations that had constituted Austria-Hungary? The empire could not have been put back together. Its advanced decrepitude had precipitated the war. If not given independence, to whom should these nations have been subjected, and how would this have made Europe more stable or the peace more secure? World War II may have broken out in Central Europe, but Central Europe's instabilities were not its cause. Its cause was German aggression and allied appeasement, an appeasement whose main ingredients were U.S. isolationism, British pacifism, and French realism.

Another instance of America's being led astray by democratic idealism may have been President Franklin Roosevelt's obsession during World War II with anticolonialism. It seemed to blind him to the difference between America's alliance with Britain and its alliance with the Soviet Union. Whether Roosevelt's feckless diplomacy at Yalta was an essential element in Soviet subjugation of Eastern Europe may be arguable, but his propensity to treat Joseph Stalin as if he were as true a friend as Winston Churchill was inexcusable. This error might as well be charged to an insufficiency of democratic idealism, however, as to an excess. Surely the main fault lay not in opposing British colonialism but in averting his gaze from the bestial antidemocracy of Stalinism.

Conversely America's democratic idealism, expressing itself in a form that many found excessive, yielded the proudest fruits of peacemaking after World War II: the transformation of Japan and West Germany. That Japan and Germany would have to be democratized to preserve the peace is a characteristically American notion. To many it seemed quixotic to believe that such a transformation was possible. Now, however, democracy has sunk deep roots in those countries, and their prosperity and domestic stability are keys to the enduring peace of Asia and Europe.

The realist critique of idealism fails to distinguish between pacifist idealism and democratic idealism. It inveighs against the latter but has brought telling evidence only against the former. To argue against one form of idealism and not against the other, as I do, may seem counterintuitive, but the two are not analogous. Pacifism is inherently self-defeating. Those who disarm for love of peace are likely to invite war. This may be a tragic comment on human nature, but history has confirmed it many times over, most vividly in this century when the policy of appeasement precipitated the very war it was intended to forestall. Conversely it is not at all rare for peace to be preserved by arms. The peace of Europe has endured longer since World War II than after any other war in centuries, largely as a result of the advent of terrifying nuclear weapons. This evokes the ancient adage, "If you want peace, prepare for war."

No comparable irony exists with respect to democracy. There is no adage, "If you want democracy, install dictatorship." Only in rare and debatable cases can it be said that democracy has been furthered by undemocratic actions (for example, arguably by the broad powers arrogated by Abraham Lincoln during the Civil War). The quest for democracy has often suffered defeat or failure, but it contains no inherent self-defeating mechanism like that of pacifism.

Another realist line of criticism of democratic idealism focuses on the way democracies, especially the United States, behave in war. Walter Lippmann and Robert Osgood each suggest that the United States was disingenuous in proclaiming that its entry into World War I was motivated by a desire to make the world safe for democracy. The true motive was to prevent Germany from upsetting the balance of power, a goal that might better have been achieved by entering the fray much earlier.[34] George Kennan criticized America for fighting "to the bitter end" in World War I and voiced his unease with the demand for unconditional surrender in World War II.[35]

The essence of this critique is that democracies are too much ruled by passion. They are reluctant to fight even when their interests clearly require it unless they have been angered, and once angered they are reluctant to make peace until they have exacted revenge. The second half of this critique is simply false. Yes, America entered each world war in anger, but each time it was the most benevolent of victors. Far from seeking vengeance, it labored to deflect the demands for vengeance on the part of its allies, especially its undemocratic ones. The criticism that democracies are reluctant to fight without passion is true, but surely it is not an unmixed evil. America's one great experiment in fighting a war without passion was Vietnam. President Lyndon Johnson conscientiously eschewed stirring passions or putting the nation on a war footing. America's objective was strictly limited: safeguard the independence of South Vietnam; do not threaten North Vietnam. The goal of combat was negotiation, and force was employed merely as a tool of diplomacy. The results were disastrous.

The Geography of Interest

The realists, however, insist that the Vietnam War serves only to prove their point. A realist knows from sheer geography, they say, that Vietnam is not vital to America's interests, as Kennan and Morgenthau argued at the time. But Henry Kissinger, another prominent realist, knew no such thing. This illustrates a critical weakness in the argument of the realists: their failure to explain convincingly the boundaries of America's genuine interests or even to agree on this among themselves. To Morgenthau, for example, "the Monroe Doctrine and the policies implementing it express that permanent national interest of the United States in the Western Hemisphere."[36] But Arthur Schlesinger, Jr., who sometimes dons the mantle of realism, denounced U.S. intervention in Central America as "imitating the Soviet model" and derided "Reagan's sneak attack . . . on Grenada."[37]

By logic, realists ought to have been much more ready to aid the Nicaraguan contras and perhaps Jonas Savimbi's UNITA in Angola (because of the strategic value of South Africa's mineral resources) than the Afghan mujahedin or the Cambodian guerrillas. Cambodia and Afghanistan are distant from the United States and empty of important resources. But despite the rhetorical vogue of realism, almost nobody in public life took such a stand.[38] On the contrary, among members of Congress and commentators the causes of the Afghan and Cambodian resistance were far more popular than those of their Nicaraguan and Angolan counterparts.

The critical flaw in the realist argument for a fixed geographic definition to America's interests is that other states do not behave according to realist maxims. Morgenthau says that "the traditional methods of diplomacy," which he exalts, "presuppose a political world peopled by approximate equals, in strength and in virtue."[39] But our world is emphatically not peopled by equals in either sense. The superpowers dwarf the power of the other industrialized nations, which in turn dwarf that of most developing states. Although all states may harken to their own interests, most democracies and some other states balance concern for their own interests with respect for those of others or for principles of world order and law. Less virtuous states pursue their own interests without such qualifications or scruples. When Arthur Schlesinger, Jr., tells us that "national interest, consistently construed, is a self-limiting motive," he only underscores the gap between realist theory and the actual behavior of states.[40]

To put it another way, the term "interest" as used by the realists obscures a critical distinction between self-defense and self-aggrandizement. All states look out for themselves, but some have limited appetites while others have unlimited ones; some have reasonable goals, others unreasonable ones. Between these two postures is an enormous difference. Granting that the traditional diplomacy of national interest may have been rendered obsolete in this century, Schlesinger ironically found that the most undermining change has been the "democratization of foreign policy."[41] Democracies do have trouble summoning the cold cynicism required for traditional diplomacy, but the far more fateful change has been the rise of aggressive, messianic ideologies. Although Britain was democratic before World War II, Prime Minister Neville Chamberlain still was able to pursue a cold, cynical policy aiming to balance what he took to be the interests of Germany with those of England and France. The problem was that German policy was driven by nothing like the traditional motives that Chamberlain imagined but by an unquenchable thirst for empire and by other impulses originating in the murkiest recesses of the human psyche.

The question that realists fail to address is what constitutes a realistic policy for the United States in a world in which many polities refuse to accept limited goals or the methods of traditional diplomacy. From the 1930s through the 1980s, international politics was driven by powers in thrall to messianic ideologies. To be realistic is always a virtue, but the self-proclaimed realists are slaves to a theoretical model that bears little resemblance to the real world.

The Illogic of Cultural Relativism

Finally, the realists are left with the argument that it is wrong to foist our ways—that is, democracy—on others. In saying this the realists suddenly are arguing in moral terms. Their point, however, entails a logical fallacy. The reason it is wrong to impose something on others, presumably, is because it violates their will. But, absent democracy, how can their will be known? Moreover, why care about violating people's will unless one begins with the democratic premise that popular will ought to be sovereign?

This argument implies that people prefer to be ruled by an indigenous dictator than to be liberated through foreign influence. The realists will have a hard time explaining this to the people of Panama who danced in the streets when U.S. invaders ousted dictator Manuel Noriega or to Aleksandr Solzhenitsyn, who wrote:

> On our crowded planet there are no longer any "internal affairs." The Communist leaders say, "Don't interfere in our internal affairs. Let us strangle our citizens in peace and quiet." But I tell you: Interfere more and more. Interfere as much as you can. We beg you to come and interfere.[42]

The examples of Panama, Japan, Germany, the Dominican Republic, and Grenada notwithstanding, to foist democracy on others does not ordinarily mean to impose it by force. Nor does it mean to seek carbon copies of American institutions. No serious advocate of democracy believes that each country ought to have a president rather than a prime minister, a two-house legislature rather than a single chamber, a two-party system rather than multiple parties, a triangular separation of powers rather than a bifurcation, quadrennial elections rather than some other schedule, federalism rather than a unitary system, or any of the other peculiarities of the American way. Belief in democracy as a universal value boils down to the conviction that adult human beings ought not to be governed without their consent. (And since universal consent on the choice of governors is impossible, its closest approximation is a system in which everyone may participate in the choice, even though not everyone's preferences are satisfied.)

This belief, it must be confessed, rests ultimately on premises about human dignity that are unprovable axioms. That human beings prefer not to be subjected arbitrarily to the rule of others is demonstrable, but that this preference ought to be honored is a value, not a truth. It is no more true than the contrary proposition that people ought to be ruled by the vanguard party or by the corporate state or by the religious authorities. But to argue, as Kennan and Morgenthau and Schlesinger do, against democratic universalism on the grounds of cultural relativism is self-contradictory. It is logically unassailable (although repugnant) to argue against democracy on the ground that Lenin or Mussolini or Khomeini ought to rule. It is, however, incoherent to argue against democracy on the ground that people somewhere do not want it, for that argument is an appeal to democratic criteria. When realists resort to such pseudomoralism, they reveal only a lack of confidence in the essence of their own position, which is the rejection of morality in foreign policy.

In drawing a sharp distinction between the morality of individuals and that of states, the realists speak as if morality and self-interest were incompatible. But what form of personal ethics demands complete self-abnegation? Even Christianity, whose messiah is the apotheosis of self-sacrifice, does not enjoin its faithful to forgo self-preservation. It and every other major creed and ethical system recognizes self-preservation as a legitimate goal of the individual. Idealism or morality insists only that self-interest is bounded, that it is not infinite. Legitimate self-regard must be balanced against sensitivity to the well-being of others and must be pursued through honorable means. Why should the same not hold for the nation? Why can't national policy attempt to combine respect for the requisites of self-preservation with adherence to honorable means and with respect for the legitimate claims of other nations?

Perhaps the mixture between regard for self and for others differs somewhat in countries and individuals, but this is a difference of degree, not of kind. National policy may require more caution than some individuals choose in governing their own lives. The realists would be on far stronger ground if they asserted only that foreign policy must be guided by an inherent conservatism, that we must keep our powder dry and be mindful of our safety.

Admittedly there is no virtue in a failed idealism, an idealism so pure it defeats its own aims. That is the error in pacifism and the reason most of the nostrums of pacifist idealism (arms control, international law, international organization) warrant skepticism. But there is nothing wrong in principle with these ideas. Were all the nations of the world democracies or even liberal constitutional regimes, these might not be nostrums at all but sound bases of world order. Indeed, if the collapse of communism does herald the end of history in the sense suggested by Francis Fukuyama, namely, the final triumph of liberal democracy, then the time for pacifist idealism may be drawing near.[43]

Neither is there virtue in a self-defeating form of democratic idealism. There are countries where it is far easier to wish for democracy than to know how to achieve it. In the 1970s Congress and the Carter administration sometimes undermined undemocratic regimes because of their human rights violations, without regard to what kind of regime might follow, and sometimes the results were disastrous.[44] But that does not prove, as the realists would have it, that idealism has no place in foreign policy. It shows only that at times one must choose lesser evils, that idealism must express itself with due respect for reality, and that policies must be judged by their consequences, not by the nobility of intentions. This is not much different for nations than for individuals. An individual who obeys a code of behavior so strict as to be self-defeating is less likely to be thought admirable than obsessive. One who asks to be judged by the intentions behind acts rather than their effects is less likely to be thought high-minded than irresponsible.

The radical distinction that realists draw between the morality of individuals and that of states fails on a second ground as well. If individuals are obliged to abide by certain moral rules, can they be exempted from those rules when they act collectively with others in the name of the nation?

Those who argue yes sometimes point out that although we exalt the sixth commandment, we send soldiers off to kill. But the contradiction here is not explained by the contrast between personal behavior and national behavior. The contradiction is between killing and killing in self-defense. Most people condone killing done in defense of one's own life. In condoning military acts we assume, or we ought to, that they are conducted in self-defense. For a nation to wage aggressive war, to engage in acts of killing for self-aggrandizement rather than self-defense is no more justifiable than homicide.

Granted, self-defense for the nation is defined more broadly than for the private individual. We condone an individual's killing in self-defense only in dire emergencies. Anyone receiving a threatening telephone call is expected to call the police, not to kill the caller. A nation cannot call the police. Thus its legitimate acts of self-defense may include acts of deterrence or collective self-defense. In acknowledging the need for a broader definition of self-defense in the case of the nation, we are acknowledging that the universe in which it acts is not precisely analogous to the universe in which the individual acts. We can acknowledge too that some acts of war may be borderline between aggression and self-defense. But that does not amount to a total inability to distinguish between self-defense and aggression, or more broadly between right and wrong.

However difficult the judgments may be on occasion, some nexus must remain between the moral principles that govern an individual acting in a personal capacity and those that govern one acting as part of a nation. That is the judgment that the civilized world rendered in the Nuremberg trials. It is one we would reverse at our peril.

4
Neorealism

Although various critics have exposed the logical inconsistencies and descriptive shortcomings of classical realist theory as exemplified by Hans Morgenthau's work, realism has enjoyed something of a rebirth in the 1980s. Indeed Stanley Hoffmann put it: "In the mainstream we are all 'realists' now."[1] This is in part a consequence of America's post-Vietnam search for a new basis for its foreign policy and in part a reaction against the activism and highly ideological content of the foreign policy of the Reagan administration.

Academic Neorealism

In the academic discipline of international relations, Kenneth Waltz has advanced a neorealist theory.[2] In essence it maintains that international politics is best explained in terms of the dynamics of the international system rather than in terms of the inner politics or motivations of individual states. Such a theory must contain at least a modicum of truth. Whatever the internal decision-making processes of each state, its external behavior is influenced by its power and situation relative to the rest of the states of the world. But such behavior is a product of internal processes as well. Why else would different leaders or parties within the same country advocate different foreign policies? The distinction between analyzing international relations in terms of the inner workings of states or in terms of their external situation, as David Singer pointed out years ago, is largely a matter of the tastes and interests of the researcher.[3]

Liberal Neorealism

Tom J. Farer. Whatever the scholarly merit of Waltz's theory, it is of limited importance to the debates between conflicting prescriptions for U.S. policy. After all, if his argument is true—that external circumstances compel states to behave as they do—our policy debates have a lot less consequence than we imagine. A wide range of other commentators, however, have adopted the neorealist label in advocating this or that approach to U.S. foreign policy. On the more liberal side of the political spectrum, Tom J. Farer has called for a new diplomacy of neorealism to replace containment as the basis of American strategy:

> The new diplomacy counsels against reflexive opposition to beneficiaries of Soviet assistance, whether they be established governments or rebels, except in those few countries where domestic violence threatens imperative U.S. interests. Some leftist governments may arise. But the experience of the last twenty years demonstrates that they will pursue their own interests and eventually accommodate with the West, which normally has far more to offer.[4]

Accordingly, Farer advocates "an open, principled rejection of the premises of global containment."

The essence of Farer's realism is to place the United States on the side of change by embracing or accommodating leftist movements that we traditionally have been inclined to oppose. This, he argues, is a realistic thing to do. But any such shift in the thrust of American policy must be justified in terms of the substantive virtues of the leftist movements with which Farer would have America align, not in terms of realism. By using the label "realist," Farer means to suggest that it is futile for Americans to resist the tide of change. But the kind of change to which Farer refers does not just happen; it is brought about by leftist movements. Why is it any less realistic for America to resist them than for them to resist America? And would Farer himself continue to counsel realistic accommodation to change if once again the winds of change began to blow in the direction of fascism as they did in the 1920s and 1930s?

Leon Wieseltier. Another liberal thinker who has raised the banner of realism is Leon Wieseltier. "If American foreign policy is to recover from the moral and intellectual intoxications of the Reagan years, it must be recalled to realism," says Wieseltier.[5] Referring to the Iran-contra scandal, Wieseltier declared, "The clandestine relationship with Iran, and its sordid link to Central America, must be considered against the climate of unreality in which President Reagan's foreign policy has been conceived for years."[6]

Wieseltier accused Ronald Reagan of adhering to idealism, which he defined as "the belief that the world is informed by ideals; that they are inscribed in the world, or can be painlessly inscribed in it; that the world is more perfect, or more perfectible, than in fact it is."[7] This definition of "idealism" rather loads the dice in favor of "realism" if the two are taken as antithetical, and Wieseltier loaded them still further by implying that the alternative to realism is not merely idealism but also an aversion to reality. Thus he called for "cleaving as closely to facts and interests as to values,"[8] as if a live issue in our foreign policy debates is how much weight to attach to facts.

Ironically, however, the decision to sell arms to the regime of Ayatollah Khomeini was the Reagan administration's quintessential act of realism in foreign policy. That decision was motivated in part by the wish to free hostages. But it was also motivated in part by Iran's geopolitical importance, and it was justified in these terms both to the public and to the councils of the administration itself. Iran's oil and its strategic location between the Soviet Union and the Persian Gulf were deemed more important than the principle of not yielding to terrorist blackmail. This was the ultimate victory of interests, or "facts," over values.

Wieseltier went on to offer four other examples of errant Reagan policies: failing to call in the Polish debt, permitting overly free trade with the Soviet bloc, and cosseting the incumbent governments of Chile and South Africa. A realist policy would do better, he said, as if each of these was not a realist policy. In each case, Wieseltier would have accepted short-term risks to U.S. interests—risks to the stability of pro-Western governments or to the prosperity of American enterprises—for the sake of the values of democratizing Chile and South Africa or liberalizing the Soviet bloc. It is Wieseltier who is the idealist.

He would presumably argue that such democratization and liberalization are not mere ideals but serve the long-term interests of the United States. And they do—if efforts to achieve them do not backfire. Idealists believe that their policies will ultimately best protect the nation's interests, just as realists believe, as Wieseltier forcefully asserted, that theirs will ultimately best protect its values. But the operational difference between the two is largely over the choice between short-term benefits and larger, but less certain, long-term ones, between a bird in the hand and two in the bush. Wieseltier might have been right in what he would have done about the Polish debt, East-West trade, Chile, and South Africa, but the changes he championed are no realist alternative. They point in fact in the opposite direction.

Arthur Schlesinger. Another liberal who has used realism as a club with which to beat Reagan is Arthur Schlesinger, Jr. Denouncing Reagan's policy as a "unilateralist, militarized, ideological, messianic foreign policy,"[9] Schlesinger advocates instead a "prudent balance-of-power foreign policy confined to vital interests of the United States" and guided by "realism, sobriety, and responsibility."[10] But Schlesinger's is a strange kind of realism. Looking toward the 1988 presidential election, Schlesinger sought a Democratic president who would "keep . . . his faith with

Woodrow Wilson and Franklin D. Roosevelt" and who "will have, I hope, a bold and generous vision of the world's possibilities when humanity begins to devote its energy and ingenuity to cooperation rather than to conflict. In this spirit the twenty-first century may yet see the realization of F.D.R.'s world of the Four Freedoms."[11] This is a strange realism.

Schlesinger's realism grew stranger still. Although chary of morality in foreign policy, Schlesinger says, "There are certain international questions with so clear-cut a moral character that moral judgment must guide political judgment—slavery, genocide, torture, atrocities, racial justice, human rights."[12] To this list he adds nuclear war. Genocide and nuclear war are indeed very extreme, one might say transcendent, issues, but what is Schlesinger's point? Are there situations in which political judgment would lead one to favor genocide or nuclear war but must be overruled by moral judgment? Such scenarios hardly leap to mind, unless Schlesinger means to associate himself with those Catholic bishops who argue that because nuclear war is immoral, the strategy of deterrence through the threat of nuclear retaliation, albeit pragmatically sound, is impermissible.

The inclusion of racial justice and human rights on Schlesinger's list adds to the confusion. These important values are at issue in many major international situations: South Africa, Central America, the Middle East, Northern Africa, to name a few. Does Schlesinger mean that moral judgment should guide policy toward each of these situations? I believe it should, but being an idealist, I believe that moral judgments should underlie all political judgments. This is precisely the view that Schlesinger means to refute in unfurling the banner of realism. But he seemed to want to have it both ways.

The importance that Schlesinger would give to moral considerations in guiding foreign policy would distress Hans Morgenthau and George Kennan. But even more than morality in foreign policy, these traditional realists scorned the quest for legality in foreign policy. In contrast, Schlesinger's brand of realism would "end the unlovely spectacle of the United States careening around the world as a law unto itself and restore the historical American conviction that a world of law is in the national interest."[13]

Most Americans would agree that "a world of law is in the national interest," but this only begs the question. We have no such world and no immediate prospect of one. We have instead a body of international law with no means of enforcement. The real question is whether America should bind itself to observe this law even while others, including its adversaries, do not. Schlesinger's implicit answer is that it should, for he criticized Reagan policies for violating international law and he argued

41

that "morality in foreign policy . . . consists not in preaching one's values to lesser breeds but in living up to them oneself."[14] Since he assuredly counts law among our values, he apparently wants us to obey regardless of what others do.

Yet if the goal is a world of law, the question is how to achieve it. This would be true even if devotion to the law stemmed from pure idealism. It is all the more true if the reason for devotion lies, as Schlesinger states it, not in ideals but in national interest. It is surely not self-evident that unilateral obedience to the law by the United States will make the world more lawful. I, for one, would argue that America will contribute less to advancing lawfulness by setting a fine example than by wielding its power to stymie the designs of the most lawless states. Schlesinger may disagree. But he was so absorbed in the music of his anti-Reagan polemic, that he did not even stop to address the question.

Alan Tonelson and Christopher Layne. The reason that such bright men as Farer, Wieseltier, and Schlesinger have made such a muddle is that they are not realists. Realism for them is a banner of convenience disguising a project whose true purpose seems to be nothing more than partisanship. Others, however, have realist convictions that go much deeper than those of these liberals. Two of the more articulate neorealists are Alan Tonelson, former associate editor of *Foreign Policy*, and Christopher Layne, both associated with the Cato Institute.

Both men seek, in Tonelson's phrase, "an interest-based policy,"[15] and both agree that it is to be found in "a realistic policy of selective containment,"[16] as Layne puts it. Such a policy, he says, "aims only at containing the expansion of Soviet political influence and military power in regions truly vital to U.S. national security."[17] It offers, says Tonelson, "a concrete idea of national interest—a finite set of intrinsically important goals."[18]

But what is that set? Where are those regions? Tonelson says, "The inability to find some common ground concerning those regions whose security affects America's very survival and those that do not would reveal a political system utterly incapable of encouraging foreign-policy coherence at all."[19]

If this is true for a political system, then it is perforce all the more true for a political faction such as the neorealists. Tonelson and Layne themselves are hopelessly at odds over the crucial regions. Tonelson's list includes Canada and Mexico, Western Europe, Japan, and South Korea, and, in a more qualified way, the Persian Gulf and Egypt. As for the rest of the world, he says, "There is hardly any security justification at present for extensive U.S. military or political engagement in the affairs of sub-Saharan Africa, the South and southeastern Pacific, or Latin America."[20]

Layne, however, reached different conclusions. He agrees with Tonelson on the least important issues like Canada and Mexico and on the negative side about sub-Saharan Africa and the Pacific. But he disagrees diametrically on the most important issues. While Tonelson sees Western Europe and Japan as vital to the United States, Layne advocates withdrawal from these areas, or, as he put it, ironically, Marshall Plan II: "a firm timetable for a phased withdrawal—perhaps over 10 years—coupled with an invitation to Western Europe and Japan to formulate their own postalliance defense plans."[21] In contrast to Tonelson's concern about South Korea and Egypt, Layne says: "The United States has few tangible interests in the Third World that compel military or even extensive political involvement. There is no Third World region or country whose loss would decisively tip the superpower balance against America. . . ."[22] What about the Persian Gulf? Its oil "is vital only to Western Europe and Japan," and therefore, says Layne with impeccable logic, its security will become their problem, not ours, under his Marshall Plan II.[23]

Not only does Layne disagree about most of the areas that Tonelson considered vital to American security, he also disagrees about the most important area that Tonelson cited as not worth American involvement—Central America. This, he says, is a special case because "the United States has a strong interest in maintaining a favorable political and strategic environment in neighboring areas."[24] Following this to its logical consequence, he concluded:

> U.S. policy must combine force and diplomacy to compel changes in Nicaraguan policies that threaten regional security. Thus the United States must support the anti-Sandinista *contra* forces and exert other forms of military and economic pressure, because, otherwise, the Sandinistas have little incentive to accommodate U.S. wishes.[25]

How can we rest American strategy on the defense of only a few selected vital areas when the people who urge this strategy are themselves so sharply divided about which those areas are? Tonelson and Layne's problem goes to the heart of the realist fallacy. It seeks in geography answers that can be found only in the human mind. Regions are not inherently important or unimportant to us. Their importance varies with time, technology, and myriad man-made variables. Granted, the degree of proximity of a region helps to determine its importance to us, but so do many other factors. The tactical significance of any area also varies according to its wealth, its natural resources in relation to contemporary science and technology, the nature of its government and political system, the configuration of power and alliances in the world, the identity of our allies and our enemies, and the nature of their goals and ours.

All of these factors are constantly changing. Technological change made petroleum important, and with it the Persian Gulf, and will probably render both unimportant during the coming century. South Korea wins inclusion on Tonelson's short list of vital places because it is "an important cog in the world economy,"[26] yet only a few decades ago it was among the poorest of nations. Canada is important to our security only in a potential sense: we would fight to prevent its falling under the domination of our enemies. This contingency is so unlikely, however, that we have long paid it little mind. Yet at one time Canada meant Britain, and Britain was our main adversary; then Canada was the most urgent focus of our day-to-day security concerns.

Tonelson and Layne might reply to this line of criticism by pointing out that their disagreements with each other are not unique to their camp. Adherents of other schools of thought about foreign policy, including democratic idealists, also disagree among themselves about particular countries or tactics or priorities. True enough, but the disagreement between Tonelson and Layne is more damaging to their underlying position. The real departure in the policy that they espouse lies not in the list of foreign commitments that they would endorse but in those they would jettison. Current U.S. policy recognizes some degree of commitment to each of the states that Tonelson regards as important to our security and each of those that Layne so regards, as well as others that neither of them list. Their prescription in short is withdrawal from existing involvements. What if we follow Tonelson's advice and turn our back on Latin America only to discover after it falls prey to forces hostile to us that Layne is right, that because of its proximity it affects us deeply? What if we follow Layne's advice and withdraw from Europe and Japan only to discover after they fall into hostile hands that Tonelson is right, that under those circumstances their economic and scientific power are deeply threatening to us? What do we do then? The policy that they urge is a gamble with the highest of stakes: world peace and our security. This kind of gamble can be justified only if we know we are making a safe bet. But just how far we are from any such certainty is underscored by the fact that Tonelson and Layne could not even agree on which bet to place.

In addition the idea of constructing a specific list of places whose security affects the United States raises the question of what affects the security of those places. Many Americans agree that Japan is important to our security, but most Japanese believe that South Korea is important to theirs. Mexico and the Persian Gulf are on most short lists of regions essential to America, but the security of these countries can hardly be separated from that of other countries in their regions. The Earth is a seamless web. Once the realists agree that America's well-being depends on the situation of certain distant countries they are foolish to believe that these can be sealed off from the fate of others.

The United States cannot as a practical matter commit itself to military action wherever its interests may be threatened. But neither can we make any part of the globe unimportant to us by fiat. Whether to resist hostile forces in any given instance and by what means are tactical questions that depend on the gravity of the threat, the costs of resisting, the prospects for success, the opportunity for compensatory gains, and other such considerations.

Conservative Neorealism

Robert W. Tucker. A group of conservative writers, gathered around the journal *National Interest,* merits inclusion under the rubric neorealists. In contrast to liberals of the Schlesinger-Wieseltier stripe who brandish the label realist while advocating policies that are not at all realist, this conservative group does not often use the label realist, but belongs to the realist tradition because of the arguments that it directs against the advocates of an ideologically animated foreign policy.

In the maiden issue of that journal, coeditor Robert W. Tucker laid out this argument for a foreign policy focused on interests rather than ideals:

> While freedom is the highest of political values, this does not make its universalization a proper interest of foreign policy in the sense that its pursuit justifies the sacrifice of blood and treasure. There are many things of value that are not the proper interests of foreign policy. Conservatives, despite their deep attachment to liberty, should be the first to recognize this.[27]

Irving Kristol. Although Tucker's sally was aimed at Charles Krauthammer, a reply could be read in another article in the same issue by the new magazine's publisher, Irving Kristol. Kristol argued that "the fundamental flaw of the academic-diplomatic vision of the twentieth century is its reluctance to admit that the basic conflict of our times—that between the USSR and the United States—is ideological."[28] From this he concluded that

> American foreign policy, hitherto reactive, is bound to become more activist. This activism, if it is to have popular support, will necessarily have a significant ideological di-

mension. Those who make American foreign policy will discover—may already be discovering—that any viable conception of the United States's "national interest" cannot help but be organically related to that public philosophy—ideology, if you wish—which is the basis of what we have come to call "the American way of life."[29]

Soon, however, Kristol reversed himself. In an article about the issue of human rights in foreign policy, Kristol went well beyond the familiar neoconservative critique of the double standards of Jimmy Carter and the Left-liberal human rights activists. He criticized the very notion of giving human rights a major place among the goals of American foreign policy. While reiterating that the American-Soviet contest is an "ideological conflict," Kristol argued that nonetheless

> it is both a simplification and a distortion to describe it as a conflict about "human rights." It is, rather, a conflict over the very *definition* of "human rights," and the point of this conflict is to determine who will have the *power* to define "human rights" for future generations. In that sense, the United States cannot evade the urgencies and the ambiguities of "power politics."[30]

Kristol seemed to say that although the U.S.-Soviet conflict is motivated by ideology, it can be waged not with ideological weapons but only with real ones. "Since the Soviet Union has its own (Marxist) conception of 'human rights,' about which it is brutally assertive and in no way apologetic," he continued, "it does seem quixotically futile to criticize it for not sharing our traditional-liberal political philosophy."[31] But as Kristol would in all likelihood now concede, in the few years since he penned these words, *glasnost* and *perestroika* have proved criticism of Soviet human rights abuses to be anything but quixotic. The Soviet system has been turned inside out by Mikhail Gorbachev, motivated in part, so he says, by his dissatisfaction with its lack of democracy.

Still Kristol scorns the idea of democratizing third world countries.[32] He also opposes giving them foreign aid. In addition long before *perestroika* he advocated jettisoning NATO and other alliances because our pusillanimous allies constantly restrained us from the bold actions befitting a superpower. For this, Charles Krauthammer labeled him a "right isolationist."[33] Kristol protested that his aim was not to withdraw from the world but to free America from encumbering alliances so that it might act more energetically. He calls this "global unilateralism."

Although Kristol is no doubt sincere in disavowing isolationism, his opposition to alliances taken together with his opposition to foreign aid and to attempts to encourage the growth of democracy gives weight to Krauthammer's charge. What exactly would constitute Kristol's globalism? Not fostering political systems similar to our own, not forming alliances, not giving aid—then what?

Patrick Buchanan. If isolationist implications can be discerned in Kristol's realism, they are unmistakable in the recent writings of Patrick Buchanan. Echoing the slogan of America's foremost pre–World War II isolationist organization, Buchanan took to the pages of *National Interest* with an essay titled "America First—and Second, and Third." Like the America-firsters of yore, Buchanan called for America to withdraw from Europe and Asia but to maintain an interest in the security of Latin America. "The Monroe Doctrine should be made again the cornerstone of U.S. foreign policy," he said.[34]

Buchanan reserves his sharpest venom for the "democratists"— those who want to promote democracy abroad. He accuses them of substituting "a false god for the real, a love of process for a love of country." There is something faintly malodorous in Buchanan's taxing his opponents with insufficient love of country. But there is a failure of logic here too. Do Americans consider democracy merely a process? Can some essence of America be separated from the American system? The Yugoslav dissident and American immigrant Mihajlo Mihajlov demonstrated a surer grasp of Americanism than the table-thumping patriot Buchanan when he wrote:

> The United States is not a state like France, China, England, etc., and it would be a great tragedy if someday the United States became such a state. What is the difference? First of all, the United States is not a national state, but a multinational state. Second, the United States was founded by people who valued individual freedom more highly than their own country.
>
> And so the United States is primarily a state of freedom. And this is what is most important. Whole peoples from other countries can say, Our homeland is Germany, Russian, or whatever; only Americans can say, My homeland is freedom.[35]

Buchanan, seconded by the journal's executive editor Mary Eberstadt, labored to draw a distinction between freedom, or liberty, and democracy. Other conservatives dwell on this point as well, but it is rather easily answered. Freedom and democracy are not synonymous, and indeed there is even some tension between the two. Democracy means majority rule, and rule of any kind implies limits on freedom, limits that are bound to be felt all the more sharply by those who are not among the majority. But in every human society some rule is necessary. No anarchist utopia has ever existed. And much human experience teaches that the approach of anarchy brings not freedom but terror. The method of rule that limits freedom least is democracy because on any issue it satisfies the wishes of the majority, if not of everybody, and because the minority retains the possibility of getting its way by becoming the majority. Thus although democracy is not freedom, it is the method of government that maximizes freedom. The founding fathers understood this clearly when they wrote "to secure these rights, governments are instituted among men, deriving their just powers from the consent of the governed."

Buchanan can celebrate putting America first, but he has yet to explain how America would be better off for withdrawing from the world. In this century we tried isolationism for one sustained period, and it led us to Pearl Harbor. We then tried internationalism, and it led to our greatest triumph. The challenge Buchanan's position faces is to refute or counterbalance this argument.

Neopacifist Idealism

As the Communist threat recedes, the currents of realism and isolationism are sure to gather strength on the conservative side of the political spectrum. As realism and isolationism grow closer, it is possible that democratic idealism and pacifist idealism will do so too. If the twenty-first century does see the majority of countries, including all the most powerful, become democracies, then the world will be a very different place. Various ideas that have sprung from pacifist idealism and that now seem utopian, such as a true regime of international law or international organization, may then become realizable.

5

Is America in Decline?

During the waning years of the presidency of Ronald Reagan, a new school of political analysis muscled its way into the center of American debate—the school of decline. The "declinists," as these analysts were dubbed by Samuel Huntington,[1] peered beyond today's headlines to capture larger historical trends. They concluded that the dominant trend of the present era is the diminution of American power.

The declinists, says the *New York Times*, are "a small but growing cadre of intellectuals who are wielding considerable political influence. . . . Their books have sparked a rousing dialogue among professors and politicians that threatens to shake Reagan's America from a decade of rose-colored, Ike-revivalist torpor."[2] In rousing America, however, the declinists do not aim to sound a clarion call, but a warning. And the *New York Times* notwithstanding, it is not torpor from which they would rescue America but the illusion of omnipotence.

Recorded history can be read as a long saga of the rise and decline of various empires. America too is an empire, argue the declinists. And it too will decline. Indeed, they say, it is already in rapid descent. The declinists adduce a long ledger of statistics showing that America's share of global wealth, output, trade, and the like is much smaller today than it was in the years immediately after World War II. Whereas once America towered over the world economy like a colossus, today it has shrunk to a stature more like first among equals.

Because America's decline is part of the natural rhythm of history, most declinists argue that it is irreversible. The worst mistake, they say, would be to resist this trend, for resistance is futile. Nay, it would be worse than futile. To oppose, or merely to ignore, what history has ordained is to invite catastrophe. If America persists in acting as if it possesses vast power all the while the economic wellsprings of its power are drying up, its empire will come crashing down like a structure whose support beams have been eaten away. Conversely, if America recognizes and accepts the inevitable and pulls back from the ambitious exercise of global power, it may be able to adjust gracefully to its dotage as an imperium.

The declinists have not addressed directly the question of exporting democracy. But the implications of their arguments are clear. This is the time for America to come to terms with its finitude and to reduce its efforts to exert influence abroad, they say. If this is right, then surely it is folly to pursue an ambitious foreign policy that takes as its mission spurring on a worldwide democratic revolution. But is it right?

Varieties of Declinism

The declinists do not speak with one voice. Far the most celebrated of the declinists is historian Paul Kennedy, whose book *The Rise and Fall of Great Powers* enjoyed startling commercial and critical success. As Owen Harries put it:

> A historical study of nearly 700 pages, with eighty-three pages of notes, a thirty-eight-page bibliography, and dozens of tables and charts does not often enjoy a vogue. But . . . . [in] best-seller lists, op-ed pages, seminars, talk shows, little magazines, and dinner-table conversations it is evident that the decline of America is an idea whose time has come.[3]

In addition to Kennedy, those identified by the *New York Times* as the leading lights of the declinist school are the political scientist David Calleo, the economist Mancur Olson, and Walter Russell Mead, a young writer from Yale and Groton who serves as a consultant to New York Governor Mario Cuomo.

Olson is placed in this group on the strength of his book *The Rise and Decline of Nations*. His approach, however, is quite distinct from that of the others. Olson argues that decline is a natural concomitant of stability, which allows for the growth of "distributive coalitions." Distributive coalitions exercise collusive or political power to secure for themselves rewards larger than an unimpeded market would afford them. With each feather added to their own nests, these coalitions derogate from the total economic efficiency of their society. As these accretions of inefficiency multiply, economic growth grinds to a halt. Today America's competitors are younger nations or those with their slates wiped clean, so to speak, by war or revolution. Hence their distributive coalitions are fewer and less powerful, their markets less distorted.

In contrast to other declinist theories, the decline perceived by Olson is readily remediable. "The most obvious and far-reaching remedy," he says, is

> simply [to] repeal all special-interest legislation or regulation

and at the same time apply rigorous anti-trust laws to every type of cartel or collusion that used its power to obtain prices or wages above competitive levels. A society could in this way keep distributional coalitions from doing any substantial damage.[4]

Olson's theory is well outside the mainstream of declinism. While others locate the root of America's problems in its imperial appetite, Olson points his accusing finger at the Norris-LaGuardia Act. Whatever the validity of this, if Olson is right, America's decline or salvation depends exclusively on whether it pursues a more libertarian domestic policy. His theory contains no implications for foreign policy.

Kennedy, Calleo, and Mead, conversely, are directly concerned with foreign policy. According to Kennedy, "there is detectable a causal relationship between the shifts which have occurred over time in the general economic and productive balances and the position occupied by individual powers in the international system."[5] In other words military and political power is a product of economic strength, which in turn is prone to be undermined by military expenditures. The present implications are these:

> The United States . . . cannot avoid confronting the two great tests which challenge the *longevity* of every major power . . . : whether, in the military/strategical realm, it can preserve a reasonable balance between the nation's perceived defense requirements and the means it possesses to maintain those commitments; and whether . . . it can preserve the technological and economic bases of its power from relative erosion in the face of the ever-shifting patterns of global production. This test . . . will be the greater because it . . . is the inheritor of a vast array of strategical commitments which had been made decades earlier, when the nation's political, economic, and military capacity to influence world affairs seemed so much more assured. In consequence, the United States now runs the risk, so familiar to historians of the rise and fall of previous Great Powers, of what might roughly be called "imperial overstretch": that is to say, decision-makers in Washington must face the awkward and enduring fact that the sum total of the United States' global interests and obligations is nowadays far larger than the country's power to defend them all simultaneously.[6]

While Kennedy's critique of imperial overstretch seems to refer primarily to American activities in the third world, Calleo takes aim at America's continued deep involvement in Europe. He writes:

> In many respects, the global changes that exacerbate NATO's

> particular difficulties may be summarized in terms of one
> fundamental change: the decline of American power in rela-
> tion to the rest of the world. Militarily and economically, the
> United States has lost the ample edge it held at the end of the
> Second World War. . . . Logically, two broad courses suggest
> themselves: reaffirmation or devolution.[7]

Although he concedes that logically two choices exist, in practice Calleo
believes only one of these is viable: withdrawing from Europe (and East
Asia) and thereby "restoring American fiscal equilibrium through military savings."[8] In sum,

> to remain a viable world system in a pluralist age, liberal
> capitalism needs discipline and self-restraint from its leading
> power. . . . A reasonable case can be made that America's
> endemic economic disorder is today a more serious threat to
> the postwar international liberal order than is any plausible
> Soviet aggression. For whereas Soviet expansionism is rea-
> sonably contained, American fiscal and monetary disorder is
> not. So long as America continues its present geopolitical
> role, containing Soviet military power and maintaining a
> viable world economy seem increasingly incompatible. A
> strategy of devolution, designed to promote and profit from
> strategic pluralism, seems the logical way out.[9]

Mead also takes the domestic economy as his point of departure.
He argues that "the erosion of the middle classes on which American
democracy originally rested—the small farmers and commercial propri-
etors plus the professional groups—has left the country divided essentially between a large group of wage earners and a small group of
investors."[10] Further,

> in all the countries of the capitalist world . . . [w]ages have
> been falling, social programs have been cut back, and in the
> Third World much of the population has endured cata-
> strophic collapses of their standard of living. We have already
> seen where these trends lead if they cannot be reversed—to
> a progressive breakdown of order and even democracy itself,
> not only in the Third World, but also in the United States.[11]

In short the rich are growing richer; the poor, more numerous; and
all of society is being reduced to these two classes. Were it not for
international factors, America might respond successfully to this economic situation through measures of liberal socialism, that is, by "sys-
tematizing the activity of government in the economy" through "national economic planning."[12] Such a benign solution, however, is
impeded by the capitalists' need to continue exploiting the third world.
This leads America to wage recurrent wars against local liberation

movements, and these wars in turn exacerbate social tensions here at home. Consequently reactionary forces may cast aside America's democratic forms in favor of rule by coercion. Mead wrote:

> It is unfortunately accurate to say that some members of the American right support the tactics, as well as the stance, of the Latin American right. They tend to view death squads and states of siege as regrettable necessities—necessities that under some circumstances might be required inside the United States, too.[13]

A happy outcome to America's mounting contradictions might be brought about by the rise of a mass populist Marxist movement that could resolve America's crisis through "an expansion of the role of government in almost every field."[14] At the same time it would resolve the international crisis by forging "a kind of global commonwealth," which would institute a "world minimum wage" that would "increase consumption in the Third World."[15]

The Main Lines of Declinism

Mead is at odds with his fellow declinists on some points. Whereas Kennedy and Calleo, for example, see America's decline as a relative process directly attributable to the ascent of the other advanced capitalist economies, Mead sees America's decline as part of the collapse of international capitalism as a whole. Despite such differences it is possible to sketch the main lines of the declinist argument that give it its coherence and its vogue, even though each point may not be shared by all the writers.

In brief this argument holds that America is already in the process of a long-term and irreversible economic decline. (To Kennedy the decline is relative; to Mead it apparently is absolute). This decline is caused largely by the overextension of America's political and military power. Economic decline will lead in time to politico-military decline. By drawing back from international engagements, the United States can husband its resources and ensure a soft landing for its empire.

Errors in Generalizations

The declinist argument is faulty both in its generalizations and in its specific application. To begin with, it tends to be highly deterministic and suggests that man's fate is largely the product of inanimate forces around him. Early in his book Kennedy says that among "the main strands of the argument which permeate this entire work" is the conviction "that to understand the course of world politics, it is necessary to focus attention upon the material and long-term elements rather than the vagaries of personality or the week-by-week shifts of diplomacy and politics."[16] In this formulation the words "long-term," "vagaries" and "week-by-week" are fudge. Stripped of them, Kennedy's argument counterposes "material elements" to "personality" and "politics." In short, material factors transcend human ones in determining political outcomes.

This is akin to Marx's argument about the "base" determining "superstructure," and it is susceptible to the same simple but decisive refutation that Raymond Aron offered against Marx.[17] What, asks Aron, is the source of the "base"? Like Marx, Kennedy implies that it is inherent or given, but in reality it is largely the product of man's scientific and technological knowledge. The growth and direction of such knowledge are in turn sharply affected by political arrangements and religious ideas that may either encourage or inhibit scientific inquiry and shape its objectives. Kennedy describes how China's Ming dynasty, acting from political and philosophical motivations, compelled that country to turn away from various maritime and industrial arts, with the result that China declined from an advanced country during the first half of the second millennium to a backward one during the second half. He makes analogous observations about the Ottoman empire, Tokugawa Japan, and imperial Spain but seems blind to the implications.[18]

Replying to objections to the materialist position, Kennedy writes: "Individuals still counted [in shaping history]—who in the century of Lenin, Hitler, and Stalin could say they did not?—but they counted in power politics only because they were able to control and reorganize the productive forces of a great state."[19] Surely, however, some individuals who have counted weightily in twentieth-century history have not commanded such resources, say, Khomeini, Ben-Gurion, Gandhi, and Mao. And as the nations of Eastern Europe consolidate their freedom and independence, with Poland in the vanguard, we ought to bear in mind how much of the inspiration for this transformation was furnished by Pope John Paul II. He has at last provided the answer to Stalin's cynical question—the ultimate statement of the materialist position—"How many divisions has the Pope?"

To the extent that what Kennedy says is true, it is almost tautological. To wield military power requires possessing the sinews of power. Although arms do cost wealth, the questions remain, How is wealth created, and indeed what constitutes wealth? (Petroleum, for example, does today, but this is a relatively recent development, the fruit of human invention, and its value will last only until its utility is superseded by new human inventions.) Kennedy also fails to answer the question, How are states—great or small—created, or even how are nations created? None is the product of nature. Most of today's great states are the artifacts of political imagination.

Kennedy is obviously aware of such questions. In discussing how European civilization surpassed those of Asia in the middle of the second millennium, for example, he writes: "It was a combination of economic laissez-faire, political and military pluralism, and intellectual liberty . . . which had been in constant interaction to produce the 'European miracle.'"[20] Europe's political ascendance rested on its economic and technological development, and these in turn rested on other factors. But in his constant drumbeat on the economic roots of power, Kennedy seems to forget that wealth is as much an effect as a cause.

Moreover he does not escape the classical self-contradiction of determinists. Namely, if our history is shaped by forces larger than ourselves, then there is little point to exhorting one another to political action. But Kennedy clearly does exhort, both in his text and in his op-ed articles, talk shows, and even congressional testimony, all generated by his book. If America can save itself by so simple and painless an act as cutting its defense budget, as he suggests, then why cannot nations that take far more taxing and energetic measures exercise control over their own destinies?

In contrast to Kennedy, Walter Russell Mead avoids this self-contradiction by adopting a more radically determinist position: "If we are correct in our belief that this decline is inevitable, our attitudes toward it matter no more than a pebble matters to the course of the Mississippi." Elsewhere he put it, "The tides of history created the American Empire. . . . Once tides began to flow against the empire, no president and no Congress could stop them."[21]

Mead's escape from self-contradiction comes, however, at the price of descent into mysticism. For it is unclear what force drives Mead's tides. His is not a religious position in which it is assumed that God is the mover. Rather, like Hegel and Marx, he seems to reify history, to treat it as if it were a being with an intent of its own, unaffected by the decisions of human beings.

A second questionable generalization in the work of Kennedy and to some extent Calleo is the assumption of a close translation of wealth to power. Although weapons cost money and money can buy weapons, the correspondence is far from one-to-one. The United States and the Soviet Union enjoy approximate military parity although the American economy is more than twice the size of the Soviet. The European Economic Community is collectively far wealthier than the USSR, but it is far from being a military match for it. Israel is one of the world's more formidable military powers although its economic strength is negligible, while Japan, rapidly moving from third to second wealthiest country in the world, is militarily weak. The People's Republic of China is a rich country according to GNP but a poor country in terms of GNP per capita.

Its military strength, accordingly, is modest for a rich country, vast for a poor one.

Once again Kennedy is well aware of the objection. He wrote:

> Military potential is . . . not the same as military power. An economic giant could prefer, for reasons of its political culture or geographical security, to be a military pygmy, while a state without great economic resources could nonetheless so organize its society as to be a formidable military power. Exceptions to the simplistic equation "economic strength = military strength" exist in this period, as in others. . . Yet in an era of modern industrialized warfare, the link between economics and strategy was becoming tighter.[22]

Kennedy cannot have it both ways. The essence of his argument is about the correlation between economic and military strength. By denying any "simplistic equation," he can mean only that the relation is a rough one, not a tightly deterministic one. A few percentage points of difference in GNP between two countries may not show which is stronger, a change of modest magnitude within a single country may not produce a change in its power, but a gross difference is bound to have consequence. If a country is many times wealthier than another, it is likely to be the stronger, or if a country's wealth increases manyfold, its power is bound to grow. If this is all Kennedy means to assert, then he is on safe ground. But clearly it is not all that he does assert. His central policy recommendation is that America can avert catastrophe by reducing defense spending. Since America's defense spending is a paltry 6 percent of its GNP, reducing it cannot ensure any particular change in American power, certainly not one so momentous as to arrest America's decline.

Moreover both Kennedy and Calleo were much too quick to assume that reducing defense expenditures will have a beneficial effect on economic performance. While such a reduction could plausibly benefit growth if the savings are directed to productive investment, the cause and effect are far from predictable. Paul Seabury put it:

> There would seem to be no necessary relationship between large defense outlays and low economic growth rates, or the reverse. In recent times, Switzerland, Taiwan, South Korea and others have successfully combined huge defense outlays, as proportion of GNP, with astonishing rises in national economic productivity. Others, like Canada (which lately has spent virtually nothing on its national defense) have experienced protracted economic stagnation.[23]

Likewise, Kennedy points to defense spending as a major cause of the ascendance of Europe. By the late seventeenth century, he says, "the balance of military strength was tilting rapidly in favor of the West. For the explanation of this shift one must again point to the decentralization of power in Europe. What it did, above all else, was to engender a primitive form of arms race among the city states and then the larger kingdoms."[24]

This arms race had two beneficial consequences. The first was an "upward spiral in knowledge—in science and technology." The second was a powerful fiscal stimulus: The "two-way system of raising and *simultaneously* spending vast sums of money acted like a bellows, fanning the development of western capitalism and of the nation-state itself."[25]

Thus, although intuition tells us that military investment drains an economy because it produces no wealth, experience tells us that it may have very different consequences. Americans can hardly forget that the forced economic mobilization for World War II, more than Franklin Roosevelt's New Deal, lifted our country out of the Great Depression. Ironically the declinists build their case on the fall in America's comparative economic strength from its peak immediately after the war. That peak was the consequence not only of the destruction of so much of Europe's productive capacity but also of America's dramatic industrial growth, which was fueled by military spending at a level never matched before or since. (Indeed Kennedy reminded us that "the U.S. GNP had surged by more than 50 percent in real terms during the war.")[26] Why then do the declinists treat it as self-evident that America can slow its decline by cutting military spending?

This irony illustrates a broader weakness in the declinists' argument. While they offer various statistics to give their case weight, they draw inferences far beyond what their evidence shows. Sometimes hard numbers can hide soft thinking. Their central premise, that America is in the process of economic decline, is open to question. They rest this premise on data showing America's shares of various economic indicators to be much smaller today than immediately after the war. Extrapolating from them, they conclude that America is in the throes of long-term and inexorable forces. But trends can be fickle. As Owen Harries pointed out:

> According to the figures [Kennedy] provides [the U.S.] share [of world manufacturing] was lower throughout the 1930's than it had been in 1929, while in the same period the Soviet share more than tripled. . . . On this basis it could have been argued then, as it is argued now, that America was on the way out and that its displacement as the dominant economic power was inevitable and not very distant. That is what many

Western intellectuals actually believed at the time, and they were hopelessly wrong.[27]

Moreover the trend on which the declinists rely has long passed and was hardly a trend at all. As Samuel Huntington explained: "The United States produced 40 to 45 percent of the gross world product in the late 1940s and early 1950s. That share declined rapidly, reaching the vicinity of 20 to 25 percent of gross world product by the late 1960s. That is roughly where it has remained."[28] In short the statistical basis for the declinists' argument lies in the extraordinarily dominant position the United States enjoyed when it emerged from the war as the only major power whose territory was essentially unscathed. That artificial position disappeared as soon as the other advanced countries had rebuilt their industry and infrastructure, with the United States left in a less overwhelming but still preeminent position, which has remained constant since. Is this decline?

Just as the declinist argument is weak in its statistical basis, so too is it weak in defining some of its central concepts, most important the idea of overstretch. The term is Kennedy's, although the same thought is present in Calleo's work and Mead's. Calleo wants the United States to withdraw from Europe and East Asia, which most analysts consider the bedrock outposts of American security commitments. Although much of his argument seems addressed to the American presence in the third world, Kennedy does not appear to disagree with Calleo about Europe: he characterized NATO as "only the beginning of American overstretch."[29] Mead too, one may infer, disapproves of virtually any overseas involvements on the part of the United States and sees U.S. policy as driven by the avarice of capitalists.

The accusation that America is overstretched raises the question of whether America should stretch itself at all, of what would be a proper degree of stretch, of whether there is any such thing as understretch. The declinists never even ask, much less answer, such questions. Are any military expenditures or any foreign alliances or bases ever justifiable? If a country can make itself vulnerable by overexerting itself, can it not also do so by underexerting itself? If this undeniable point is granted, then the debate must turn to concrete evaluations of needs, interests, and strategies. Such evaluations cannot be waved away with airy generalizations.

For forty-odd years, the presence of American forces in Western Europe deterred any Soviet encroachment. The advent of Gorbachev's new thinking alleviates this threat, and yet Europeans are all but unanimous in wanting American forces to remain. They are seen as a stabilizing force in the face of new anxieties about German reunification and possible upheavals within and between the countries of the disintegrating Warsaw Pact. Perhaps the old fears were exaggerated; perhaps the new ones are. But the need to think through the military and political contingencies is in no measure obviated by the concept of overstretch. If indeed the price of withdrawal from Europe would have been a profound shift in the balance of power to America's detriment or if today it would be severe instability, then the costs of remaining there were and remain quite tolerable in comparison. It is better to be overstretched than underdefended.

Errors of Particulars

In addition to the weaknesses of the generalizations in the theory of decline, there are numerous flaws in the application of that theory to present American reality. First, it is hardly clear that America is suffering from economic decline. During the 1980s it enjoyed the longest period of sustained growth since World War II, outpacing most other countries. To cite Huntington again:

> During the past five years (1983–87) the U.S. and Japanese economies grew at almost the same rate, with the United States leading in three of these years. In all five years U.S. growth exceeded that of the European Community. The biggest economy has been getting bigger, absolutely and relatively.[30]

It is true that America's economic growth rates were lower in recent years than in the 1960s, but this decrease has affected most of the world more than the United States, and America's relative standing is the focus of the declinists.

Moreover a comparison of growth rates in various decades and various countries demolishes another central idea of declinism, namely, that whatever economic decline America has suffered results from excessive defense spending. As Herbert Stein has explained:

> This is a quite incredible idea. For one thing, the slowdown in economic growth that began in 1973 affected all the industrial countries, including Japan, whose military burden was and is trivial. For another thing, in the period of our most rapid growth, from 1948 to 1973, defense expenditures were a much larger fraction of GNP than they have been in the slow-growth period since 1973. In the earlier period, defense expenditures averaged 8.6 percent of the GNP. Between 1973 and 1987 they have averaged 5.7 percent. In 1987 they were 6.6 percent.[31]

Cutting defense spending is the panacea of the declinists. Indeed it may even be the ulterior motive of their entire argument. Stein demonstrated, however, how minuscule would be the impact of defense cuts on our economic circumstances. For the sake of illustration, he estimated defense spending under President Reagan at the somewhat exaggerated figure of 7 percent of GNP, private consumption at 67 percent, and GNP growth rate at 2.8 percent. Reducing the share for defense from 7 to 6 percent of GNP means a 15 percent cut in the military budget. If the whole amount were applied to investment and brought a 20 percent return, it would push the growth rate up from 2.8 to 3.0 percent. This hardly seems enough to make the difference between America regnant and America in decline. The same effect, Stein pointed out, can be achieved by reducing private consumption from 67 to 66 percent, which, given the rate of growth, means "we would reach any given level of per capita consumption about eight months later than we would otherwise have reached it. That is, we would reach in October 1988 the consumption level we would otherwise have reached in February 1988."[32] Even if the U.S. military were virtually abolished, and our defense budget cut to the 1 percent of GNP spent by Japan, whose constitution decrees it a disarmed state, this would boost the rate of GNP growth only to 4 percent if we invested every penny of the savings and received a rate of return of 20 percent.

Whatever America's difficulties, past empires have not declined in a vacuum but have been defeated or surpassed by other emerging powers. What power looms as the successor to America? The nations whose strong economic growth accounts for most of the decline in America's relative economic status are lightly armed and show little interest in translating their new wealth into major military or political power. They are especially disinclined to topple American power since most are allies of the United States and most rely on it for their security.

The sole military competitor of the United States, the USSR, is suffering genuine economic decline and political disintegration. It retains the might to incinerate the United States in a nuclear holocaust. But short of this far-fetched apocalypse, it has no chance of displacing American preeminence.

How long will that preeminence endure? We cannot know. One thing that differentiates it, however, from the fallen empires of yore is that, properly speaking, America has no empire. The term "empire" is defined by *Webster's* as "an extended territory usually comprising a group of nations, states, or peoples under the control or domination of a single sovereign power." The *Oxford English Dictionary* gives the meaning as "an aggregate of subject territories ruled over by a sovereign state." By any such definition the United States is not and has not an empire.

I do not mean to quibble over definitions. The United States is the world's most influential state, with influence that is especially strong among those states that are economically or militarily dependent on it. But influence is not the same thing as rule or control or domination. The term "empire" is sometimes used more loosely than its dictionary definition would suggest, and some would use it to characterize the group of states where American influence is strong. If we are to speak in this sense of an American empire, however, we must recognize what distinguishes this from, say, the Roman or British or Soviet empires.

Those empires consisted of nations conquered by the imperial sovereign and ruled by it (or by those whom it designated) by means of force or the ever-present threat of force. The American "empire," conversely, consists of states that trade with America, some that receive aid from America, and some that have mutual defense treaties with America. But none lacks the freedom to govern itself, and none fails to defy American wishes when it wishes. No country is more militarily dependent on the United States than Japan, yet this inhibits the Japanese little from pursuing aggressive export policies and restrictive import policies that create serious economic woes for America. Few countries are more economically dependent on America than Israel, the largest recipient of U.S. foreign aid; yet this aid has not made Israel accept U.S. proposals for resolving the Palestinian issue.

Mead calls America "the greatest empire in history."[33] He claims that "the most successful conquerors have been those who disguised their rule, employing local figures as functionaries and allowing the conquered to continue their daily lives"; he argues that "like all successful empires, the American empire ruled by consent and cooperation when it could."[34] But this is tendentious to the point of childishness. The British or Romans may have employed local functionaries, but they scarcely disguised their rule. Queen Victoria was declared the empress of India. The empire that went furthest to disguise its rule was the Soviet empire, but the presence of thousands of Red Army troops in each of the Soviets' East European colonies rendered the veneer rather thin. If the United States is disguising its rule over Japan, West Germany, France, or Israel, it has succeeded remarkably, for it is invisible to the naked eye.

The tortured discussions of the American empire reveal the heavy political freight that the declinist theories carry. Kennedy and Calleo are accomplished scholars, to be sure. Yet their writings on this subject reveal a strong bent toward viewing America as an unjust and unsuccessful power. Declinism sounds as though it was formulated in explicit rebuttal to Ronald Reagan's reelection theme of 1984, "It's morning in America." The declinists want to convince us that in truth it is evening. They want especially to convince us that Ronald Reagan's presidency was not the success that it appears to have been (and to prove that George McGovern was right after all with his call to "come home, America"). Indeed the *New York Times* may have given such prominence to this school of thought because, as the *Times* author Peter Schmeisser put it, it "mixes a concern over relative decline with a rejection of eight years of telegenic, Republican palliatives."[35]

Mead carries this same bent to extremes and reveals a world view that is Marxist, anti-American, and pro-Communist. He opined that "the resemblance between South African society and the American empire is not merely casual. South Africa is a microcosm of the empire as a whole."[36] He also says that former UN Ambassador Andrew Young's "statements about the constructive role of Cuban troops in Angola and his sympathy for the Palestinians were close to the minimum required of a United States that hoped to be taken seriously in the world as an ally of peoples aspiring to freedom and nationhood."[37] And he predicts that

> if the United States is truly facing an era of stagnant or falling real wages combined with a succession of vicious little wars in the Third World [which Mead argues is indeed the case], then Marxism is going to be a much more attractive ideology than it has been in the recent past. Millions of people rather than hundreds of thousands will begin to think in Marxist terms. This shift will not be limited to youth culture or to minority groups; it will take place generally among those who have reason to fear for the future.[38]

This may prove the most imperishable piece of Mead's work, for it is bound to be immortalized in anthologies of ridiculous prophecies.

If the Declinists Are Right?

Showing that declinist theory arises from political or ideological motivation does not prove it false. I have already explained what I believe to be numerous major flaws in the declinist argument, which, taken together, make nonsense of it. But even if the declinists are right, the case for an internationalist, assertive U.S. foreign policy seeking to promote the growth of democracy around the world would not be weakened.

Because I believe that the declinists yearn for a reduction of American global influence as a goal in itself, I suspect that they would oppose such a foreign policy. But such opposition does not flow logically from the main points of their argument. Their central argument is that America cannot afford the level of military spending necessary to fund its current defense policies and foreign alliances. Fostering the growth of democracy abroad is the least expensive method of strengthening America's security. Success at this effort will make the world more peaceful and a safer place for America. Hence it will allow us to lessen our military investment and still be adequately defended.

The dollar costs of democracy-building programs are quite small. The National Endowment for Democracy operates with annual budgets in the low tens of millions. The part of the U.S. foreign aid budget that has been devoted to fostering political development has been small. The operating costs of the State Department's Human Rights Bureau are insignificant. Radio Liberty and Radio Free Europe spend $228 million annually. A small share of the budget of the U.S. Information Agency goes to activities that may encourage the growth of democracy, as may a small share of the covert operations expenditures of the CIA. All told, these programs probably do not exceed 1 or 2 percent of the defense budget in cost, nor would they even if some of their appropriations were increased (as, for example, the NED's richly deserve to be).

The declinists have difficulty in making a convincing case that defense expenditures at a level of 6 percent of GNP are an intolerable drain on the U.S. economy. Surely they will not argue that democracy-promoting programs that might cost one-tenth of 1 percent of GNP are beyond our means, especially if these programs help to reduce other burdens. The democratization of Eastern Europe has already begun to reduce the costs of NATO defense. Still larger benefits would accrue from continued democratization of the Soviet Union itself.

Ironically, if the United States is successful in fostering the growth of democracy, it may well exacerbate the trend that so alarms the declinists. If democratization brings in its train economic growth, as it probably will, then its spread will cause a decline in America's share of growing global wealth. A world that increasingly mirrors America's ways will be a world that increasingly matches America's success. America's preeminence will perforce diminish. This may serve to reconfirm the declinists in their convictions. But it will not make them right. Such a decline will not be a setback for America but a triumph. America's telos is not to be an imperium but a "shining city on a hill," a model and inspiration for people everywhere. Decline should ever be so sweet.

6

Can Democracy Flourish around the World?

In preceding chapters I have argued two points about the relation between democracy and America's foreign policy strategy. First, I have argued that the spread of democracy tends to make the global environment more congenial to America because democracies tend to be peaceable and pro-American. Second, I have argued that it is advantageous for America to be democracy's advocate, even apart from the benefits of creating a more democratic world, because playing this role enables America to rally support for its policies and actions from large numbers of people both at home and abroad.

These arguments lose their force, however, if as some believe there is no practical prospect for the spread of democracy. If democracy can thrive only in rich countries or Western countries or English-speaking countries, as is variously suggested, then it has already spread about as far as it can. To work for its extension would be futile. Nor would advocacy of democracy win America much credit if everyone could see that the cause had already reached its furthest horizon.

Skeptics from All Sides

The skeptics of democracy's prospects come from all points on the political spectrum, and their voices can be heard both in scholarly writings and in topical debates. Here, for example, is the liberal academic Robert Dahl commenting in 1984 on U.S. policy toward Central America:

> Much of the debate over Central America has been based on what increasingly appears to be a faulty assumption: that the region's nondemocratic regimes—El Salvador, Guatemala, Honduras, and presumably Nicaragua as well—can all be converted into democracies by means of American assistance, guidance, and intervention. . . . But the truth is that these countries are no closer to the Administration's goal than

they were four years ago, and that they are not likely to achieve stable democratic institutions for a long time to come.
. . .

It is a disagreeable, perhaps even tragic, fact that in much of the world the conditions most favorable to the development and maintenance of democracy are nonexistent, or at best only weakly present.[1]

A more conservative scholar, the Latin Americanist Howard Wiarda makes a similar point: "I doubt that democracy U.S.-style can be exported. I doubt that Latin America wants it, or wants it all that much." He elaborates:

There are alternative legitimate routes to power in Latin America besides elections, and democracy itself often is of tenuous legitimacy. Second, Latin America has traditionally meant something different by democracy than we do. Where we have always emphasized the mechanical processes of democracy (elections and the like), Latin America is more apt to judge a regime democratic—regardless of its route to power—that governs for and in the name of the common good, that is broadly representative of society's major interests, that evidences a degree of populism and nationalism, that provides for economic and social development, that is not brutal and oppressive, etc.[2]

The same point made by Dahl about Central America and Wiarda about Latin America is applied more widely. The conservative commentator Irving Kristol says:

We should not pretend in our foreign policy statements that we can look forward in the near future to democracy conquering the world. The world is not like that. I am not one of those who is thrilled by the success of democracy in Argentina or in the Philippines or . . . in Korea. I am a betting man, and I will lay odds that democracy will not survive in those countries. The preconditions of democracy are complex—certain strong cultural traditions, certain strong cultural attitudes. So far as I can see, those countries do not have them, and therefore, a democracy in any of them would shortly be discredited and be replaced by some sort of authoritarian regime of either the left or the right. That is apparently their norm, and I refuse to feel guilty about it.[3]

Kristol's views are not much different from those of political scientist Robert Packenham, who describes himself as part of the leftish "revisionist" school of historical interpretation and who probably agrees with Kristol about few other topics. He wrote that the chances for liberal democracy in most Third World countries in the foreseeable future are not very great; and the chances that the United States can be effective in advancing the cause of democracy through positive action are probably even smaller. The attempt to promote liberal constitutionalism is often both unrealistic from the point of view of feasibility and ethnocentric from the point of view of desirability.[4]

While some on the Left agree with some on the Right that the prospects for democracy are bleak, the two sides diverge sharply when it comes to drawing implications for U.S. policy from this assessment. Kristol would view more favorably undemocratic regimes of the Right that accommodate U.S. security interests: "If we have an authoritarian ally, we have to say we have an authoritarian ally, not pretend that it is a democratic ally, and we should explain why it is useful to us, or necessary to us, to have an authoritarian ally."[5] Packenham, on the other side, wishes the United States were more sympathetic to undemocratic regimes of the Left, which he believes are more responsive to the dictates of social justice. Describing Fidel Castro's Cuba in the 1970s, he said, "Its achievements in several spheres, including education, health, women's rights, distribution of income and status, national identity and pride, have few if any parallels in Latin America during the last decade."[6]

Some of the skeptics of democracy's prospects reach their conclusions reluctantly or regretfully. But for others the belief that democracy is not in the offing is welcome news. To Packenham, for example, democracy would only get in the way of the things that third world countries need to do:

In poor countries relatively authoritarian regimes are usually less likely than democratic ones to fail in advancing the ends of economic development and socioeconomic justice. . . . This is why relatively authoritarian regimes are often a better, if not the best, alternative for poor nations. For the "best" alternative may be utopian and quite inappropriate if it means political democracy "at any price" while ignoring the negative consequences of this democracy for other desirable goals—such as economic and social democracy—which may compete with it.[7]

Left or Right, regretful or gratified, the skeptics of democracy all speak in the tone of wisdom and experience rebuking democratic globalists for their juvenile enthusiasm. In particular the skeptics point to the record of the many new nations created in the decolonization that followed World War II. Most were endowed at their birth with democratic constitutions, but democracy failed to take hold. Reinhold Niebuhr and Paul Sigmund captured that experience:

The picture in *Life* magazine at the time of the independence of Ghana in 1957 showing a bewigged African speaker presiding over a replica of the House of Parliament, with Government and Opposition facing one another in solemn array, symbolized the hopes of the colonizers for a transfer of democratic institutions to the former colonies. Yet within a few years, the English wigs gave way to African tribal symbols, the shape of the parliament was changed to a semicircle, and the leaders of the opposition were in jail.[8]

Special Cases?

For all their pretensions to dispassionate empiricism, the skeptics tend to be dogmatic. They ignore a wealth of evidence that contradicts their wisdom. Germany and Italy are not Anglo-Saxon countries. Japan is not a Western country. And India is certainly not a rich country. Democracy flourishes in each of them. True, many poor and non-Western countries are not democratic. True, democracy does not come easily, and it has often been destroyed. But this does not prove the skeptics' case that democracy is virtually impossible outside the first world. One need not believe that universal democracy can come easily to believe that such examples as Japan and India show that it is reasonable to work for the growth of democracy in non-Western, nonrich countries.

The skeptics sometimes reply that Japan, or one of the other late-developing or non-Western democracies, is not really democratic. Japanese politics, they point out, have long been dominated by one party. That party's internal dynamics are driven by factional divisions based not on ideology but on personality. Relations within each faction, moreover, are rigidly hierarchical.[9] In short the texture of Japanese politics differs markedly from the democratic norm that derives from the American or British experience. Indeed it differs in some of the very things that we feel give our democracy its democratic quality, such as egalitarianism.

In this argument the critics are coming at the democratic globalists from opposite directions. They often say that it is absurd to expect other societies to adopt or imitate American structures. ("Democracy U.S.-style cannot be exported," says Wiarda.)[10] Surely this is a straw man because nobody seriously advocates that democracy U.S.-style even be encouraged abroad, much less exported. (The efforts of some overly zealous occupation officials forty years ago to impose U.S.-style federalism on Japan despite that nation's legal unity and ethnic homogeneity quickly fell by the wayside.) Then these same critics or others turn around and dismiss the use of Japan as an example of Asian democracy because its structures so differ from our own that they ought not to be labeled democratic.

What the Japanese have, not surprisingly, is Japan-style democracy rather than U.S.-style democracy. This is exactly what they ought to have. Its personalistic factions and emphasis on loyalty and hierarchy reflect Japanese culture. These features may seem repugnant to us. But the system retains the essential features of democracy; namely, the main government officials are chosen in honest, open, competitive elections and the citizens enjoy the right to hear and take part in unfettered political discourse. These features are the bedrock of what democratic globalists want to universalize. The fact that they may be achieved within a myriad of legal and conventional forms is more than tolerable; it is desirable.

Another retort of the skeptics is that Japan and India are special cases, the one having been democratized at gunpoint by the American (officially the Allied) occupation, the other by decades of British tutelage. Perhaps so, but each country in the world is a special case, in some sense unique. And Japan and India, though powerful examples, are not the only ones to which democratic globalists can point. Freedom House each year publishes a "Report on Freedom," which rates every country in the world on a scale of one to seven in terms of its political freedoms and civil liberties and then groups them into three broad categories: free, partly free, and not free. In its most recent report, issued in January 1990, Freedom House found that sixty-one countries deserved to be called free. They included about 39 percent of the world's people, a higher percentage than ever before. The proportion living in free countries has crept steadily upward in recent years, although the share of the world's population living in the advanced Western countries has steadily declined.[11]

Of Freedom House's list of free countries, nine are in Latin America, twelve in the Caribbean, fourteen in Asia and the Pacific, three in Africa, and one in the Middle East. In other words thirty-nine free countries lie outside North America, Europe, Australia, and New Zealand. Many of these thirty-nine besides Japan and India can be called special cases. Israel, for instance, is not entirely a non-Western country. Some Pacific countries in this list are small. Some Caribbean ones are prosperous, and some have a heritage of British tutelage. But given the numbers, can these all be dismissed as special cases? Thirty-nine countries constitute a substantial portion of the non-European, non-Anglo-American world. How many such exceptions are required before we dismiss the skeptics' denial that democracy can work in such countries? The list includes a wide variety of countries, showing that democracy can exist under many different conditions. Significantly, although some are prosperous, many on the list are poor. Twelve of the thirty-nine, according to figures furnished by Freedom House, have per capita annual gross national products of less than $1,000—for example, India, the Philippines, Bolivia, Botswana, and the Dominican Republic.

Further, the argument that many of these non-Western democracies are special cases, even if true, implies less than first appears. Many non-Western countries that are not among these thirty-nine but among the partly free might also be considered special cases. Turkey, for one, is a European country; Pakistan shares India's tutelary history; the Republic of China is prosperous; and so on. The point is, the United States could fashion a busy program of fostering democracy abroad merely by focusing on such countries. A substantial part of the world might be democratized before we exhaust the special cases.

As much as these tabulations dramatize the growth of democracy, they in fact understate it. For one thing, they have not yet caught up with the changes in the Communist world. Poland and Hungary are counted in this survey as partly free, as is Nicaragua. East Germany, Czechoslovakia, Bulgaria, Romania, the USSR, and Mongolia are all counted as not free. Yugoslavia is listed partly free, which is still accurate albeit more literally than intended: parts of it—Slovenia and Croatia—have become free. Nor did the 1990 survey record some recent changes outside the Communist world. Thus it lists Namibia as partly free and Panama as not free.

The Growing Appeal of Democracy

Neither do the Freedom House data measure the enormous growth of prodemocracy sentiment in countries that are still far from being democratic. In Nepal, South Africa, Mozambique, Nigeria, and Haiti popular pressures have led to promises or processes of democratic reform. Elsewhere democratic movements have been cruelly repressed, as in Burma (which now calls itself Myanmar, a change promulgated in the hope of deflecting prodemocracy sentiment), but how long will the repression succeed? That question presents itself most forcefully in regard to the People's Republic of China, where reform was severely set back by the government's bloody massacre at Tiananmen Square and its subsequent purges, arrests, and executions. But this reversal does not cancel the astonishing display of prodemocracy sentiment that occurred in the spring of 1989. However many are imprisoned or killed, the millions of student and worker demonstrators, with their papier-mâché statues of liberty, have stamped the issue of democracy indelibly on the Chinese political agenda.

Driven by the American model, the democratic idea steadily increased in appeal through the nineteenth century but then suffered a decline after World War I, under the challenge of philosophies that seemed newer and more promising. Now, after a seventy-year detour, democracy again seems to capture the imagination of intellectuals, students, and workers in all corners of the world.

Chai Ling, a leader of the democracy movement, emerged in the West, courtesy of China's underground railroad, despite being on Beijing's most wanted list. The twenty-four-year-old female psychology student explained her cause simply: "[We] aspire to human dignity and to democratic freedoms, like people everywhere aspire to."[12] Even the Arab world, which has seemed least affected by global democratization and which alone possesses a still vibrant rival ideology in Islam, has begun to feel the tremors. In the early months of 1990, according to the *New York Times*, "Kuwaitis have taken up the slogans of pro-democracy movements, demanding the return of their parliament, abolished by the ruling Emir in 1986, and the lifting of press censorship."[13] And the Dalai Lama, surely one of the less Western of world leaders, recently proposed that his successor be elected rather than chosen by the traditional examination of children to find the one whose birthmarks reveal that he is the reincarnation of the deceased Dalai Lama. The Tibetan spiritual leader also expressed optimism about his nation's future despite the harsh treatment it now suffers from Beijing. "Rigid oppression can't work in a human society. . . . The love of freedom and democracy is human nature," he said.[14]

Democracy is also growing stronger in the democratic world, including the United States. The victories of the civil rights movement in the 1960s alleviated the most egregious deficit of American democracy. Since then, other minority groups and women have gained in their struggle for equal rights of citizenship in America. Similar progress has occurred in other Western democracies.

Earlier Doubts about Democracy

Yet the recent surging of the democratic tide leaves many of the skeptics unmoved. Outside America and Europe democracy has its ups and downs, they say. Today's rise is tomorrow's fall. Elected governments in Latin America are not much to get excited about. Latin America, they say, has had elected governments and then reverted to dictatorship. While they boast a long historical memory, the skeptics forget the record of their own forerunners. Many of the doubts expressed about the prospects of today's fledgling democracies were expressed a few decades ago about democracies now considered stable and enduring. As World War II drew to its end and America began to contemplate what to do with Japan, President Harry Truman received a briefing from Joseph Grew, the State Department's leading Japan expert, who had served there as U.S. ambassador until the war. Grew told him that "from the long-range point of view, the best we can hope for is a constitutional monarchy, experience having shown that democracy in Japan would never work."[15]

When the Western occupation of West Germany ended in 1952, the eminent political scientist Heinz Eulau toured that country and wrote despairingly about the prospects for democracy there. "In so many ways—despite the changed setting and the changed cast—the Bonn Republic seems like a second performance of Weimar. The spirit that animated the performance is traditional, and gives rise to the same old, vague forebodings," he wrote. "The state of political discourse is worse today than it has ever been," he lamented, adding that "German politics is . . . grounded not on democratic experience but on a deep emotionalism. . . ."[16]

Japan too regained its independence in 1952, and it continued to evoke skepticism about its democratic prospects. As one Japanese journalist put it in an essay in the *New Republic:*

> I fear that the outlook for its future as a democratic country is dark.
>
> The real danger lies not so much in the increasingly reactionary tendencies of the Japanese Government but in the lack of change in the minds of the Japanese people during six and a half years of occupation. Generally speaking, the people remain fundamentally the same in their ways of thinking as in the prewar days when the nationalists and militarists were allowed to rule the destiny of that nation.[17]

The British historian David Thomson wrote in 1959 that democracy was collapsing in Asia because

> Asiatic countries still mainly lack the social and educational foundations, as well as the political habits and traditions, of sound representative parliamentary institutions. . . . To transplant full-fledged the electoral devices and the parliamentary procedures which Western European nations gradually and laboriously developed in peculiar economic conditions has usually been to court disaster.[18]

As Thomson in part acknowledged, his doubts about democracy in Asia mirrored doubts expressed a generation earlier about Europe. Waldo Frank wrote in *Foreign Affairs* in 1943:

> In Western Europe, where the religion of democracy was nurtured through its hazardous childhood, it is today engaged in a great struggle for survival. . . . on the whole Continent—its very existence is threatened. And the threat will

outlast Hitler, since Fascism itself is a mere end-product of deep-grained anti-democratic forces within the very texture of modern European thought, and of the whole industrial West. . . .[19]

A decade earlier Arnold Toynbee had written much the same:

The vague and abstract Greek word "democracy," by which this peculiar institution of the medieval kingdom of England and its political offspring had come to be known, slurred over the fact that parliamentarism was a special local growth which could not be guaranteed to acclimatize itself in alien soil. . . . [N]o parliamentarian can close his eyes to the significance of the portent of Fascism in post-war Italy; for Italy lies near the heart of our Western world; she has made one of the greatest single contributions made by any country to our common western civilization; and in the nineteenth century her adoption of Anglo-French parliamentarism seemed to be of the essence of her national resurrection. In these circumstances, her repudiation of "democracy" (in our conventional use of the term) has made it an open question whether this political plant can really strike permanent root anywhere except in its native soil.[20]

Doubts about the suitability of democracy have in the recent past extended all the way to America itself, or at least to parts of it. As Senator Strom Thurmond explained to the Harvard Law School in 1957:

Many Negroes simply lack sufficient political consciousness to spur them on to participate in political and civic affairs. I might point out here that a great number of those who lack this political consciousness probably also lack certain other qualities prerequisite to casting a truly intelligent ballot, and thus that the cause of good government would not necessarily be served by a sudden vast swelling of the registration lists through artificial politically-inspired stimuli.[21]

Within a few years after the adoption of the Voting Rights Act, however, Senator Thurmond had reevaluated the level of Negro political consciousness to the extent of announcing his decision to become the first southern senator to hire a Negro professional staff member. Why should today's skepticism about democracy in Latin America or Asia prove any more perspicacious than that of a couple of generations ago about Japan, Europe, or South Carolina?

Gradual Advance of Democracy

Democracy is fragile and does need time to take hold. It would be amazing if the current democratic momentum were unbroken by disappointments and reversals here and there. Many states where democracy is now entrenched once experienced failures at establishing democratic rule, for example, France. Many newer nations are likely to have similar experiences. But history shows a gradual and ragged advance of democracy. Indeed to call democracy's growth gradual may concede too much to the skeptics. When modern democracy was born in 1776, the free population of the United States was not much more than 2 million. The all-male, and in some states property-qualified, electorate amounted to less than 1 million. Today according to Freedom House's figures some 2,034,000,000 live in democratic countries.[22] In short, over the past 200 years, while the population of the world has grown six times larger, the population of the world that is self-governing has increased 2,000 fold.

The American Revolution inspired revolutionary activity in France and the colonies of Latin America, which smashed the old regimes—and in the Latin case won independence from Spain—but failed to achieve democratic government. Although constitutionalism also advanced in Scandinavia and elsewhere in Europe, democracy made few gains until the 1830s.

In 1830 Belgium won its independence from Holland and established a largely democratic constitution providing for a parliamentary monarchy. In France, after Charles X was forced to abdicate, the "bourgeois" Louis Philippe took the throne proffered by Parliament. This method of selection, as well as his title, king of the French, signified the rise of the idea of popular sovereignty. Nonetheless the outcome was a triumph for constitutional monarchy, not republicanism. Upheavals in Iberia resulted in the replacement of absolutism by nominal constitutionalism in both Spain and Portugal, but in practice rule in both countries remained highly autocratic, attenuated mainly by severe instability. Outside Belgium, the most enduring consequence of the revolutions of 1830 was the 1832 reform law in England, which abolished the rotten boroughs, reduced voting qualifications, and extended the franchise from the aristocracy to the rising bourgeoisie.

The next revolutionary spasm in Europe, in 1848, was the greatest of all—until 1989. Again it began in France, where rebellion forced the abdication of Louis Philippe and led to the proclamation of the Second Republic. The fever spread to Vienna and the Austrian empire, to Prussia and the rest of Germany, to Italy and parts of northern Europe. The rallying cries were national independence, constitutionalism, parliaments, expanded suffrage, and abolition of serfdom. But all the sound and fury left the political map of Europe little changed. In France the democratic embryo matured into Louis Napoleon's misshapen empire. Thoughout central Europe the revolutionary surge collapsed as quickly as it had risen. The old order was restored, with only a memory of 1848 left as a heritage—Louis Kossuth, for instance, as a symbol of Hungarian independence, and the Frankfurt Assembly as a model for the writers of the Bonn Constitution a century later. Lasting gains were achieved in Switzerland, which adopted a federal constitution that was essentially democratic, and in Denmark, Holland, and Sardinia, which became constitutional monarchies, more or less liberal. Prussia too moved in this direction, and even Austria, the apotheosis of reaction at the end of 1848, did not restore serfdom.

The second half of the nineteenth century saw a steady growth of liberalism and to a lesser extent democracy. In 1853 Argentina adopted a constitution on the American model, with a federal system, a bicameral legislature, and a president chosen by an electoral college. Ten years later Colombia did likewise. In the 1860s Italy and Germany achieved unification under constitutional monarchies with parliaments and limited suffrage. In the decades that followed, the electorate was expanded. In Austria the empire was reorganized in 1867 into the dual monarchy, with a single sovereign ruling concurrently as the emperor of Austria and the king of Hungary. Each of the two component nations was endowed with a constitution and parliament of its own. In 1866 Sweden created a bicameral parliament as a rein on royal authority. In England the reform bill of 1867 extended the franchise to more than one-third of adult males, including many workingmen. That year Parliament also adopted the British North America Act, which united four of the provinces of Canada and provided for their self-rule under the British crown in a manner "similar in principle to that of the United Kingdom." In the United States the Civil War brought the Emancipation Proclamation and the Thirteenth, Fourteenth, and Fifteenth Amendments, which in theory guaranteed to blacks full rights of citizenship.

In the 1870s the Franco-Prussian War ended the rule of Louis Napoleon and gave birth to the Third Republic, establishing democratic governance for France that has endured despite the many instabilities of the Third and Fourth Republics. Spain became a republic briefly during the internecine broils of the 1870s but reverted to a constitutional monarchy, as it had been intermittently since 1812.

During the last quarter of the nineteenth century and the first years of the twentieth, few dramatic political transformations occurred. In 1884 parliamentary government was established in Norway when the high court of the realm deposed the government and clipped the king's power. Elsewhere the most important developments in democratization were reform acts that extended the franchise to larger portions of the citizenry of various countries. In 1874 Switzerland adopted universal manhood suffrage. A decade later Great Britain's Third Reform Act did almost the same, and in the 1890s Spain, Belgium, and the Netherlands followed suit. In the years that followed, Denmark, Sweden, Norway (which separated from Sweden in 1905), Greece, Bulgaria, Serbia, Italy, and Portugal did likewise. By the outbreak of World War I, the large majority of European states practiced universal male suffrage. Although all of them were not democracies, the growth of democracy in Europe was steady.

And Europe was not alone. Latin America also made notable democratic progress in the decades before World War I. In 1891 Brazil adopted a federal constitution on the American model. The same year, in a civil war in Chile, forces allied with the congress defeated those allied with the president, ushering in a long period of parliamentary rule. In 1895 Peru began twenty-five years of orderly constitutional rule with one brief interruption. During this "aristocratic republic," politics rested on peaceful electoral competition, but the electorate remained narrow. After a civil war in Uruguay ended, orderly electoral processes were established, which were bolstered by a new constitution in 1917 and lasted almost uninterrupted until 1973. Between 1905 and 1914 Costa Rica adopted reforms that extended the franchise, provided for direct public election of officials, and encouraged participation by commoners. In 1910 Colombia adopted constitutional reforms creating a long era of stable government, called "oligarchical democracy."[23] And in 1912 Argentina adopted universal male suffrage and a secret ballot, leading in 1916 to a peaceful transfer of power to the opposition radicals, led by Hipólito Yrigoyen, Argentina's first democratically chosen president.

A Democratic Decline

The war that America entered "to make the world safe for democracy" almost had the opposite consequence. World War I so shook the foundations of civilization as to make the prospects for democracy unsafe indeed. A burst of democratization followed the war, as most of the independent sovereignties born out of the old empires became democracies, but in the next two decades, democracy collapsed in almost all of them.

Russia foreshadowed what happened elsewhere. In February 1917 it became democratic, or incipiently so, all at once. In October it succumbed to a new tyranny more imperious than czarism at its worst. In the war's aftermath Germany became a democratic republic, as did Austria. Hungary did too but only for a moment; the republic was brushed aside by the Communist Bela Kun, who in turn was deposed by the authoritarian regime of Admiral Horthy. Czechoslovakia emerged from the Hapsburg empire as a democracy. Poland regained its independence as a democracy. The state of Yugoslavia was born as a constitutional and essentially democratic monarchy. Romania followed a similar pattern. Finland, Estonia, Latvia, and Lithuania emerged as independent democratic states. In 1924 Greece, Turkey, and Albania became republics. Sweden, Denmark, and Iceland further democratized. In 1918 Uruguay adopted universal male suffrage, and although Costa Rica that year suffered a military coup, it was reversed two years later. In Japan in the 1920s the political parties, which were popularly based and fairly prodemocratic in ideology, gained enough strength to dilute significantly the rule of the Meiji oligarchs.

Before this democratic tide had fully run its course, however, countercurrents began to flow. In 1922 Benito Mussolini seized power in Italy and destroyed a democracy that had grown up over decades. Eleven years later his pupil and ally, Hitler, took over in Germany. In between, democracy had succumbed in Poland, Yugoslavia, Albania, Spain, Romania, and Lithuania. Following Hitler's rise, democracy collapsed in Austria and Latvia, and the democratic features that remained in Bulgaria, Greece, Spain, and Portugal were obliterated. In Eastern Europe democracy survived only in Czechoslovakia—until that country was gobbled up by Nazi Germany.

The antidemocratic tide of the 1930s also swept the shores of Latin America. In Argentina President Yrigoyen was ousted in a 1930 coup that established a military dictatorship, influenced by European fascism. Much the same happened in Brazil that year. In Chile Colonel Carlos Ibáñez seized power in 1927 and abolished parliamentary government, but he was ousted after four years and democratic government renewed in 1932.

One lasting feature of the democratic tide that followed World War I was women's suffrage. In 1920 the Nineteenth Amendment to the U.S. Constitution extended the vote to women. Two years earlier it had been given to British women above the age of thirty. The democracies of northern Europe and the temporary democracies of central and eastern Europe followed suit. Although democracy disappeared in many of those countries, the principle of female suffrage became firmly established, and virtually wherever democracy survived or revived, it became a matter of course.

The decline of democracy during the years between the world wars was compounded by the initial conquests of Hitler and his allies (including for a time Stalin), which wiped out several existing democratic governments. Even before the war's end brought a renewal of democracy, two small democratic gains occurred in former colonies of states Hitler had conquered. Lebanon in 1943 and Iceland in 1944 gained independence from, respectively, France and Denmark, as democratic republics.

Postwar Democratization

After the war, democratization of the aggressor countries was a key goal of the United States. Democratic systems were restored in Germany, Austria, and Italy, and one was created in Japan. Korea gained its independence from Japan but was divided into two separate states. A democratic system installed in South Korea by the Americans did not last long.

In 1946 Turkey undertook various democratic reforms; these included legalizing the opposition Democratic party, which won the presidency in 1950. Also in that year the Philippines was granted the independence that had long been promised by the United States, and it became a democratic republic. The autonomy of New Zealand was formalized in 1947. Ceylon became an independent British Commonwealth state in 1948, while the Irish Free State left the Commonwealth in 1949 to become the Irish Republic. Also in 1948 the state of Israel was founded. All of these were democracies.

Latin America in the immediate aftermath of the war presented a mixed picture. Liberal constitutions were adopted in Brazil and Panama in 1946. Venezuela enjoyed the birth of democratic rule in 1945, but it lasted only three years. Meanwhile Colombia descended into a protracted, bloody civil war, known as La Violencia. Even Costa Rica suffered civil war, but unlike in Colombia, this brief affair soon left democratic institutions more firmly planted than before. In the 1950s notable democratic progress occurred in two countries. In Venezuela the dictatorship of Marcos Pérez Jiménez was overthrown in 1958 by the military, which organized free elections the following year, restoring democratic rule that has endured ever since. In Colombia a decade of civil war was brought to a close by an agreement between the two warring parties to create a national front and to alternate in power. This arrangement brought peace, not democracy, but it proved a steppingstone to democracy.

In 1947 India and Pakistan gained independence within the British Commonwealth. In 1950 India became a republic. In 1956 Pakistan declared itself an Islamic republic, but within two years martial law was declared for the first of several times. In the late 1950s and 1960s, other colonies in Asia and Africa that had been given independence after World War II and that began with democratic constitutions also devolved into dictatorships. Botswana and Mauritius, which have remained democratic since becoming independent in 1966 and 1968 respectively, are the most striking exceptions in Africa. Senegal, which became independent in 1960, and the Gambia, which became independent in 1965, remain fairly democratic (although Senegal was a one-party state from 1966 through 1974).

The late 1960s and 1970s were also a grim time for democracy in Latin America. Military dictatorships seized power in Brazil, Peru, and Panama in the 1960s and in Guatemala, Uruguay, and Chile in the 1970s. In contrast, all the small colonies of the Caribbean, almost all of which received their independence in the 1960s, 1970s, and 1980s, have remained democracies. The same holds for several of the small island states of the Pacific: Nauru, Kiribati, Tuvalu, Papua New Guinea, Western Samoa, and the Solomon Islands.

The current trend of democratization began in the mid-1970s in Mediterranean Europe. After the military junta that had ruled since 1967 released its grip, Greece resumed democracy in 1974. Also that year the Caetano dictatorship of Portugal (heir to the long authoritarian rule of Salazar) was overthrown by the Armed Forces Movement. For two years Portugal's fate hung in the balance as its Communist party, abetted by some elements of the revolutionary military, grasped for power. But after the Communists took a drubbing in the 1976 free elections, democratic rule was established. Meanwhile in Spain, after the long-time dictator Francisco Franco died in 1975, Prince Juan Carlos took the helm of government as king, inaugurating a transition to a democratic parliamentary monarchy.

Perhaps influenced by events in Iberia, the states of Latin America in the late 1970s began to slough off military regimes and return to elected governments. This trend quickened in the 1980s, until almost all of the Western hemisphere became democratic. The exceptions were Guyana, Cuba, Haiti, Suriname and perhaps Paraguay, which seemed on its way to democracy, and Mexico, a rather open society with an elected government but a long tradition of vote rigging. As the 1980s gave way to the 1990s, even these recalcitrant states, except Cuba and perhaps Guyana and Suriname, seemed headed toward democracy.

In the 1980s the democratic trend also spread to Asia, where important changes occurred in four countries. After dictatorial President Ferdinand Marcos was ousted in the Philippines in 1986, democratic rule was restored. In 1987 free elections were held in South Korea and restored democracy there. The same happened in Pakistan in 1988, after that country's military ruler, President Zia ul-Haq, died in a plane crash. In 1986 the Republic of China in Taiwan announced a plan of democratization, which included legalizing opposition parties and removing restrictions on the press. Its peculiar history leaves Taiwan saddled with a legislature of octogenarians chosen before 1949, when the Nationalists lost power over the Chinese mainland to the Communists, but a fairly elected government may evolve early in the 1990s. A step in this direction was the legal participation of thirty-eight opposition parties in local elections held in December 1989. In 1990 an uprising in Nepal elicited promises of a democratic transition.

In the late 1980s the trend of democratization reached even the Communist world. Under Mikhail Gorbachev the Soviet Union began a dramatic process of liberalization. Externally it released its grip on the states of Eastern Europe that it had subjugated at the end of World War II. In 1989 Poland held elections, which were more democratic than they were intended to be. Although the lion's share of seats was to have been reserved for the Communists, the opposition scored such a dramatic victory in balloting for the open seats that it formed Eastern Europe's first non-Communist government in forty years. Then the governments of Hungary and Bulgaria agreed to democratic transitions. Under the impact of peaceful popular protests, East Germany, Czechoslovakia, and even Mongolia followed suit. The dictatorship of Romania was overthrown. In 1990 free elections were held in all these countries (except Romania, where irregularities made the voting something less than free) and in Nicaragua and parts of Yugoslavia as well.

A Historical Pattern

This brief sketch of the history of democracy should make two things clear. First, the road to democracy is not a one-way street. Many countries have experienced democratic rule only to revert to dictatorship. In many of these countries, democracy has then risen again. Some countries have been through this cycle more than once. Second, on the whole the domain of democracy has grown ever larger.

We may gain some perspective by considering the world in arbitrary fifty-year intervals. In the world of 1800, one democracy existed, the small United States of America. The French Revolution, though inspired in part by America, had failed to establish democratic government. If we look next at 1850, America had been joined in the democratic camp by Belgium, Switzerland, and to some extent England, which had an elected government although a majority of males still lacked the franchise. By 1900 England was almost fully democratic. France too was a democracy. Italy, the Low Countries, and Scandinavia were all in varying degrees democratic or well on their way to being so. By 1950 all of western Europe, except Iberia, was democratic, including West Germany although its elected government still functioned under the aegis of the Allied occupation. The same was true for Japan. Newly independent India was democratic, as were the new states of Israel and Lebanon.

The next half-century interval, the year 2000, is still a decade away. Today we find all of western Europe democratic with inroads being made into Eastern Europe. We also find nearly all of Latin America and the Caribbean democratic, as well as many of the Pacific island states and large chunks of Asia. According to the ratings of Freedom House for 1990, 61 of 167 of the world's sovereign states, comprising about 39 percent of its population, lived in free states, that is, democracies.[24] By the year 2000 some of these states may have fallen off the list, but this list may also expand over these years. Indeed, taking this 200-year vantage point, we can see not only that democracy has spread dramatically, but also that it seems to be growing at an accelerating pace.

7

The Export of Democracy and the Force of Example

Even if it is reasonable, as I have been arguing, to hope for the spread of democracy, the United States is not necessarily able to help the process along. Can we export democracy? The term "export" can be a kind of straw man. Democracy is not a product that we can sell or barter. Nor can the United States control the political future of other nations. The real question is whether the United States can influence the political development of other nations to make them more democratic or to make the achievement of democracy more likely or its advent sooner.

When put this way, the answer is yes. Could the enormous growth of democracy of the past two hundred years have occurred anyway had the American Revolution failed and the colonies returned to the rule of King George III? Or if it had never occurred? Democracy might then have begun somewhere else, some decades or generations later, perhaps in England, perhaps in France. But who would argue that absent the American Revolution democracy would have unfolded in the rest of the world as it has?

Although this point is unarguable, it has bearing on other points that often are argued in discussions of democracy, especially by the skeptics. Democracy is often discussed as if it were organic or, in the language of social science, as if it were a dependent variable. Democracy arises from certain social circumstances, it is said. A solid case can be made that literacy, affluence, national unity, peace, and the like are factors that make democracy easier to create or preserve. It is equally true, however, that democracy is created; it does not just arise. It is created as a result of political, cultural, or intellectual processes that persuade a body of people to create democratic structures. Those processes are manifestly subject to external influence.

Can America export democracy? It can. Senator Daniel Patrick Moynihan raised a skeptical voice at the moment of the American invasion of Grenada: "I don't know that you restore democracy at the point of a bayonet."[1] No? Look at Japan, West Germany, Austria, Italy, Grenada, the Dominican Republic, and Panama. All have democratic systems imposed by American arms. The systems, to be sure, are now maintained by their own dynamics and popular support. American forces have long since departed. But would those polities be the same had U.S. troops never landed?

The limitation of these examples is obvious. In each case the United States took to arms for reasons of self-defense or national security, not for the purpose of spreading democracy. Once the adversary was subdued, democracy was implanted either because America believed it essential to cure the conquered foe of its belligerent tendencies or because America's sense of right demanded that it leave behind the only political order it views as legitimate. These acts are a far cry, however, from initiating aggressive war for the purpose of imposing democracy. Neither international law nor world opinion would accept that. Nor would the American public long agree to shed its blood for so selfless a cause.[2]

Although the United States cannot spread democracy through the world by conquest, these cases show that democracy implanted from without rather than grown organically from within, can take hold. In 1939 Assistant Secretary of State Adolph A. Berle declared that "a nation coerced into democracy is not a democratic country."[3] Although this makes sense intuitively, experience has proved it wrong. It is nearly four decades since occupation forces left West Germany and Japan. In that time nothing external has prevented the authoritarian traditions of those societies from reasserting themselves. Instead democracy has grown constantly stronger, its popular support deeper.[4]

Even though these cases prove that democracy can be fostered from abroad, the question remains how such influence can be exerted without conquest. But countries do influence one another all the time in innumerable ways. In particular, America has influenced other countries in the direction of democracy by methods less intrusive than military intervention, such as diplomatic representations, foreign aid, education, propaganda, and even nonaction. The sheer force of its example has been a powerful prod to the rest of the world.

Impact of the American Revolution

The impact of the American example began with the Revolution. The historian Robert R. Palmer put it:

> There were many in Europe . . . who saw in the American Revolution a lesson and an encouragement for mankind. It proved that the liberal ideas of the Enlightenment might be

put into practice. It showed, or was assumed to show, that ideas of the rights of man and the social contract, of liberty and equality, of responsible citizenship and popular sovereignty, of religious freedom, freedom of thought and speech, separation of powers and deliberately contrived written constitutions, need not remain in the realm of speculation, among the writers of books, but could be made the actual fabric of public life among real people, in this world, now.[5]

The impact of the American Revolution on Europe was initially surpassed by that of the French. France, after all, was Europe's dominant country. America was small, weak, and far away. France's revolution was more imitable by other European states, which were monarchies as France had been, not colonies like America. Nonetheless America's influence remained profound, as on the French revolution. In 1786 the eminent philosopher Condorcet published his essay "The Influence of the American Revolution on Europe." It declared that "it is not enough that the rights of man be written in the books of philosophers and inscribed in the hearts of virtuous men; the weak and ignorant must be able to read them in the example of a great nation. America has given us this example."[6]

France's inspiration from the American Revolution was embodied in the Marquis de Lafayette. As historian John Simpson Penman described it, Lafayette

> came back to France at the close of the war with many of his brother officers imbued with ideas of liberty and equality. His democratic sympathies were so strong that he affected even its spirit in his dress and his speech, saying, "We and other Republicans." An anecdote which he related about himself at this time shows the strength of his democratic opinions: "In the military reviews under Louis XVI, Lafayette was seen wearing the American uniform, of which the baldrick, according to a fairly common custom, was decorated with an emblem at the choice of each officer; and the king, having asked him an explanation of this, discovered that this emblem was a tree of liberty planted above a crown and a broken sceptre."
>
> In 1783, he placed in his own house the Declaration of Independence and by its side a vacant frame which he said boldly was "awaiting the Declaration of the Rights of France."[7]

Lafayette lionized George Washington, who was a surrogate father to him. Other leading American revolutionaries enjoyed immense prestige in France as well. Benjamin Franklin served as the new nation's first ambassador to France. According to Simon Schama his "popularity was so widespread that it does not seem exaggerated to call it a mania. Mobbed wherever he went . . . he was probably better known by sight than the King, and his likeness could be found on engraved glass, painted porcelain, printed cottons, snuffboxes and inkwells. . . ."[8] Franklin was succeeded as ambassador by Thomas Jefferson, who held the post during the French Revolution. He collaborated with Lafayette in drafting the Declaration of the Rights of Man and Citizen. In the summer of 1789 when divisions broke out in the Patriot party over provisions of the constitution being drafted for the revolutionary government, a negotiating session was convened in Jefferson's home.[9] In 1792 the National Assembly conferred honorary French citizenship on Washington, Hamilton, and Madison, although only the last accepted it.

They surely were all great men, but their cachet in France resulted not from their individual virtues but from the fact that they represented America. As the French historian George Lefebvre, described a half century ago as "the most distinguished living authority on the period of the Revolution,"[10] put it, "The revolt of the English colonies may in fact be considered the principal direct cause of the French Revolution."[11] Simon Schama's more recent magisterial chronicle differs from Lefebvre's view of the revolution but reaches the same conclusion about the importance of America's example: "For France, without any question, the Revolution began in America." He explains:

> The consequences of French involvement in the revolutionary war were, in fact, profoundly subversive and irreversible. . . . [One] can hardly fail to register the extraordinary importance of the flirtation with armed freedom to a section of the aristocracy that was rich, powerful and influential. On their own they could not conceivably have constituted any kind of independent "revolutionary" opposition to the crown. But once the money crisis of the monarchy was transformed into a political argument, the vocabulary of "liberty" was apt to take on a life of its own . . . .
> . . . writers like the Abbé Gentil saw the American example as contributing in some warm and woolly way to the "regeneration" of France or even, more generally, the whole world.[12]

Hamilton, polemicizing in favor of U.S. neutrality between France and England in 1794, replied to the argument that the combined European powers, after subduing France, would turn on the United States because they "will never forgive in us the origination of those principles which were the germs of the French Revolution." He conceded the premise of their antipathy but argued that they would not undertake such an aggression because it would depend on Great Britain, where public opinion "would disrelish and oppose the project. . . . many, not improbably a majority, would see in the enterprise a malignant and wanton hostility against liberty, of which they might themselves expect to be the next victim."[13]

This point of the argument may have been a bit fanciful on both sides, but Hamilton was right to suggest that the American Revolution had European friends outside France. The American colonists were moved to rebellion in defense of their rights as Englishmen, and many Englishmen back home agreed with them. In 1775 John Horne-Tooke advertised in the newspaper his intention to raise funds for the relief of the families of the colonists "murdered" at Lexington and Concord.[14] The *London Evening Post* reported that "the prevailing toast in every company of true Englishmen is, 'Victory to the Americans, and re-establishment to the British Constitution.'"[15] In 1776 members of the radical party pressed in the House of Commons for universal suffrage and annual parliaments, and several books advocated democracy in England.

Democratization of Britain

The most important book in advancing the democratic cause in England was published fifteen years later. It was written by an American, although British born: Tom Paine. George Trevelyan put it: "The democratic movement in England . . . owed its origin to the spectacle of the French revolution and to the writings of Tom Paine."[16] Paine's *Rights of Man*, written in reply to Edmund Burke's *Reflections on the French Revolution*, caused a great stir, forcing Paine to flee the country. Among those affected by Paine was William Cobbett. At first a bitter critic, Cobbett became such an ardent admirer that after Paine died, Cobbett carried his bones home to England. After his own leftward political evolution, Cobbett became a firebrand publicist for the grievances of the common man. He "was the man," said Trevelyan, "who diverted the working-class from rick-burning and machine-breaking to agitate for parliamentary reform."[17] In the repressive atmosphere of 1817, Cobbett fled to America "to breathe the air of a free country for once."[18] But he returned and resumed his leading role in the agitations leading to the reform acts of 1832.

Nor was this the last time the influence of America lent weight to the democratization of Britain. It could be observed again late in the 1830s in the six points of the Chartist movement and in the impetus that the North's victory in the American Civil War gave to the Second Reform Act of 1867, which extended the franchise. Trevelyan called these the "adaptation of our institutions to the new theory that Britain was a democracy no less than her own Colonies or America."[19]

A Pull on Europe

Elsewhere in Europe the American model also exerted a strong pull. In 1789 the Belgians of what was then the Austrian Netherlands rebelled against Emperor Joseph II's efforts to centralize authority in Vienna. As Palmer recounted:

> The declaration of independence of Flanders (each province announced its independence from the Hapsburg emperor separately) reproduced certain phrases of the American Declaration of Independence. The democratic party which briefly existed in Belgium in 1790 pointed to some of the American state constitutions for examples of what it wanted. The act of union of the United Belgian States resembled the American Articles of Confederation in its provisions and even occasionally in language. These new United States of Belgium even called their central body a Congress.[20]

In 1830 Belgium rose again, this time against Dutch rule, and secured independence under a constitutional monarchy. One of the drafters of the constitution, Desire de Haerne, later said:

> We are the only nation that has . . . followed America from the foundation of her political establishment and her liberal institutions. Yes, we looked upon England, . . . but, at the same time, we were conscious that there were certain customs in the institutions of that country we could not adopt, and we cast our eyes beyond the Atlantic, where we found a great people worthy of our entire imitation, and it is the institutions of that people we have chiefly inscribed upon our organic charter. We have followed their example in all that regards public liberty, the distribution of power, the election of representatives and decentralization of rule.[21]

Thaddeus Kosciuszko fought in the American Revolution and then returned to Poland to lead its unsuccessful rebellion of 1794. The Irish, moved by the American example, secured various reforms in 1778–1782 including an independent parliament; most, however, were reversed in the harsh repression of the rebellion of 1798. In Norway C. M. Falsen, known as the father of the Norwegian constitution, which was written in 1814, named his son George Benjamin, after Washington and Franklin.[22]

In 1848 the Swiss adopted a new constitution resolving several years of internecine broils by imitating the American model of federalism and a bicameral legislature. As the eminent Swiss jurist Max Huber put it: "Where was this possibility of a synthesis of Freedom and Power? The North American colonies of Great Britain had found it in their struggle for independence: the federal state. . . . Switzerland was the first country that followed the example of the United States."[23] That same revolutionary year the Hungarians led by Lajos Kossuth issued a declaration of independence inspired by the American original.[24] The invocations of the American example were not even limited to the revolutionaries. François Guizot, the French scholar turned politician, was ousted as premier in the revolution that overthrew his sovereign, Louis Philippe. He used his forced retirement to write a warning to his countrymen that their new republic would do better to follow the model of Washington than of Napoleon.[25]

The history of democracy in Germany until the Bonn Republic was a tragic one, but the German democratic tradition that finally flowered in West Germany had its roots in the Frankfurt Assembly of 1848. Of that gathering Carl J. Friedrich wrote:

> Perhaps the most general influence of the American federal concept as of the presidential one in the thought of constitutional draftsmen, at least in Europe, is to be found in the German constitutional assembly which sat in Frankfurt in 1848. Dubbed derisively the "assembly of professors," it did indeed gather the most learned, if not the most experienced or practical-minded, of constitution-makers. Many of them were close students of the American experience, and the records are replete with references not only to the Constitution and *The Federalist*, but also to the leading commentators. . . .[26]

Closer to Home

While the American example influenced many Europeans, it was even more strongly felt closer to home, in Latin America, where it helped to inspire rebellions against Spanish rule beginning in 1809. Initially unsuccessful, these rebellions culminated in independence in the early 1820s. Although democracy failed to sink secure roots in Latin America in the nineteenth century, all of the newly independent Latin states began as constitutional republics, many even adopting variants of the American constitution.[27] The Venezuelan constitution of 1811, the Mexican of 1824, the Central American Federation's of 1825, the Argentine of 1826 and 1853, and the Brazilian of 1891 all bear this stamp.[28] Although Mexico lost a huge portion of its territory to America and has long borne resentment toward its overpowering northern neighbor, it has been deeply influenced by America's democratic example. A recent essay by Mexican historian Enrique Krauze, whose main point is to chastise America for insufficient dedication to democracy, recalls some of that influence:

In 1824 Mexico adopted a constitution inspired by the Founding Fathers of the United States which the contemporary Mexican newspaper *El Sol* considered "one of the most perfect creations of the spirit . . . the foundation on which the simplest, most liberal and contented government in history rests." Among some Mexican liberals, this admiration for U.S. institutions and political ideas overshadowed even the most basic feelings of nationalism. . . .

In the nineteenth century Mexico experienced a civil war with marked ideological connotations. On one hand, conservatives sought the continuation of the Spanish political tradition. . . . On the other, and in spite of the War of 1847, the liberals struggled to implement a democracy like the one to the north.

. . . . [In the early 1900s a] young entrepreneur, Francisco I. Madero, led an innocent and purely democratic revolution against Diaz. Madero had studied at Berkeley, where he learned the progressives' message. He devoutly applied this message in Mexico upon his return. Democracy was not an ideology for Madero, but a religion.[29]

Postwar Influence

With the turn of the century and then World War I, the United States emerged as a great power. Its influence accordingly grew more ubiquitous and often more direct. The cause of democracy became widely identified with the American president Woodrow Wilson. His speeches in translation became a bestseller in China.[30] After World War II America championed the cause of national independence for the colonial world, and its example as well as more direct forms of its influence made a mark on the new nations. Even in India, whose democratic system was shaped by its British former rulers, the new constitution incorporated important ideas borrowed from America, notably a federal structure and a system of separated powers in which a supreme court may rule upon the constitutionality of legislation.[31] In addition it contains an enumeration of rights, "almost every [one of] which," according to Indian scholar P. V. Tripathi,

> has its counterpart in the United States Bill of Rights. In most cases the text is deliberately altered because the true import of the guarantee as it now obtains in the United States after about one hundred and sixty years of judicial application will be—or so it was thought—more truly captured by an altered text.[32]

In the first five years after World War II, the constitutional authority Karl Loewenstein could count more than fifty states that had "equipped themselves with new constitutions." He noted that "practically all new constitutions are surprisingly alike in structure in that they operate uniformly with the traditional tripartite division of functions into legislative, executive-administrative, and judicial organs of the state. Almost without exception they have a comprehensive and ambitious bill of rights."[33] By division of functions Loewenstein does not necessarily mean a separation of powers as in the American system; the bills of rights, he explained, often include things that would not qualify as rights in the vocabulary of American legal philosophy. Nonetheless the influence of the American model is palpable in his account. And in the four decades since, scores of additional nations have adopted new constitutions of this sort. As Friedrich put it: "Wherever men have gathered to draft a constitution, they have drawn upon American constitutional theory and practice."[34]

After World War II the UN Universal Declaration of Human Rights was adopted and established democratic norms as a universal standard for mankind, even if honored largely in the breach. The universal declaration was drafted largely by Americans, under the chairmanship of Eleanor Roosevelt, and clearly the idea behind it was derivative in part of the American Bill of Rights, although it diverges in many ways from it. In this postwar period America became the world's preeminent status quo power, at least insofar as it took upon itself the task of building and sustaining a structure of world order. Nonetheless the year 1989 furnished dramatic evidence that America's example still constitutes a potent inspiration for the rise of democracy in other parts of the world.

The students who marched for democracy in Beijing and Shanghai took as their symbol the Statue of Liberty. Yan Jiaqui, a close adviser to Zhao Ziyang and a principal patron within the Chinese power structure of the democracy movement, fled the country after the Tiananmen massacre. In Hong Kong he published a booklet that advocated "that China should follow the American system of a three-way division of power, 'depoliticize the military, make the Constitution supreme and obey the rule of law.'"[35] When protesters in Czechoslovakia called a general strike in the fall of 1989, the *New York Times* reported this scene from Prague:

> Soon after the strike began today, Zdenek Janicek, a brewery worker, rose on a platform in grimy overalls and began to speak.
> "We hold these truths to be self-evident," he said, "that all men are created equal, that they are endowed by their creator with certain unalienable rights, that among these are life, liberty and the pursuit of happiness."[36]

When Romania's hated dictator Nicolae Ceausescu was overthrown, Ioan Grigorescu, a writer and filmmaker active in the rebellion, told the *Washington Post*, "[We] live at the moment of 1776."[37]

In the wake of these revolutions, the Post reported that "a flood . . . of official and unofficial guests—principally members and administrators of newly elected parliaments—. . . come to Capitol Hill to take what amounts to a graduate seminar on the day-to-day operations of a democratic legislature. . . . they come from Warsaw, Prague, Budapest, Moscow and other capitals to see for themselves how Congress operates, down to the smallest detail of its rules and procedures." A *Post* interviewer asked one Soviet parliamentarian "what did not impress him favorably about Congress." He replied: "We're not really in a position to reject anything because you have such a profound experience of 200 years of running a legislature, while we've only been at it for a year or so. We're trying to learn what you've accumulated over 200 years."[38]

8

Imposing Democracy through Military Occupation

A significant part of the democratic world is democratic as a result of direct American coercion. In the course of war the United States has occupied more than a dozen countries at one time or another. In most cases America did not aspire to reshape the nation it occupied. In the cases it did, the U.S. goal invariably was to foster democratic government. In many of them, although not all, America's efforts have proven successful and durable.

Japan

The single most remarkable example is Japan. With a population of more than 120 million people, it commands an economy that may be the world's second largest. Japan embodies a distinct and highly articulated culture marked by a tradition of extraordinary insularity. General MacArthur, by far the single most important American in this process, pointed out that "history has given us no precedent of success in a similar military occupation of a defeated nation."[1] And if nothing like the American occupation had ever succeeded before, Japan certainly seemed an unlikely place to begin. When the concept of rights was imported into Japanese politics in the late nineteenth century, it was so foreign that it was not easily translated into Japanese: it required a compound word consisting of four characters to express it.[2] The indigenous prodemocracy movement that arose there in the late nineteenth and early twentieth centuries under foreign inspiration had petered out in the face of what Robert Scalapino described as "an overwhelmingly hostile tradition,"[3] of which the hallmarks were hierarchy, conformity, and obedience.

The measure of what the occupation accomplished was summarized by Robert E. Ward:

Prewar Japan had a notably authoritarian political system

> while postwar Japan, by any realistic standards of judgment, must be considered democratic . . . . this transition is remarkable enough in its own right. But added interest and significance flow from the further facts that practically all of the basic institutional changes involved—and many of the associated attitudinal and behavioral changes—originated during the Occupation period and that the initiatives underlying these changes, and a very substantial portion of their content as well, stemmed from American officials. . . .[4]

The occupation, to be sure, disposed of absolute power. It could do with Japan what it wished. But what it could not do, in the truism expressed at the time by the anthropologist Ruth Benedict, was "to create by fiat a free, democratic Japan."[5] Indeed many then believed that Japanese leaders would simply go through whatever motions were demanded of them until the conquerors departed "and then bring to naught as soon as possible much of what the foreigners accomplished," as John M. Maki put it.[6]

Some of the occupation's measures were indeed undone almost as soon as sovereignty was restored, for example, the purge of Japanese tainted by association with the militarist regime. Yet the main thrust of the reforms, amounting to a fundamental shift in Japan's political history, remained firmly intact. "Never before," says Edwin Reischauer, "had one advanced nation attempted to reform the supposed faults of another advanced nation from within. And never did the military occupation of one world power by another prove so satisfactory to the victor and tolerable to the vanquished."[7]

To call the results of the occupation satisfactory from America's viewpoint is something of an understatement. Democratization of Japan, though valued in itself by the Americans, was an instrumental goal. "The ultimate objective" read MacArthur's instructions, was "to foster conditions which will give the greatest possible assurance that Japan will not again become a menace to the peace and security of the world."[8] Americans believed that the best way to accomplish this was to make over Japan's political system. In this scheme—so visionary, so typically American—the United States succeeded, one is tempted to say, beyond its wishes. Japan has remained a democratic American ally; it has also remained so pacifistic that U.S. leaders are forever goading their Japanese counterparts to enlarge their military forces. And whether or not the occupation may have seemed tolerable in the eyes of the Japanese, the outcome cannot too much displease them. From the depths of physical devastation and exhaustion that made it one of the poorest nations on earth in 1945, Japan has risen to such towering heights of economic power and performance as to dwarf anything it might have achieved through the Greater East Asia Co-Prosperity Sphere, in the name of which it fought the war.

The accomplishments of the occupation are all the more remarkable for its brevity. In all, the occupation lasted six years and eight months. It might have ended sooner had not cold war tensions complicated the diplomacy of arranging a peace treaty. In practice the occupation exercised little power after the beginning of the Korean War in 1950. Moreover the political reforms of the occupation were mostly carried out within its first two years. As early as March 1947 General MacArthur suggested that "the time is now approaching when we must talk peace with Japan," meaning end the occupation. "The political phase [of restructuring Japan] is approaching such completion as is possible under the Occupation," he added.[9] By late 1948 the occupation's government section began to produce its account of its activities, a report written from the perspective that the task was in essence complete.[10]

It is true that the vast changes effected by the occupation were not fashioned from whole cloth. Robert Ward has said, "The fundamental importance of the [American] plans was in stimulating, reinforcing, and giving direction and form to forces for change that were endogenous to Japan."[11]

Forced Modernization. Japan's era of rapid, one might even say forced, modernization began with the Meiji restoration of 1867, a kind of coup d'état touched off by humiliation at the hands of American naval power. This era saw the rise of forces and institutions that encouraged democratization. Probably the most important were the various political parties, which individually rose and fell but collectively shifted the locus of politics from the oligarchy to the public. This political party movement was, in the words of Scalapino, "fundamentally dedicated to Western liberalism."[12]

Under pressure from the party movement, Japan's first constitution was promulgated in 1889 as "a gift from the emperor." This constitution was modeled in large part after the Prussian, specifically in emulation of its authoritarian character. The Diet was created and was first elected in 1890, but the government was accountable to the emperor, not the Diet. The emperor was accountable to no one. Ironically, although his authority was in theory absolute, he did not in truth rule. The principle of imperial sovereignty was sacrosanct, but in practice power rested with a small oligarchy who ruled in the emperor's name, even though the Meiji restoration had abolished the centuries-old shogunate, so it claimed, to restore imperial rule.

Although the powers of the Diet were severely circumscribed, it provided an arena for prodemocratic forces. "Through persistent and clever exploitation of these [legislative] powers," says Ward, "the leaders of Japan's political parties were able, over a period of thirty-odd years, to liberalize appreciably the political institutions inherited from the Meiji oligarchs."[13] In 1925 tax qualifications for voting were abolished, effectively establishing universal male suffrage.[14] For all the weakness of the Diet and the authoritarian forms of the Meiji constitution, by the time of the occupation the Japanese, in Ward's words, "were in no sense strangers to the mechanics of a democratic political system."[15]

The mechanics of democracy may have become familiar, but the philosophy of democracy had not taken hold. Even the liberals of the late nineteenth and early twentieth centuries tended to advance their beliefs on the grounds not that they were integrally valid but that liberal reforms could help to strengthen the state.[16] Such arguments were too weak to stand up against the rightist, militarist tide that gained strength in the 1920s and 1930s in Japan as well as in Europe. "Long since weakened by its many shortcomings, the Japanese democratic movement was no more than a hollow shell by the 1930's," says Scalapino. By 1940 the political parties all manifested their devotion to the state (and their own fundamental failure) by dissolving themselves.[17]

In short, although the occupation built on existing traditions or impulses within the Japanese body politic, those forces had proved incapable of establishing democracy on their own. To cite Ward again:

> The . . . period from 1932 to 1945 is somewhat embarrassing for those who claim that Japan was gradually evolving into a democratic society. It lasted too long to be shrugged off as merely an episode; it was too dramatic and disastrous in its consequences to be ignored. It marked a reversion to authoritarian and militaristic ways that were certainly far more in the main stream of Japan's political traditions than were the brief years of "liberalism."[18]

The Occupation's Purge. What then did the occupation do to overcome this discouraging history? Although brief, the occupation was intense. General MacArthur took to heart his mission to "guide [the Japanese] . . . to higher principles, ideals and purposes, to help them rise to the full measure of new and loftier standards of social and political morality."[19] This would entail, he said, "a complete reformation of the Japanese people—reformation from feudalistic slavery to human freedom."[20] Sometimes zealous underlings took this mandate for complete reformation too literally. As Theodore Cohen, head of the occupation's labor section who stayed on after the occupation, related:

> Absent any idea of constraints, the Civil Information and Education Section of Occupation Headquarters felt free to

sponsor square dancing and billiards for the Japanese as obviously more democratic than geisha dances and *kendo* sword-fighting. The Civil Transportation Section's Chief had no compunctions about explaining to the Transportation Ministry . . . that pricing second-class rail tickets at triple third-class fare and first-class at triple second-class fare was not democratic. . . . The imposition one fine day of daylight savings time by the executive officer of the Economic and Scientific Section . . . was even more distantly related to [the] "purpose of war."[21]

Such excesses were exceptional (and each of these examples was countermanded), but the occupation did intrude deeply into Japanese life. It ruled indirectly, however, keeping in place Japanese governmental institutions from the emperor on down. This method made its tutelage in democratic procedures more like a practicum than a lecture. The occupation communicated its requirements, for example, for a new constitution, a new electoral law, new elections, or new labor law and then encouraged Japanese authorities to carry them out themselves. Ultimate power lay with the Americans, and sometimes, as in drafting the constitution, it was wielded with a heavy hand. In the main, however, a process of give and take characterized the relations between the Japanese functionaries and their counterparts or overseers in the occupation administration. The functionaries went through the motions of democratic procedures even without exercising true sovereignty.

Although the ocupation left Japanese government structures in place, it strongly influenced who would administer them, not by directly selecting personnel but by purging from public life those associated with the militarism of the 1930s and the war years. Prime Minister Shigeru Yoshida was probably correct in saying later that the purge was "on a scale seldom paralleled in any country outside the Communist nations."[22]

The purge began with figures in national politics and worked its way down to local officials, then branched out to other realms such as the economy and mass media. Those purged included many leaders of the first postwar government, including most of the cabinet and a big share of the legislators elected to the first postwar Diet. Hundreds of thousands were screened and thousands were purged. Countless others removed themselves from posts, or from consideration for posts, to avoid subjecting themselves to the purge.

In addition to individuals, organizations that had abetted militarism were banned. Not only were existing organizations dissolved, but a prohibition was declared against

any future organizations any of whose principal officers were members of organizations abolished in accordance with the [purge] directive, former commissioned officers of the Imperial Japanese Regular Army or Navy or the Special Volunteer Reserve, who served on active duty at any time since January 1, 1930, or persons who served in or with the military police or naval police. . . . [And] any society whose membership included more than 25 percent former members of an organization or organizations abolished or prohibited in accordance with the directive.[23]

This provision gives some idea of the thoroughness of the purge, as does the provision that forbade "any relative of a purgee within the third degree by blood, marriage or adoption from succeeding to the appointive office from which the purgee had been removed." The purpose of this provision was to "prevent any purgee from subverting family loyalty into a device for maintaining his own power." But the Allied command conceded somewhat dryly that "The justice of this article had been questioned by the Japanese Government."[24]

Not surprisingly, given its Draconian character, the purge was one of the measures of the occupation most resented by the Japanese. In its latter stages the occupation began to back away from it, and as soon as the Japanese regained their independence, they repealed it. The occupation's 1948 report on the political reorientation of Japan, prepared under MacArthur's direction, vigorously defended the purge as "a vital part of the whole program of democratic reform. . . . Without it, all subsequent attempts at reform would have been futile."[25] But one of his biographers noted that MacArthur later "played down the purge. . . . not proud of [his] part in it."[26] In his memoirs the general sought to deflect all responsibility for it:

The Potsdam declaration . . . contained a purge provision requiring all Japanese who had actively engaged in militaristic and ultra-nationalistic activities prior to the war to be removed from public office and excluded from political influence. I very much doubted the wisdom of this measure, as it tended to lose the services of many able governmental individuals who would be difficult to replace in the organization of a new Japan. I put the purge into operation with as little harshness as possible, but it was the one issue in which popular support by the Japanese people was lacking. The punitive feature of such a policy always outweighs all other attributes and invariably breeds resentments which carry the germs of future discord.[27]

The retrospective consensus against the purge seems especially broad in condemnation of its extension to the economic realm. Prime

Minister Yoshida complained in his memoirs that the rebuilding of Japan's decimated economy was stalled by "a serious lack of available men experienced in [foreign trade] because of the large numbers eliminated by the purge."[28] U.S. Ambassador William Sebald (representative to and chairman of the Allied Council for Japan) reached the identical conclusion:

> In 1947 and, indeed, for the next two years, the Japanese lacked both the means and the will to revitalize their economy. This was due, in considerable measure, to the so-called economic 'reforms' which, in my view, barred the very men upon whom we would have to rely to improve the economy.[29]

The application of the purge to leaders of the economic world may have been misconceived: the surprisingly strong influence of Marxism on some of the personnel of the occupation probably led to an overestimation of the role played by the captains of industry. And the purge in its entirety certainly bruised Japanese sensibilities; it ran counter to MacArthur's cardinal principle of showing careful respect for the Japanese even while ruling over them. Still the purge of political leaders played an important part in Japan's transformation by debilitating the old, nondemocratic political elite and hastening the emergence of a new elite more disposed or receptive to democratic philosophy. Even Prime Minister Yoshida, though highly critical of the purge, said:

> We have to admit that [it] did exert a considerable influence in bringing about the democratisation of all spheres of activity in Japan. Most of the former leaders in the walks of life concerned were removed from the national scene; new men were promoted to key positions in their stead, and this new personnel, operating new systems, caused a complete break with things as they were before. . . .[30]

The New Constitution. If the purge is the one occupation action for which MacArthur in retrospect was least eager to claim credit, endowing Japan with a new constitution seems to have been the reform of which he was most proud. He called it in his memoirs "probably the single most important accomplishment of the occupation."[31] The constitution is most famous for its unique provision (article 9) renouncing war and the maintenance of military forces. A visionary step, this language expressed Japan's determination to shut the door on militarism (as well as MacArthur's determination that it should do so). Putting this into the constitution, however, has had the awkward effect of forcing Japan to maintain its modest but not negligible defense forces in defiance of the letter of its own law, a contradiction that it must disingenuously deny.

Far more important than article 9 or any of its other specific provisions is the influence of the constitution as a whole, which, as one occupation official put it, "marked the undoing of the powerful minority that had ruled since the Meiji Restoration and the rise of the masses from the rank of *shimmin* (subjects) to the rank of *jimmin* (the people)."[32] Formally the constitution makes Japan a constitutional monarchy, but in effect it makes it a republic. Article 1 deprives the emperor of sovereignty—which had been proclaimed in the Meiji constitution of 1889 and in immemorial Japanese understanding—and declares him instead "the symbol of the State and of the unity of the people, deriving his position from the will of the people with whom resides sovereign power."[33] The articles that follow declare flatly that the emperor "shall not have powers related to government," that "the advice and approval of the Cabinet shall be required for all acts of the Emperor in matters of state," and even that "no property can be given to, or received by, the Imperial House . . . without the authorization of the Diet." So radical a departure was this from Japanese tradition that none of the Japanese leaders, powerless though they were in the face of the occupation, were prepared to accept it until Emperor Hirohito himself commanded them to do so.[34]

Another major innovation in the constitution is a bill of rights comprising thirty-one articles, including the assertion of equal rights and suffrage for women. In contrast to the Meiji era, the current constitution makes the cabinet (which is appointed by the prime minister) accountable to the Diet. The Diet consists of two popularly elected houses. It chooses the prime minister from among its members. Other important liberalizing provisions of the constitution grant greater independence to the judiciary and greater authority to local governments than Japan had known.

More than most other reforms of the occupation, the constitution was forced on the Japanese government. Prime Minister Yoshida later commented wryly that "there was a good deal of the American spirit of enterprise in the undertaking of such a fundamental piece of reform . . . within two months of Japan's defeat."[35] Nevertheless the Japanese government, as instructed, appointed a committee to recommend constitutional revisions. These fell so far short of the degree of change that occupation officials viewed as essential that they concluded that the Japanese were acting in bad faith. MacArthur then ordered his own staff to write a constitution behind closed doors, which was presented to the Japanese in English. In theory this was a model for their own draft but in reality they were allowed to deviate from it little.

When he read the American draft, Dr. Joji Matsumoto, chairman of the Japanese drafting committee, protested: "A juridical system is very much like certain kinds of plants, which transplanted from their native soil degenerate or even die. Some of the roses of the West, when culti-vated in Japan, lose their fragrance."[36] To make matters worse in the eyes of Matsumoto and those who thought as he did, once the document had been agreed to in English, the Americans insisted that it be translated into Japanese literally rather than idiomatically because they feared that otherwise their recalcitrant Japanese interlocutors would subvert the meaning in the translation. As a result their constitution reads poorly in their own tongue, an irritant to the highly esthetic Japanese and a constant reminder of its foreign origins.

Writing a few years after the occupation, the Japanese scholar Kazuo Kawai forecast:

> However desirable the contents, this constitution suffers from the fatal stigma of being an alien-imposed document. As the Occupation recedes further into history, it is inevitable that the revival of national independence and self-respect will give increasing rise to the demand for a truly indigenous constitution.[37]

Although Kawai's prognostication seemed quite plausible at the time, it has been dramatically confounded. Revision of the constitution to make it more in keeping with Japanese tradition did indeed become a theme of Japan's right wing after the occupation. Although amendment of the constitution is not easy, it is less onerous than in the United States (in Japan a two-thirds vote of each house is required and then approval in a national referendum by a simple majority of those voting). The de-mands for changes failed, however, and they have grown weaker through the years. American occupation officials who have written about their experiences insist that although the Japanese government was disconcerted, the Japanese public was enthusiastic about its new freedoms and welcomed the constitution.[38] Its subsequent endurance lends some weight to their argument.

Other Structural Reforms. In addition to the new constitution, parlia-mentary reforms were adopted under the aegis of the occupation putting more services and resources at the command of legislators and creating standing committees. A meritocratic civil service replaced a system based on personal bonds. The larger goal of these two sets of reforms was to raise the power of the Diet over that of the bureaucracy, a reversal from the Prussian-inspired heritage of the Meiji era. In the realm of the economy, the occupation broke up the vast *zaibatsu* conglomerates, encouraged the unionization of labor, and distributed land to those who had been tenant farmers.

Not surprisingly some of these changes endured, while others did not. Trustbusting was a failure. Theodore Cohen explains, "Just or unjust, the Japanese could see no workable substitute for the *zaibatsu* in rebuilding industry and particularly in expanding exports on the scale needed to regain Japanese economic independence in a harsh world."[39] He illustrates the point by describing what happened to Japan's two most famous enterprises:

> When [the occupation] broke up the Mitsui and Mitsubishi trading companies into hundreds of fragments—213 successor companies in all—six months after the order, the employees loyally rallied round the new fragments formed by their old section or subsection chiefs . . . , who in turn adhered to the companies organized by their old division chiefs . . . and directors, and all of them recombined as soon as they could. Within five years, like droplets of mercury coalescing into ever bigger drops on contact with each other, both the Mitsubishi and the Mitsui trading companies were substantially reconstituted as before. Two hundred thirteen became two again. Their staffs had been held together by personal relations in the meantime.[40]

In contrast the encouragement of labor unions was a big success. According to Cohen, the head of the occupation's labor section, "By the end of 1946, a total of 4.5 million Japanese—ten times the prewar peak—were union members."[41] Land reform was also a success. In the four years from 1946 to 1950, the proportion of Japanese farms that were worked by tenants declined from 39 percent to 12 percent.[42] The newly self-employed peasantry brought about a sharp increase in agricultural production and provided a social base for the stable and conservative politics characteristic of Japan's ruling Liberal Democratic party.

The occupation also aimed beyond structural change. MacArthur himself said that "an acceptable constitution does not of itself establish democracy, *which is a thing largely of the spirit*" (emphasis added). The larger goal, he said, was "reshaping of national and individual character . . . to form the strong foundation of popular support upon which a democratic state must rest."[43] MacArthur hoped that structural reforms would stimulate spiritual change, but the occupation undertook other measures to encourage reculturation.

Curriculum reform was introduced into the schools and millions of new texts were issued. "The great efforts to teach democracy and civics in the primary and secondary schools were highly significant in inculcating the new values," says Japanese scholar Tanaka Hideo. "Educating the population about the constitution early in life meant that the basic concepts became a common ground for analyzing and discussing social issues. . . . its concepts have become part of our *Zeitgeist*."[44] For those beyond school age the occupation sought to foster democratic sensibilities through "adult education projects, libraries, community activities, and the like. Even more it sought to ensure that the press, radio, theater, and other media of mass communication would contribute adequately to the formation of an enlightened public opinion."[45] For mass education (or propaganda), posters depicting the transformation from old ways to new were placed in public places. In the old the emperor was elevated above the people; in the new he was the symbol of the people. Similarly the old family was depicted with the father ruling supreme; in the new the family was more of a partnership.

As the posters reflected, the reculturation process sought to attenuate Japan's extreme sense of hierarchy in favor of civic equality. This was also the goal of the principal structural reforms, which emasculated the role of the emperor, encouraged labor organization, gave land to the peasants, and enfranchised women. Occupation forces also spread the message of civic equality by their example. American soldiers made a strong impression on the Japanese because their humane and self-disciplined actions contrasted with what the Japanese had been told to expect. The sense of civic equality embodied in the day-to-day behavior of these Americans toward the Japanese and toward one another was also not lost on the Japanese. All in all a deep change was wrought in Japanese political culture. The Japan scholar Robert Ward studied whether the lines of continuity or of discontinuity between the prewar and postwar eras were stronger. He concluded that comparing "popular attitudes, behavior, and values in the 1920s or 1930 [the apex of Japan's indigenous liberalization] with those in present-day Japan, there is no doubt that the verdict would come down on the side of a pronounced discontinuity."[46]

Reasons for Success. The expectations of the U.S. officials who carried the occupation out were in many ways not reasonable, Ward suggests, but a measure of their own ignorance and arrogance. "Had they known more, they might have accomplished less," he says.[47] Why did it work so well?

It succeeded first because the devastating defeat not only had wrecked Japan physically but had shaken the Japanese loose from their cultural and spiritual moorings. As General MacArthur saw it:

> They suddenly felt the concentrated shock of total defeat; their whole world crumbled. It was not merely the overthrow of their military might—it was the collapse of a faith, it was the disintegration of everything they had believed in and lived by and fought for. It left a complete vacuum, morally,

101

mentally, and physically. And into this vacuum flowed the
democratic way of life.[48]

The occupation succeeded by breaking the grip of tradition in many
areas of Japanese life: that grip had already been weakened by the
outcome of the war. Theodore Cohen put it: "The Japanese [were]
inclined to believe that 'traditional behavior' was somehow responsible
for their defeat." They were "in a mood to question everything to which
they had been loyal," and conversely "everything the Americans did
was food for thought."[49]

Such openness to foreign things was quite uncharacteristic of the
Japanese, who are remarkable for their homogeneity and insularity.
Interestingly, however, it was not unprecedented. At two other mo-
ments in their national history, albeit under different circumstances, the
Japanese engaged in great spasms of cultural borrowing. The first oc-
curred in the seventh and eighth centuries, when, as anthropologist Ruth
Benedict described it,

> the Japanese Emperor and his court set themselves the task
> of enriching Japan with the customs of the high civilization
> that had greeted the amazed eyes of their envoys in the great
> kingdom of China. They went about it with incomparable
> energy. Before that time Japan had not even had a written
> language; in the seventh century she took the ideographs of
> China and used them to write her own totally different
> language. . . . Japan adopted Buddhism wholesale from
> China. . . . She had had no great permanent architecture,
> either public or private; the Emperors built a new capital city,
> Nara, on the model of a Chinese capital, and great ornate
> Buddhist temples and vast Buddhist monasteries were
> erected in Japan after the Chinese pattern. The Emperors
> introduced titles and ranks and laws their envoys reported to
> them from China. It is difficult to find anywhere in the history
> of the world any other such successfully planned importation
> of civilization by a sovereign nation.[50]

Japan's second era of borrowing came in the late nineteenth century following the Meiji restoration, when Japanese political, military,
and educational systems were entirely redesigned along European lines,
primarily Prussian. The occupation was thus Japan's third episode of
borrowing, this time from America. The occupation differed from the
two earlier episodes in that they were voluntary and this time Japan had
no choice. Still the Japanese were to some extent willing to explore new
ways, their old ones having failed them so catastrophically.

Another source of the occupation's success was its chief, General
MacArthur, whose brilliance was fortified by a fine feel for the Japanese.

One of his biographers spoke of his having a "deferential regard for the Japanese way of life."[51] It is easy to see how the courtesy, orderliness, self-discipline, and other values of the Japanese might have appealed to him. The general himself, although effusive in his rhetoric about the virtues of democracy, exhibited a sensibility that was deeply traditional, one might even say premodern. An ironic mixture, it may have been well suited to the ironic task of imposing freedom on a subjugated people. And MacArthur's admiration for the Japanese was without doubt reciprocated.

There was much paternal in the way MacArthur set about to mold the Japanese. He was secure in his authority and did not hesitate to have things his way when he thought it important, as with the constitution. Conversely, absolute as it was, he usually tried to exercise his power with a light touch,[52] sensitive to Japanese feelings. Even in his first speech to them, accepting their surrender aboard the *Missouri*, he offered words of hope and encouragement, not recrimination. He directed his subordinates to respect Japanese ways insofar as they were compatible with specific objectives of the occupation, and where they were incompatible, he sought to let the Japanese back down with minimum loss of face.

When the occupiers arrived, Japan was decimated and hunger was widespread. The Americans, by MacArthur's order, brought in their own food rather than living off the land, as occupiers normally do. And they soon brought in food for the Japanese, too. At the same time MacArthur protected Japan from paying reparations that the Allies had agreed should recompense the nations it had victimized in the war. Since Japan had no money and meager production at the war's end, the reparations were to be taken in the form of industrial plants, just as the Soviet Union did in Germany and Manchuria. Largely devised in Washington, this scheme had the support of the U.S. government but not of MacArthur. He sabotaged it through procrastination and bureaucratic machination for the better part of four years until the U.S. government reversed its policy.[53]

He also protected the emperor, whom some of MacArthur's superiors wanted to try as a war criminal. Instructed by the Joint Chiefs of Staff to gather evidence against the emperor, MacArthur cabled back, disingenuously, that "the decision as to whether the emperor should be tried as a war criminal involves a policy determination upon such a high level that I would not feel it appropriate for me to make a recommendation." His opinion about the likely consequences of such a step, however, was calculated to chill their ardor:

> The whole of Japan can be expected, in my opinion, to resist the action either by passive or semi-active means. They are disarmed and therefore will represent no special menace to

trained and equipped troops; but it is not inconceivable that all government agencies will break down, the civilized practices will largely cease, and a condition of underground chaos and disorder amounting to guerrilla warfare in the mountainous and outlying regions result. I believe all hope of introducing modern democratic methods would disappear and that when military control finally ceased some form of intense regimentation probably along communistic lines would arise from the mutilated masses. This would represent an entirely different problem of occupation from the one now prevalent. It would be absolutely essential to greatly increase the occupational forces. It is quite possible that a minimum of a million troops would be required which would have to be maintained for an indefinite number of years. In addition a complete civil service might have to be recruited and imported, possibly running into a size of several hundred thousand. An overseas supply service under such conditions would have to be set up on practically a war basis embracing an indigent civil population of many millions. . . .[54]

The cable had its intended effect: plans for a trial proceeded no further. This may have been MacArthur's single most important act. He liked to say later that he "found that [the emperor] had a more thorough grasp of the democratic concept than almost any Japanese with whom I talked."[55] Whether this assessment was accurate, MacArthur himself seemed to grasp better than other U.S. officials that the emperor could be an asset to democratization, not an impediment. Although he probably realized this intuitively rather than through systematic historical study, the political sociologist Seymour Martin Lipset subsequently pointed out the "absurd fact" that a disproportionate share of the world's democracies are monarchies.[56] Presumably the monarchy confers legitimacy upon the nascent democratic institutions and discourages their overthrow by the power hungry. That seems to have been the case in Japan. Prime Minister Yoshida concluded that "it was the attitude adopted by General MacArthur towards the throne, more than any other single factor, that made the Occupation an historic success."[57]

Some other aspects of Japan's pre-occupation history also conduced to democratic development and helped the occupation succeed. Ward has pointed out that in the areas of bureaucratic, constitutional, and electoral reform

Japan's own pre-Occupation experience was rich, deep and varied. . . . It is equally notable that the Japanese populace was already at the outset of the Occupation a remarkably literate, well-educated, and politically experienced national group. All of the mass media and educational apparatus for reaching them, presenting a case, and attempting to influence their views and practices were ready at hand.[58]

Perhaps the most important available asset was preexisting democrats. The democratic movement had lost out in the political battles to control Japan's destiny in the 1920s and 1930s, but democratic ideas had survived even while their advocates were silenced during the years of war and militarism. "It was widely anticipated that the Japanese people would be politically apathetic," says Nobutaka Ike,

> and that a long interval of tutelage would be required to implant in them a desire for democratic government. Yet hardly had the military government removed the restrictive laws that had been acting as a political straightjacket than there emerged a popular movement, the vigor and scope of which surprised the occupation authorities.[59]

The occupation thus reversed the outcome of the prewar political battles and raised the democrats above the authoritarians. Although a large part of this job was accomplished through the purge, the occupation, says Ward, also showed "the favoritism [to] some political parties, politicians, and scholars."[60] Those Japanese whose democratic convictions or credentials seemed most compelling to the Americans had the greatest chance of influencing decisions taken by occupation officials. The Americans, says Ward, "held the field for those who at least professed democratic sentiments and excluded all others."[61]

In addition to aiding indigenous democrats, the occupation created new constituencies of its own, less by design than by a natural political process. Those who benefited from occupation reforms had a vested interest in the new order. Women were liberated by the new constitution, in comparison with their subordinate and disfranchised status under the old regime. A substantial portion of the peasantry became freeholders instead of tenant farmers as a result of land reform. Industrial workers flocked to labor unions by the millions. In addition to these large social groups, a new political elite emerged during the occupation, including national legislators and local officeholders who gained their positions in part from the openings created by the purge. These politicians worked with the occupation in designing the new institutions and were in turn shaped by them. By the time the Americans left, this group had a stake in the system under which it rose.

In addition to such vested interests, a large, amorphous group of Japanese discovered in the new order a self-interest of a more general kind, namely, the sense of relief at being freed from war and dictatorship. This spiritual gain might have been vitiated had the harsh privations that followed the war lasted long, but the political changes were accompanied by material benefits. First, these came from American charity, then from an almost bottomless American market for Japanese goods once the Korean War began. Since then, the Japanese economy under the new order has provided the Japanese people with unprecedented affluence.

A final reason for the occupation's success is that although the occupation ended in 1952, American influence did not. When they regained their sovereignty, the Japanese were free to amend or discard the system that had been imposed on them. They declined to do so because that new system quickly established its roots in Japanese life, tapping into some old ones and sinking some new ones. The special relationship with America had important economic, military, and psychological dimensions, as the United States became Japan's protector and largest market. Japan could not sacrifice this relationship without radically affecting its international position, and it could not abandon its new democratic ways without deeply disturbing its relations with America.

Refining the Changes. Not every reform sponsored by the occupation endured, nor did every one deserve to endure. Many Americans and Japanese have expressed doubts about the large scale of the purge, for example. The economic purge and trust busting aimed at the *zaibatsu* probably hampered Japan's economic recovery (though obviously not fatally). No doubt these actions reflected a degree of American naiveté. After forty-odd years of U.S.-Soviet cold war, we forget how sensitive we were in 1945 to threats to democracy in Japan emanating from the Right, rather than the Left. Many U.S. officials were inclined to overrate the harm that giant corporations might do and to underrate the contribution they might make. The same naiveté was evident in actions on Japan's institutions of communications and scholarship. As Edwin Reischauer described it:

> The American occupation left the intellectual field open to
> [communists and socialists], and they came to dominate the
> magazines, newspapers, university faculties, and student
> bodies. . . . Though the reforms of the occupation and the
> Japanese institutions these helped to produce were grounded
> in liberal, democratic tradition, Japanese thought took on a
> heavily Marxist flavor.[62]

As the cold war took shape, some U.S. occupation officials became concerned about the mounting strength of Japan's Communists, especially in the new and powerful labor unions. General MacArthur responded by turning the purge against the Left. Like many other belated reactions, this one overreacted and claimed many non-Communist leftists as well as Communists.[63] In addition new civil service laws were written to curtail the power of public employee unions. Although Communist power was diminished, the wellsprings of anti-Americanism were replenished in labor and intellectual circles.

When the occupation ended, the Japanese revised some of the legislation that had been passed. The purge was lifted, and the anti-monopoly law was weakened. Rules governing the organization of the Diet were changed, mostly to narrow the autonomy of individual legislators. A new law partially reversed the complete dispersal of police powers to local governments, which had been demanded by the occupation. Although the police law and some others involved bitter controversy, they merely trimmed the edges of the system put in place by the occupation.

Over the years that system has taken on a uniquely Japanese cast, and the many new institutions that have grown up also have a Japanese look. In particular, as Scalapino says, "the use of the cardinal guideposts of filial piety and status was extended to all economic and political organizations."[64] Political parties have their own peculiar configuration. Ike describes them as groupings of hierarchical factions based more on personal loyalty and careerism than on ideology or issues. This constitutes "yet another type of democracy—patron-client democracy—which is somewhat different from the Western models."[65]

Some have taken Ike's argument well beyond his conclusions. They say that because of its hierarchies and other idiosyncrasies, Japan's system is not a democracy at all. The effective answer was given by the occupation itself some forty years ago:

> The sovereignty of the people, the supremacy of law, the absolute guarantee of basic rights and liberties, the independence of the courts, the recognition of the individual—these must of necessity be the fundamental requirements. Through what machinery they are provided, how they are to be obtained and assured, presents a problem the solution of which may differ widely among men.[66]

Democracy in Japan is no less genuine for having acquired a peculiarly Japanese character than for having been initiated by Americans. It is one of history's greatest and most constructive feats of social engineering.

Measuring the importance of the various actions taken by the occupation or judging which, if any, were decisive is impossible. Listing what appear to have been most important, however, is not so hard. One is the replacement of elites: purging old leaders, most with little affinity for democratic ways, and elevating new ones, some with backgrounds of liberal conviction and all with a stake in the new system. A second is the adoption of a new constitution and other basic legislation. The constitution not only provided rules of the game within which democratic experience could begin to grow; it also gave a sense of definition and coherence to the new order.

A third major effect of the occupation was to stimulate pluralism. By enfranchising women, by encouraging the growth of labor unions, and by removing restrictions on expression, the occupation helped to disperse political power more widely in Japanese society allowing its various elements to counterbalance one another. Fourth, through educational reforms and various kinds of prodemocratic propaganda, the occupation directly encouraged new ways of thinking. Finally, the occupation left Japan with a new relationship with the United States. It was a relationship that the Japanese were loath to disturb, and they knew that few things would be more likely to disturb it than to revert to a dictatorial political system.

Germany

Many of these effects are also evident in the occupation of West Germany, the second most important case in which the United States (together with its Western allies) succeeded in implanting democracy through military rule. The transformation of Germany is slightly less remarkable than that of Japan in that Germany was a part of Western civilization and shared the Christian religion and other cultural values with the democracies of Europe. Moreover Germany had experienced fifteen years of self-generated democratic government under the Weimar constitution. Although Japan had enjoyed a period of indigenous liberalization in the 1920s and early 1930s, it never reached the point of democratic governance. Indeed the liberalization occurred within the context of an authoritarian structure modeled after the one that Germany discarded in its 1918 revolution and replaced by the Weimar system.

Nonetheless indigenous democracy within Germany had collapsed of its own weight largely because it evoked so little popular enthusiasm. Even the "rational republicans," as Peter Gay put it, "could not see that the Republic might deserve wholehearted support—or rather that it might become deserving if enough deserving persons supported it."[67] The prospects for democracy's revival in Germany at war's end can hardly have been favorable. The hardships of war and the agony of defeat had soured Germans on the glories of nazism, but had not made them democrats. Indeed the task of democratization faced two enormous psychic barriers. The first was in the minds of the Germans, who were crushingly demoralized in defeat, and absorbed by the problems of day-to-day survival. The second barrier was in the minds of the Allies, which, though proclaiming democratization as one objective, were determined above all that Germany should never rise again. Even the Americans, who had less direct cause to be vengeful or insecure than the other occupying powers, toyed with the idea of returning Germany to a pastoral condition.

Within a few years, however, increasing conflict with the Soviet Union brought a realization that Germany might play an essential part in the new configuration of European politics. Led by officers on the scene who began to develop, in Peter Merkl's words, a "fatherly regard for their German charges,"[68] the Americans turned more earnestly to the task of reconstructing a democratic Germany. As in Japan, a key part of American activity was to put in place a new, prodemocratic elite.

Like the purge in Japan, the American program of denazification resulted in controversy. It was so broad as to be unwieldy, and it was criticized for penalizing insignificant individuals while allowing important Nazis to slip through. Whatever the merit of this criticism, denazification did vacate most of the political offices from which Nazi officials had not already disappeared in anticipation of the defeat. The Americans sought to ensure that from top to bottom these offices would be filled by Germans of democratic temper. Again to cite Merkl:

> Thousands of Nazis and Nazified members of the traditional elites were removed from public positions and replaced with reliable democrats. In the long run, this result meant a considerable set-back and often the permanent demotion of ex-Nazis in public careers, whereas the antifascists enjoyed what has turned out to be a durable headstart. The new political elites admitted by the Allies in the first occupation years remained dominant for decades after the end of military government.[69]

In Germany, as in Japan, the occupation saw to the writing of a new constitution. The U.S. role in Germany, however, was less heavy-handed (although it still seemed too heavy-handed to the Germans). In directing the Germans to write a constitution, the Allies required that it provide a system of government broadly democratic and federal in character. The drafting was done by a parliamentary council of representatives of the various *Länder* (state governments). The views of the Allies on more detailed points were taken into account but were not determinative. When an initial draft was completed, the occupiers objected to some items; ultimately these disputes were resolved by compromise. Because of the Germans' sensitivity to their lack of sovereignty and their reluctance to consecrate the division of Germany, they insisted on calling the document the basic law rather than constitution, which sounded more august and permanent. Yet despite the awkward circumstances of its genesis, the German basic law, like the Japanese constitution, has become an ever firmer foundation of the nation's politics and identity. Indeed, it has outlasted the division of Germany to become the charter for the reunited nation.

In Japan the occupation encouraged pluralism by empowering certain social groups that had previously been impotent; in Germany pluralism was advanced primarily by means of federalism. Regional particularism, that is, the distinct cultural or political identity of once-independent principalities, was a pronounced feature of German history, long impeding the nation's unification. When unification was at last achieved under Bismarck in 1871, it was effectuated top-down through Prussian hegemony. When the Hohenzollern Empire was replaced by the Weimar Republic after World War I, power was democratized but was further concentrated in the central government. The Nazi Reich then wiped away the last vestiges of regional independence in favor of the pitiless uniformity of totalitarian rule.

The occupation reversed this process, although the decentralization it brought only partially heeded traditional regionalism. Its main purpose was to prevent reestablishment of a strong central government in Germany. The Allies redrew boundaries, truncating some of the old German states and merging others, and they abolished Prussia. The result was ten *Länder* of various size, with no single *Land* dominant. The basic law divides power between the central government and those of the *Länder*. The upper house of parliament, or Bundesrat, far more powerful than most secondary chambers, consists of members chosen by the governments of the *Länder*, not by popular vote. This gives the *Länder* governments a measure of direct power over the central government to counterbalance those powers it holds over them.

The federal structure of the Bonn Republic was built from the bottom up. At first the Allies were reluctant to allow the reconstitution of any central government in Germany. The Americans took the lead in encouraging the formation of *Land* governments in their zone and the adoption of *Land* constitutions, which, according to Merkl, became a model for those in the other Western zones as well as "to some extent" for the basic law.[70]

One of the important American-inspired features of the new German constitution that got its start in the *Land* constitutions is the principle of judicial review. As Carl J. Friedrich explained:

> Allied and more particularly American occupation policies were deliberately directed toward strengthening these forces [that is, judicial review]. This policy bore fruit in *Land* consti-

tutions in the American zone, discussed and adopted in 1946 on American initiative. They could and did serve as models for the Basic Law. . . .

[There are] marked differences between the American Supreme Court and the Federal German Constitutional Court. What matters is that the latter, like the former, has acted as a guardian of the constitution, has gradually enhanced respect for it, and has brought home to Germans at large that they have a "basic law."[71]

Another feature of the basic law that has served to solidify democracy in Germany is the electoral system, which has steered the country toward a two-party system (or one dominated by two parties) as opposed to the multiparty system of Weimar. The Weimar system aimed for exquisitely proportional representation, which may have maximized a kind of fairness but also maximized instability and polarization. The Bundestag of today's Federal Republic of Germany is elected in part by single-member districts and in part by party lists. Seats chosen by list are allocated proportionally only to parties that pass a threshold of electoral popularity, discouraging splinter parties. In addition a provision of the basic law empowers the federal constitutional court to outlaw parties that attempt to subvert the democratic order, and it has in fact outlawed both Nazi and Communist parties.

In the realm of reculturation the occupation attempted a sweeping reform of the educational system, which most experts now agree was not entirely successful. It did succeed, however, in purging a large number of teachers who had been compromised by Nazi activities and thus in counteracting the considerable efforts of the Hitler regime to nazify the teaching profession. The occupation also had millions of new textbooks published, replacing those of Nazi provenance as well as pre-Nazi texts tainted with chauvinist sentiments. The Americans also were instrumental in the founding of the Free University of Berlin, while the Universities of Mainz and Saarbrücken were set up by French occupation authorities.

In addition the U.S. authorities created a network of America Houses, cultural centers with reading rooms, and sponsored films, newsreels, radio broadcasts, periodicals, and newspapers, one of which, *Die Neue Zeitung*, retained a large readership for most of a decade. A still more important influence on the intellectual climate of Germany may have been the occupation's licensing of German newspapers and other communications media. This power was used to place prodemocratic individuals at the helm of German journalism. The occupation also sponsored the regeneration of German broadcasting along lines that ensured competition among broadcasters rather than a state monopoly.

In addition to direct methods of reculturation, the occupation achieved a beneficial pedagogical effect as the Germans went through the process of constructing democratic constitutions, first in the *Länder* and then at the federal level. In the opinion of Friedrich, "Probably the most positive legacy, politically, of the occupation of Germany by the Western Allies is the conversion of a majority of Germans to a democratic constitutionalism. . . . the lion's share of the credit for bringing about this change falls to the United States."[72]

Finally, as with Japan, at the conclusion of the occupation Germany found itself facing a new geopolitical order in which it was involved economically, politically, and culturally in an American-led Western alliance, which has exerted a strong pull on Germany's thinking and behavior ever since. Merkl put it, "The later identification with the west . . . had a powerful reinforcing effect that continued the work of the occupation."[73]

Austria

American and Allied occupation authorities also oversaw the reestablishment of democracy in Austria after World War II. Austria's indigenous democratic history was roughly equivalent to Germany's: a democratic system installed after World War I collapsed into dictatorship in 1934. The clericalist, nationalist dictatorship of Engelbert Dollfuss and Kurt von Schuschnigg was, however, a far cry from Nazi rule. The Austrians did not feel the boot of totalitarianism until Hitler imposed Anschluss—the union of Austria and Germany—in 1938.

The Allies had declared their intention long before the war was over to sever Austria from Germany. Although nazism enjoyed a large popular following in Austria, many in the West saw Austria more as a victim of Germany's than as a culpable part of the Third Reich. As a result, Austria was not subjected to as rigorous a program of democratization as was Germany. More attention was given to the problem of keeping Austria out of Soviet hands, and this proved sound policy. Austria was successfully rescued from the brink of the Soviet empire, and it has remained firmly democratic ever since the war.

The occupation encouraged the early renewal of democratic government in Austria. The constitution of 1929 was restored and national elections were held as early as November 1945. Only three parties were allowed to compete: the Socialists, the People's party (a reincarnation of the prewar Christian Socialists), and the Communists; Nazis were barred from voting. Not only did elections establish a legitimate government, the outcome furnished two bonuses. The Communists were trounced so humiliatingly, garnering a mere 5 percent (as against 50 percent for the People's party and 45 percent for the Socialists), that the

Soviet drive to install a Communist regime was hampered. The other bonus came from the close finish between the two major parties; it led them to form a coalition government, which helped to diminish the sharp Left-Right polarization that had undermined Austria's earlier democratic experience.

Austria's elected government remained for a time under the Allied Control Authority, which had a useful tutelary function in getting democracy working smoothly.[74] As a result of cold war divisions between the occupiers, a basis for the restoration of Austrian sovereignty was not agreed to until 1955. During the intervening decade the occupation progressively lightened its intrusions into Austrian politics.

In addition to facilitating democratic institutions, the U.S. occupation sponsored information and communications programs to help shape attitudes. They were described by Austrian authority Oliver Rathkolb:

> Among the most important tools used in influencing public opinion was a German-language daily newspaper under American management. In the late 40s (1947) it reached a peak circulation of 300,000, which made it the biggest daily in the German-speaking area. In the 50s, its influence declined sharply, so that from 1954 onwards it had to be issued as a weekly. In contrast to the newspaper, the US radio station . . . with its modern, Austria-oriented programming and US-biased political news and commentaries, which reached between 2 and 3 million listeners . . . or almost half of the entire Austrian population, was certainly more popular, when it was closed down in 1955, than the public Austrian radio station RAVAG. These propaganda tools were supplemented by 11 information centres (with an average of 200,000 monthly visitors in 1951), a film section, which in the distribution sector was soon replaced by private companies, and a special theatre and music section, which had a decided influence on programming in the 40s.[75]

As in Germany, the occupation insisted on a purge of Nazis from Austrian public life, an objective shared by many of the postwar Austrian leaders who had been victimized by the Nazis. The half-million Austrians who had been members of the Nazi party were divided into two categories according to the depth of their Nazi involvement. Both groups were barred from various positions, including such things as teaching history, and the more active Nazis were also subject to other penalties. By 1948 the less active Nazis (90 percent of the total) were amnestied. Although this purge, like those in Japan and Germany, has been criticized, it did, according to Frederick Engelmann, "result in considerable housecleaning at official levels."[76]

Finally, the American occupation helped to stimulate the growth of democracy in Austria by facilitating the country's economic recovery. At the Potsdam Conference in 1945 the United States rejected reparations from Austria, and during the occupation period it battled Soviet efforts to expropriate from Austria substantial assets that the Soviets claimed were actually German.[77] In addition to protecting Austria against Soviet pillage, the United States donated $1.4 billion in Marshall Plan aid that helped the country recover.

And Elsewhere

Italy too was occupied by the United States at the war's end although the situation was complicated because Italy had changed sides, shifting from enemy to cobelligerent. The occupation fostered defascistization, the formation of an interim government led by the Christian Democrat Alcide De Gasperi, and the reconstitution of democratic forms. In a referendum in June 1946 the Italians voted to establish a republic rather than to preserve the monarchy. At the same time a constituent assembly was elected to write a constitution. Although the occupation formally ended at the close of 1945, the United States continued a heavy involvement in Italy; it contributed $1.75 billion to aid Italy's economic reconstruction and used myriad political means to support the Christian Democrats against their principal rivals, the Communists.

Other countries that the United States has occupied militarily include South Korea after World War II; the Philippines and Cuba after the Spanish-American War; Haiti, Nicaragua, and the Dominican Republic in the second and third decades of this century; the Dominican Republic again in 1965; and Grenada in 1983; and Panama in 1989. In each case the United States tried to leave behind a democratic government, although the degree of its efforts has varied.

The one case that may be compared to the post-World War II occupations—in the sense of a prolonged conscientious effort to foster the infrastructure of democracy—is the Philippines. Whatever America's motives were in seizing the Philippines during the war with Spain and holding on to them subsequently, U.S. policy almost from the beginning included the goal of preparing the islands for self-government in accordance with American sensibilities, that is, democratic government.

By 1902 the Americans began adding Filipinos to the Philippine Commission, the colonial governing body.[78] Later that year the first Philippine Organic Act was passed by Congress. It made the Philippine Commission the upper house of a bicameral legislature, with the lower house popularly elected. As recounted by Claude Buss, a scholar and former high official of the U.S. colonial administration:

> Within a decade, significant progress was made in secularizing the government and the schools. The existing Spanish legal system was modified to accommodate American concepts based on the common law. Civil rights and equality before the law were guaranteed and an independent judiciary was created on the American pattern. Filipinos were admitted to the civil service in the lower ranks. Popular election of Filipino officials was introduced at the local level and the formation of political parties was permitted. In 1907, the Nacionalista party, the champion of immediate independence, won control of the first popularly elected National Assembly.[79]

In the decades that followed, the Americans encouraged economic development, strengthened public education, sponsored a small and apparently unsuccessful program of land reform, and increasingly tranferred authority into the hands of Filipinos. In 1935, under American aegis and as part of a transition to full independence mandated by the U.S. Congress, the Filipinos drew up their own constitution. The exceedingly strong presidential powers that it set out allowed President Ferdinand Marcos to subvert Philippine democracy nearly forty years later.

Although the United States governed the Philippines for more than forty years, it was ambivalent, even embarrassed, about its role. Thus it never attempted as thorough a reorientation of Philippine society as of Japanese society within a brief seven years. For example, Americans wrote the Japanese constitution, whereas Filipinos wrote the Philippine constitution—at American instance.

In South Korea the United States fostered the establishment of a government led by Korean nationalists of presumed democratic persuasion, rewrote textbooks to teach democratic values to schoolchildren, initiated a land reform through the redistribution of lands that had been held by the Japanese, and encouraged the writing of a democratic constitution, which was adopted in 1948, the year the U.S. occupation ended.

The cases of the Philippines and South Korea show something about the force of U.S. influence as well as its limitations. Both countries were democracies when the American occupiers departed. Democracy collapsed within South Korea after a few years and within the Philippines after a few decades. At one time these collapses seemed to show that democracy imposed by foreigners may not last. Yet both countries have now restored elected government; perhaps some American influence did indeed endure. The Philippines is far poorer than Korea; it is subject to powerful centrifugal forces of geography, religion, and ethnicity; and it has a fierce guerrilla insurgency. All these factors militate against the stability of its present democracy. Yet popular democratic currents seem stronger in the Philippines than in Korea, perhaps a product of its far deeper American influence.

That U.S. influence implanted by force of arms does not always have a lasting beneficial effect is demonstrated by the cases of Nicaragua, Cuba, and Haiti, three countries ruled intermittently by American forces in the early part of this century. Ironically, until the Nicaraguan elections of February 1990, these three were the most *undemocratic* countries in the Western hemisphere. They prove, if anyone doubted it, that U.S. military occupation is not a sufficient condition to make a country democratic. In these cases the American occupiers brought law and order and fiscal propriety and supervised fair elections. But they did not attempt programs of democratization as in Japan or Germany. They did attempt to create nonpolitical guards or constabularies on the theory that politics in these countries had been blighted by the depredations of rival partisan military bands. A nonpartisan, professional force seemed just the cure. But in Nicaragua a cunning and ruthless Anastasio Somoza used the guard to impose his own dictatorial rule on the country (to be succeeded by that of his two sons). Much the same was done in the Dominican Republic by Rafael Trujillo, and that country's current political history might be just as unhappy as Nicaragua's were it not for a second sequence of U.S. interventions, beginning in the 1960s.

In 1961, American officials were complicit in Trujillo's assassination after he had been in power more than three decades. In the next few years the United States intervened first with a show of force to prevent the overthrow of the elected government of leftish president Juan Bosch and later with the use of force to thwart an insurrection against the officers who had ousted Bosch. The United States then supervised fair elections in which the rightish Joaquin Balaguer defeated Bosch. In contrast to the early part of the century, when fair elections sponsored by U.S. forces were followed by coups and usurpations, the 1966 elections in the Dominican Republic inaugurated an era of democratic government that has endured and included peaceful transfers of power. In 1978, when election returns indicated a victory over Balaguer by Bosch's heirs, the military threatened momentarily to abort the process. Heavy pressure by the Carter adminstration, however, induced the officers to relent, and Dominican democracy escaped interruption.

The most recent cases in which American force served the cause of democracy were the 1983 invasion of Grenada and the 1989 invasion of Panama. In Grenada the Americans toppled the governing New Jewel Movement, which had seized power four years earlier and was attempting to solidify a Communist dictatorship. Although more symbolic and political weight has been invested in these events than a tiny island with fewer than 100,000 inhabitants can sustain, the invaders did leave behind a democratically elected government, which has endured. In Panama the Americans oversaw the installation of the duly elected government that had been prevented from assuming office by the thuggery of military boss Manuel Noriega.

Taken together, these diverse cases show that democracy can indeed be spread by the sword. Where efforts at reculturation and restructuring were most vigorous, Germany and especially Japan, they were most successful. Italy, whose own democratic experience was only slightly deeper than Germany's, restored democracy with only modest efforts by its occupiers. We cannot know whether Italy, or for that matter Austria or even Germany, would have found its way back to the path of democracy on its own after the defeat of fascism. Just as American activities may not always have been irreplaceable, they were also not always successful. Sustained American efforts to influence the Philippines yielded only mixed success. Nonetheless it seems doubtful that democracy would be nearly as strong as it is in the Philippines absent the American occupation. On the whole, however, the military method of building democracy has been quite successful, even though it has rarely been more than a secondary objective of U.S. engagements.

Lessons from Military Occupations

What can be learned from this? No one advocates that the United States take it upon itself to subdue other countries solely to democratize them. I certainly do not. Peace ranks with democracy among the highest desiderata and must not be violated except for the most compelling reasons. This is not to say that we should accept a blanket prohibition against military interventions to change the internal order in another state. It would have been a blessing if outside powers had overthrown Hitler and Pol Pot and Lenin before they had done their worst. The justification, however, is not merely that they were undemocratic but that their rule wrought extreme horrors. Even international law recognizes to some degree humanitarian intervention under extreme conditions. This is a different thing from intervention solely for democratization.

Conversely, if in the future as in the past the United States finds itself drawn into military occupation for reasons of self-defense or collective security, then it should not forgo the opportunity to build democracy in the country under its sway. And in policy deliberations over whether to use force in response to certain security threats, U.S. officials can factor into their considerations an optimistic assessment of America's capacity for implanting democratic systems.

117

Perhaps more important, lessons can be learned from America's experience as an occupying power that may help guide our efforts to spread democracy by other means. We have seen, for example, that raising to leadership individuals of proven democratic convictions was a key means by which U.S. occupations brought democratization. Without military occupation, the United States cannot appoint leaders of other countries, but we can identify and strengthen individuals of democratic belief. Sometimes we can aid their ascent to office. If they reach power, we can seek to stabilize their regimes, through the kind of economic aid, for example, that was so instrumental in establishing democracy's grip on the loyalties of Japanese and Germans. We can encourage pluralism, constitutional reform, and the propagation of democratic ideas and knowledge. We can involve countries in relations with us so that the desire for our good graces will encourage them toward democratic behavior. The salient point about the successful occupations is that democracy endured long after America ceased calling the shots. This durability was the fruit of changes wrought during the occupation. We may well learn to achieve similar effects by more peaceful means.

9

Covert Action

Just as the United States has spread democracy as a byproduct of war, it has done so as a byproduct of the cold war through the covert activities of its intelligence service. America entered World War II to defend itself, not to democratize Japan and Germany. Once it was engaged, however, it concluded that the best way to preserve the peace would be to convert Japan and Germany into democracies. Similarly America joined the cold war to defend itself, not to spread democracy. Nonetheless it has often found or assumed that the best way to build a bulwark against Communist advances in other countries is to strengthen democracy.

The problem has not ordinarily been to create democracy from scratch in countries that are entirely unfamiliar with it. The problem has been to nurture democracy in countries that had some democratic experience or have fledgling democratic institutions but that also have an organized force working instead for dictatorship. The main obstacle in these situations has been not social or economic or cultural factors but the local Communist movement and its backers in Moscow. A significant part of the CIA's covert political work has consisted of subsidizing publications, organizations, training programs, and conferences aimed at spreading democratic ideas to a multinational audience. To the extent they were effective, these programs have fortified democratic currents in a variety of countries.

Covert action has not always served to further democracy, and sometimes it may have had the opposite effect. In Iran in 1953 and in Guatemala in 1954 the CIA engineered coups that overthrew legitimate governments. Neither of those governments—that of Mohammed Mossadeq in Iran and Jacobo Arbenz in Guatemala—was a democratic government, but the autocracy that the CIA helped to install in Iran and the string of military dictators that followed Arbenz in Guatemala brought decades of undemocratic rule to each country. The CIA's actions were both motivated by American fears that the country would fall under Communist rule, which might have meant a more despotic outcome. Even if these fears would have been realized, the two coups were hardly a boon to democracy.

The CIA has also been blamed by some for the overthrow of the Allende government in Chile in 1973. A Senate committee (the Select Committee to Study Governmental Operations with Respect to Intelligence Activities, or the Church committee) examined these charges to ferret out improper or controversial acts by the agency. It concluded that "there is no hard evidence of direct U.S. assistance to the coup, despite frequent allegations of such aid," but it also said that the United States "probably gave the impression that it would not look with disfavor on a military coup."[1] The committee suggested too that the CIA's support for the Chilean opposition had contributed to the climate of social dislocation in which the coup occurred. These anti-Allende actions aimed at a worthy cause insofar as they sought to forestall the creation of a Cuban-type regime in Chile, but the coup itself had tragic results: sixteen years of military dictatorship in a country with one of the strongest democratic traditions in Latin America.

Despite these negative examples, covert action has probably more often served to advance democracy than to retard it. This judgment cannot be made with great confidence because the bulk of covert actions remain secret. We can judge only from that small fraction about which some information has seeped into the public record. Of these, more positive than negative examples appear. Even if we cannot rely on such totals, the positive cases demonstrate that covert action can encourage democracy in some situations.

Postwar Europe

The beginnings of such covert activities followed the inauguration of the cold war. From D-Day until the Czech coup in 1948, as Stalin consolidated an empire in Central Europe, Western nations swung from gullibility to alarm over Soviet intentions. Suddenly it seemed likely that the devastated countries of Western Europe would be next on the Soviet dictator's menu. In the words of the Church committee:

> The Soviets had powerful political resources in the West—the Communist parties and trade unions. Provided with financial and advisory support from the Soviet Union, the Communist parties sought to exploit and exacerbate the economic and political turmoil in postwar Europe. As the elections in 1948 and 1949 in Italy and France approached, the democratic parties were in disarray and the possibility of a Communist takeover was real. . . .
>
> The United States responded with overt economic aid . . . and covert political assistance. . . . Clandestine support from

the United States for European democratic parties was regarded as an essential response to the threat of "international Communism."[2]

The impetus for this covert political aid, as for so much of America's response to the challenge of that day, came from George Kennan. He has recalled being

> alarmed particularly over the situation in France and Italy. We felt that the Communists were using the very extensive funds that they then had in hand to gain control of key elements of life in France and Italy, particularly the publishing companies, the press, the labor unions, student organizations, women's organizations, and all sorts of organizations of that sort, to gain control of them and use them as front organizations.[3]

America's response to Moscow's covert aid to its supporters in the West was a pipeline of its own to help those who upheld the democratic cause. The first major use of this pipeline (as far as the public record reveals) occurred in the Italian elections of April 1948.

Italy. The Communist party of Italy emerged from World War II strong and with high prestige from the contribution of its cadres to the antifascist resistance during the war. As Nazi armies and their Italian henchmen were routed, Communists moved quickly to assume control of enterprises and local governments, while the Allied occupation authorities tried to contain this pell-mell accumulation of power. In late 1945 and early 1946 Italian sovereignty was restored under a coalition government headed by the Christian Democrat Alcide De Gasperi. In 1947 De Gasperi excluded the Communists from his government. Later that year the Marshall Plan was initiated; it was denounced by the Soviet Union, then by the parties beholden to it. In Italy unions under Communist leadership staged strikes against the Marshall Plan in the autumn of 1947.

With the approach of the parliamentary elections of April 1948, the first under the new postwar constitution, the Communists' prospects were strengthened considerably by developments within the Socialist party, the third major Italian party that emerged from the war. (The Communists, Socialists, and Christian Democrats eclipsed a handful of monarchist, neofascist, and other minor parties.) Although a minority split over the issue, the Socialists decided to merge their efforts officially with the Communists in support of a joint list of parliamentary candidates.

The stakes in the Italian polling were dramatized just two months before the election when the Communist coup in Czechoslovakia completed the absorption of Eastern Europe into the Soviet empire. The United States, responding with considerable overt pressure, publicly threatened to cut off aid if the Communists won. Italian-Americans were encouraged by the Catholic church to write their brethren in the old country and urge a vote for the Christian Democrats.[4] In addition, a sum of money, apparently on the order of $1 million, was secretly channeled to the non-Communist parties, mostly to the Christian Democrats.[5] The Christian Democrats, outdrawing the Communist-Socialist slate by 48.5 to 31 percent, won a decisive victory.

Given the margin of their victory, the Christian Democrats might have won the 1948 election without the CIA's financial help, but U.S. officials believed the assistance had been of critical importance. After exhuming this history twenty-five years later, the Church committee seemed to concur and allowed that "considerable success" had been achieved.[6]

After 1948 aid to prodemocratic forces in Italy became a major item on the CIA's agenda of covert action. According to William Colby, who was in charge of this project from 1953 until 1958 and later became director of the CIA, the funds were used for

> publication of newsletters, leaflets, posters, and other propaganda materials, staging congresses and public rallies, conducting membership drives and voter registration campaigns and the like. In addition, though, perhaps because of my earlier experience in the New York Democratic Party movement and my studies of the Communist "organizational weapon," I was particularly concerned with the fundamentals of party organization and operation, and so I insisted that not only funds but also advice be given for training programs, research and study groups, local party offices and activities, and so on.[7]

This activity continued until the early 1960s, when it was phased out, according to Colby.[8] Apparently under the impetus of Communist electoral success it was resumed sometime in the 1970s, until news leaks in early 1976 embarrassed both the Ford administration and the Christian Democrats. All told, the subsidies are said to have amounted to $65 million over the span of a quarter-century.[9]

In addition to questions about its efficacy, an obvious ethical issue presents itself, namely, whether the spending of money by one government to influence the outcome of elections in another country is itself an adulteration of the democratic process. The U.S. government felt that it was doing no more than leveling the playing field in light of the "Moscow gold" that the CIA concluded was flowing to the Italian Communists. Colby wrote that "Moscow was covertly pouring in massive support to the Italian Communist Party—according to our estimates at the time, to the tune of over fifty million dollars a year."[10]

Certainly it is hard to quarrel with the assessment of U.S. officials that electoral victory by the Communist-Socialist slate would have led Italy down the sorry path of Poland, Hungary, and Czechoslovakia. To be sure, Italy, unlike Eastern Europe, was not occupied by Soviet armies, a difference of no small moment. But it is unimaginable that the Communists, once in office, would have left without a physical fight. With the government in their hands they would have in all likelihood transformed Italy into a totalitarian state. At a minimum their efforts would have shifted the locus of political competition from the parliament and polling places to the streets and barracks.

Other Countries. Italy was by no means the only scene of CIA covert operations designed to support democratic forces against the Communists in that period. The political situation in France was similar. The Communists had emerged from the war with their image burnished by courageous service to the anti-Axis underground and enjoyed a hold on the organized labor movement. Here too the CIA began to subsidize other political forces.[11]

Soon other countries joined the list. "In Germany, both major political parties, and most of their leaders, received secret CIA subsidies," according to Morton Halperin and his far-Left coauthors.[12] Although they are a dubious source, especially as they offer only an anonymous source for this assertion, their claim, at least as far as the German political parties are concerned, gains plausibility from other evidence. The Church committee reported that "the German branch of the European Division was the Agency's largest single country component."[13] The exact meaning of this description is unclear because the CIA's operations across the iron curtain were apparently run from its German offices and the report does not say whether these were included. Elsewhere the committee report asserts that "by 1952 approximately 40 different covert action projects were under way in one central European country alone."[14] This presumably means either Germany or Austria: no doubt the CIA was active in both countries in the postwar years. All in all, CIA activities in Europe in the aftermath of the war constituted, in Harry Rositzke's phrase, "a covert annex to the Marshall Plan."[15]

Labor Unions. This covert annex involved more than campaign contributions. Another major area of activity was support for labor unions. Throughout the continent the thriving unions of the prewar years had been destroyed: the industries flattened by bombs, the members called off to war, and the leaders targeted for repression by Nazi or fascist rulers. The Communists had always enjoyed a strong position in the labor movement, even in America, where the Communist party was much weaker than in Europe. When the war ended, the Communists rushed to participate in the resurrection of the labor movements in the hope of gaining a dominant role. Their efforts were abetted by the naiveté of U.S. occupation officials, who rarely appreciated the political importance of labor.[16] Some seemed to view unions as a disruptive element and adopted a cold and restrictive attitude toward them, which only played into the hands of the Communists. Others thoughtlessly assigned labor problems to underlings who were sympathetic to the Communists. (In the 1940s the American Communist party still boasted the better part of 100,000 members.[17] Many joined the armed services, especially after Hitler invaded the Soviet Union, and at war's end served in the occupation. Their political training made them eager to work on labor affairs, an area that seemed more exciting to them than to most of their colleagues.)

A response to this Communist gambit came initially not from any agency of the U.S. government but from leaders of American unions who held strong anti-Communist beliefs. Their views had been shaped by their awareness of the fierce suppression of labor within the Soviet Union, the abuse that many of them had suffered personally from American Communists in power struggles within their own unions, and the bitter disillusionment that some of them experienced after having been drawn to communism themselves. Two particularly instrumental figures were Jay Lovestone, who was the executive secretary of the American Federation of Labor's Free Trade Union Committee (FTUC) and one-time general secretary of the American Communist party, and Irving Brown, who was the FTUC's European representative and who had been a Communist disciple of Lovestone's.

Brown and Lovestone set themselves the task of reviving or recreating non-Communist unions in France, Germany, Italy, Greece, and elsewhere. They furnished the non-Communists with advice and encouragement and in the countries under U.S. occupation represented their interests to the occupation officials. They also offered material assistance, often at so elementary a level as supplying paper for fliers and food packages for the families of union organizers. Support for their activities was contributed by American unions, but only a small number of them pitched in.[18] As a result Lovestone and Brown felt badly overmatched in material resources by the Communists, who could rely on ample support from the Soviets. Once again the CIA entered the breach and provided secret funds to the FTUC to even out the competition. Consequently non-Communists came out on top in the German labor movement. Although the Communists continued to dominate the largest labor federation in France, its power and theirs were diluted by the emergence of a competing organization, the Force Ouvriere.

Congress for Cultural Freedom

The Church committee summarized the CIA's efforts in postwar Europe:

> the Agency concentrated on developing anti-Communist political strength. Financial support to individual candidates, subsidies to publications including newspapers and magazines, involvement in local and national labor unions—all of these interlocking elements constituted the fundamentals of a typical political action program. Elections, of course, were key operations, and the Agency involved itself in electoral politics on a continuing basis. Likewise, case officers groomed and cultivated individuals who could provide strong pro-Western leadership.
>
> Beyond the various forms of political action and liaison the Agency's program of clandestine activities aimed at developing an international anti-Communist ideology. . . . activities included operations to assist or to create international organizations for youth, students, teachers, workers, veterans, journalists and jurists. This kind of activity was an attempt to lay an intellectual foundation for anti-Communism around the world. Ultimately, the organizational underpinnings could serve as a political force in assuring the establishment or maintenance of democratic governments.[19]

This is a good summary, but it is flawed by the phrase "developing an anti-Communist ideology," which misses the point of the activities it characterizes. Much of Western intellectual discourse in the 1930s had revolved around the issue of communism, bringing forth a plethora of pro-Communist intellectuals and eventually of anti-Communist intellectuals as well. The Communist parties were adept at harnessing their supporters for maximum political impact. The anti-Communist intellectuals, like intellectuals generally, were often politically feckless or indifferent to the political impact of their work. The CIA's programs aimed not to develop an ideology but to provide a platform and megaphone with which to amplify the voice of the anti-Communist intellectuals.

By far the most ambitious of such projects (at least insofar as the public record now shows) was the Congress for Cultural Freedom, whose history, including its CIA connection, has been painstakingy reconstructed in Peter Coleman's book *The Liberal Conspiracy*.[20] The congress was founded in 1950, a "pathological moment in Western intellectual history," as Irving Kristol put it. The United States, despite all it had just done for Europe, "was regarded with a mixture of contempt and hatred" by most European intellectuals[21] and by many of their American counterparts as well. In 1949 a Communist-run "peace conference" at New York's Waldorf Astoria drew such celebrities as Albert Einstein, Charlie Chaplin, Leonard Bernstein, Norman Mailer, Clifford Odets, Aaron Copeland, and Paul Robeson, not to mention such Stalinist warhorses as Lillian Hellman.

To offset this, the Congress for Cultural Freedom was launched with a 1950 conference in embattled Berlin that attracted its own stellar collection of literati including Arthur Koestler, Ignazio Silone, Franz Borkenau, Denis de Rougement, A. J. Ayer, and Sidney Hook. Its five honorary presidents were Benedetto Croce, John Dewey, Karl Jaspers, Jacques Maritain, and Bertrand Russell. During the ensuing decade the congress grew, by dint of the energies of the anti-Communist intellectuals and the funds of the CIA, to such a size that it employed a staff of 280, with representatives in thirty-five countries.[22]

> It sponsored a network of magazines including *Encounter*, *Survey*, *Preuves*, *Tempo Presente*, and *Cuadernos* and helped others ranging from *Quest* in Bombay to *Quadrant* in Sydney. It conducted large and small international seminars, which J. K. Galbraith (for one) said were "by a wide margin, the most interesting, lively and informative I had ever attended." It orchestrated international protests against oppression of intellectuals, most frequently in the Soviet bloc but also in Spain, Argentina, and Indonesia. It organized festivals and helped refugee writers. . . . Above all, the Congress in this period helped to shatter the illusions of the Stalinist fellow-travelers. It did not have the impact of Nikita S. Khrushchev's "secret speech" and the Soviet suppression of Hungary in 1956 (or of Aleksandr Solzhenitsyn later), but it prepared the ground.[23]

The congress collapsed in the late 1960s, embarrassed by revelations of its secret CIA funding. It had already begun to falter before the CIA revelations as the community of anti-Communist intellectuals broke apart under the impact of the war in Vietnam. Moreover by the 1960s its main mission had been accomplished: the democracies of Western Europe were stable. True, the congress had sought to nurture anti-Communist intellectuals in the developing countries and behind the iron curtain as well, but the driving force behind its formation had been the sense that Europe itself stood in danger of absorption into the Soviet empire.

The impact of the words spoken and written under the auspices of the congress is impossible to measure. But it seems reasonable to assume that in almost any society the ideas embraced by intellectuals come to influence those of the public and of political elites, and that this in turn shapes political structures and policies. In the aftermath of World War II, communism enjoyed a dramatic spurt of expansion, and no one could judge where this would end. The willingness of influential Western thinkers to lend themselves to its cause was surely an important asset. Underwriting the activities of prodemocracy intellectuals was a concrete measure to safeguard young democracies, even if the effects can never be proved. Peter Coleman concluded accurately that the congress "placed some severe limits on the advantages of Stalinist Russia."[24]

Scope of Covert Actions

In addition to the activities in Western Europe, published references can be found to CIA covert projects in Eastern Europe; Japan, Indonesia, the Philippines, Korea, Tibet, and Indochina; and Chile and elsewhere in Latin America. The accuracy of these references is impossible to assess, and no authoritative public record exists. The Church committee reported that "by 1953, there were major covert operations in forty-eight countries, consisting primarily of propaganda and political action."[25] It reports too that in 1952 the Office of Policy Coordination (then the name of the CIA branch in charge of covert action) employed 2,812 people "plus 3,142 overseas contract personnel" and disposed of a budget of $82 million. These employees manned forty-seven stations.[26] Moreover, this was just an early stage. "Covert action expanded significantly in the 1953 to 1961 period.... concentrat[ing] ... on political action, particularly support to electoral candidates and to political parties."[27] In this span the covert action staff expanded by 2,000.[28]

Elsewhere in its report the committee states that during this same period "the international labor, student, and media projects of the International Organizations Division constituted the greatest single concentration of covert political and propaganda activities."[29] This seems to contradict the assertion that the electoral programs were the biggest ones. Regardless, the work with international organizations added another layer of covert activity, much of it designed to advance the democratic cause, in addition to that of the covert action personnel stationed in forty-seven or forty-eight countries. These figures strengthen the impression, despite the uncertainty of our knowledge, that the covert effort was a substantial one. Gregory Treverton, who worked on the Church committee's staff, wrote that "between 1951 and 1975 ... there were some nine hundred major or sensitive [covert action] projects, plus several thousand smaller ones."[30]

Philippines. CIA covert action began in Europe but soon spread. The Philippines was the site of one early project that helped nurture democracy. Soon after the country was granted its independence in 1946, its young government was confronted with a formidable Communist insurgency, the so-called Huk rebellion. (*Huk* in Tagalog is short for People's Liberation Army.) Edward Lansdale was dispatched there by the U.S. government in 1950 to help counteract the insurgency. Although his memoirs imply that he was working for the Defense Department, other sources say that his true employer was the CIA.[31]

Lansdale soon concluded that the key to Huk success was popular support, and that this in turn was the product of deep alienation from the government in Manila. The alienation was produced by extraordinary corruption, brutality, inequities and the widespread belief that President Elpidio Quirino and his colleagues had stolen the 1949 election. Lansdale summarized the popular view:

> The farmers were losing everything they possessed through high rentals, decisions in the land courts that always favored the landlords, the usurious moneylenders who charged farmers mounting interest on the the original small debts of their fathers. The townspeople had gone to the polls in 1949 and voted for representatives who could change all this. What had happened? Nothing. They had been cheated. The election had been rigged, bringing the corrupt to power. Of course the people were joining and helping the Huks. The Huks were right.[32]

In Ramon Magsaysay, a young, charismatic politician who had just become secretary of national defense, Lansdale saw two virtues that would be a tonic for the Philippine government's faltering fight. First, he was apparently incorruptible. Second, he came from humble origins and retained a sympathy for the common people and easy rapport with them. Lansdale helped Magsaysay to assume control over the counterinsurgency, despite some friction with military commanders. In 1953 he helped him campaign successfully for president.

Magsaysay won the presidency by a landslide against the aging, corrupt incumbent, Quirino. The greatest fear of Magsaysay's supporters had been that, as in 1949, the election would be stolen. Against this possibility, the agency helped to build NAMFREL, the National Movement for Free Elections. The group, which had been started to safeguard the integrity of the 1951 legislative elections, expanded its efforts in 1953. Former CIA officer Joseph B. Smith described some of its activities:

> They preached the virtues of ensuring there would be no tricks at the polls and showed the practical ways to prevent them. They taught people how to make proper thumbprints on ballots—the system used to verify registration certificates.

One method of throwing out ballots was for government-appointed polling supervisors or protesting-party poll watchers, who feared ballots were being cast for their opponents, to claim thumbprints were illegible and declare the ballots invalid. Many times these same officials did a little ballot smudging themselves in order to accomplish their mission. People were alerted to look out for this.

Other people were taught photography and instructed to take pictures of all persons entering polling places in order to identify for prosecution the squads of multivoters that corrupt politicians used around town. A second team of photographers were instructed to go along and take pictures of any strong-arm types who might try to prevent the first group from photographing the people entering the polls.[33]

In addition the CIA encouraged as many journalists as it could influence to cover the Philippine elections. "The purpose," said Smith, "was to scare Quirino out of trying any last-minute tricks under the eyes of so many trained observers who would have liked nothing better than a good story or two about Philippine corruption, which they had been hearing about for months."[34]

Magsaysay's election was a positive step for Philippine democracy. It also set the stage for a successful completion of the counterinsurgency against the Huks. Alas, the victory did not endure. Magsaysay died in a plane crash in 1957 while seeking reelection. He was succeeded by men of modest ability until Ferdinand Marcos won the post in 1965. Marcos was a more able man but no democrat. In 1972 he established a virtual dictatorship under martial law. By then a new generation of Communist insurgents resumed the struggle of the Huks. Nonetheless something positive from the CIA's efforts did endure. In 1986 a new civic association emerged as the key force that thwarted Marcos's design to steal reelection. It took the name NAMFREL, suggesting its linear descent from the group that played the same role in Magsaysay's election. And the crusading spirit of the presidential campaign of Corazon Aquino, which succeeded in toppling the corrupt and devious incumbent, was in some ways reminiscent of the campaign of 1953.

Chile. After Fidel Castro took power in Cuba in 1959, the CIA began to devote a greater share of its energies to Latin America. Although the agency was probably active in several Latin countries, its activities in Chile have been documented most amply.

In 1958 Salvador Allende, running as the candidate of a popular front of the Communist and Socialist parties, lost the election for president of Chile to Conservative party candidate Jorge Alessandri by a surprisingly narrow margin of 3 percent. It created alarm in some parts of Washington, which was reinforced by events in Cuba the following year.

Although Allende was a Socialist, his party was not equivalent to the European social democratic parties; it was closer to the Communists. Allende served as a vice president of the World Peace Council, characterized by the CIA as "the major Soviet-dominated international front organization."[35] He maintained close ties to Castro's Cuba,[36] and when his government was ousted in 1973, top leaders of his party and of the popular front chose to take their exile in East Germany.

As early as the 1950s, according to the Church committee, the CIA had conducted projects in Chile "among peasants, slum dwellers, organized labor, students, and the media."[37] In the early 1960s the agency began to look ahead anxiously to the presidential election scheduled for 1964. Allende would have a second chance, and the incumbent Alessandri could not seek reelection under Chilean law. Initially the agency decided to channel financial support to two other parties, the moderately left-of-center Christian Democrats and the moderately right-of-center Radicals. As the election grew nearer, however, a decision was reached that the strongest choice against Allende was the Christian Democrats, with their attractive candidate Eduardo Frei.

More than half of Frei's campaign budget was eventually contributed by the U.S. government, although Frei apparently was unaware of the source.[38] In addition, according to the Church committee, the CIA worked secretly to divide the Socialist party and to prevent the Radical party from backing Allende.[39] It also

> mounted a massive anti-communist propaganda campaign. Extensive use was made of the press, radio, films, pamphlets, posters, leaflets, direct mailings, paper streamers, and wall painting. It was a "scare campaign," which relied heavily on images of Soviet tanks and Cuban firing squads and was directed especially to women. Hundreds of thousands of copies of the anti-communist pastoral letter of Pope Pius XI were distributed by Christian Democratic organizations.[40]

Frei won a decisive victory. In the CIA's own analysis its efforts had made the difference between what would have been a mere plurality and the clear majority that he polled. The victory, however, was of limited duration. After the election the agency continued its activities with the media and in the various social arenas, and it kept alive some of its polling and propaganda mechanisms.[41] But Frei could not succeed himself. While Allende's popular front prepared to run him for president again in 1970, the anti-Allende forces were again divided.

This time the U.S. government could not decide between the

Conservative Alessandri, seeking another term (nonsequential second terms were legal), and Frei's successor as leader of the Christian Democrats, Radimiro Tomic. Instead the agency was instructed to mount an anti-Allende propaganda campaign, somewhat similar to its ancillary activities in the 1964 campaign but this time without backing any candidate. The effort failed: Allende won a narrow plurality. Under the Chilean constitution this threw the election into the hands of the Congress.

The U.S. government tried desperately to sway the Congress against Allende, but it would not budge from the tradition of awarding the office to the leading vote getter. The administration also instructed the CIA to try to stimulate a coup against Allende in 1970, but these efforts also failed. During Allende's presidency, from 1970 to 1973, the agency channeled funds to various opposition groups, especially the leading newspaper, *El Mercurio*. When Allende was finally deposed in 1973, the CIA apparently was not directly involved although the Church committee concluded that it may have indirectly helped to stimulate the coup.

It was entirely proper for the CIA to support opposition forces during Allende's reign, but if the agency did contribute to the 1973 coup, it contributed to the destruction of democracy in Chile, even though Allende himself might have endangered it. Certainly the preponderant forces in his popular front party had no commitment to democracy, and it is doubtful that he did either. During his tenure in office pressure was applied against opposition media, Cuban secret service agents were used to train Chilean counterparts, and extralegal expropriations of property were carried out.[42]

In light of this, the agency's 1964 activity in behalf of Frei seems to have been a positive contribution to safeguarding Chilean democracy. Its inability to duplicate that effort in 1970 put Chilean democracy in jeopardy. All told, the agency's Chilean operations during the Allende's candidacies and presidency reveal both the better and the worse effects of covert action on democracy.

Latin American Political Training. Another covert program that aimed to encourage democracy in Latin America was political training institutes that the CIA secretly underwrote. The Institute of Political Education was founded in Costa Rica in 1959 under the aegis of the Institute for International Labor Research, a U.S. group headed by the famous Socialist party leader, Norman Thomas. It was sponsored by seventeen Latin American political parties of the non-Communist Left.[43] Those associated with it included Víctor Haya de la Torre of Peru, Rómulo Betancourt of Venezuela, José Figueres and Luis Alberto Monge of Costa

Rica, Luis Muñóz Marín of Puerto Rico, and Juan Bosch of the Dominican Republic. The parties sent their young leaders there in groups of around fifty for ten-week courses in democratic political theory and pragmatics.

Bosch was at the Costa Rican institute in 1961 when he received word of the assassination of the Dominican dictator Rafael Trujillo. Before dispatching a team of PRD colleagues to renew political work in their homeland (where they had been harshly repressed under Trujillo), Bosch asked the institute's director, Sasha Volman, to travel there "to feel out the atmosphere."[44] Almost at once Volman organized a two-month course for some fifty young cadres, most from the PRD and a few from other parties to its left and right.

At about this time, Thomas's organization withdrew its support from the Costa Rican institute and threw it instead behind a similar organization that was established by Volman in the Dominican Republic, the Inter-American Center for Social Studies (Spanish acronymn: CIDES). After Trujillo's thirty-one-year reign, the political landscape of the Dominican Republic was a vast wasteland. As Howard Wiarda described it, the dictator had

> eliminated whatever early stirrings of democratic rule—nascent political parties, interest groups, and the like—had begun to emerge in the early part of the century and in the 1920s. By the end of the long Trujillo era, there was no foundation—no leaders, no institutions—on which a new democratic order could be based. . . . In terms of democratic institutions, the Dominican Republic was only slightly more advanced in 1961 . . . than it was in 1844.[45]

Volman and CIDES sought to fill this vacuum. As Bosch recounted:

> The school taught cooperativism and Latin American political history. . . . It also offered courses for schoolteachers. The students came from all over the country, with no discrimination by class or political party. . . . The objective of these classes was to help create in Santo Domingo a democratic consciousness and an awareness of Dominican problems and how to go about solving them by democratic measures.[46]

In addition, during Bosch's brief tenure as president before being ousted in a coup, Volman organized a crash program of mass immunization against polio. CIDES provided training for the young staff of Bosch's National Planning Board. It conducted a study aimed at the reorganization of the republic's chaotic customs regulations, and it laid plans for cooperatives and industrial development.[47]

Although Bosch's election drew the institute's attention strongly toward the Dominican Republic, it continued to try to fulfill its regional mission. It "recruited Cuban exiles, Puerto Ricans sent by their government, Venezuelans, Peruvians, Argentines, people from all over the Americas who shared a known democratic viewpoint, a desire for public service, and experienced technical skills," said Bosch.[48]

The ouster of Bosch by a military coup in 1963 crippled the institute's activities, although it managed to survive for a few more years. It closed after the first revelations that its benefactor, the J. M. Kaplan Foundation, had served as a CIA conduit and shortly before it was publicly established that the institute itself had received such funds.

Portugal. In 1974 a group of young officers overthrew the military dictatorship that had ruled Portugal for nearly half a century under António Salazar and his successor, Marcello Caetano. Some members of the victorious Armed Forces Movement sought to put their country on a democratic path, but some had other ideas. Their rebellion had been fueled by the frustrations of colonial service, where many of them were influenced by the Marxist ideology of the African independence movements that they had been sent to suppress. The radical elements in the Armed Forces Movement were reinforced by a Communist party that quickly emerged from the political underground after the 1974 coup.

As is so often the case, this highly disciplined party had maintained far more cohesive organization than the democratic opponents of the old regime had. Communist party chief Alvaro Cunhal was made a minister in the provisional government. He boasted that Portugal would not take the path of parliamentary democracy. With allies in key positions in the revolutionary military junta, including Premier Vasco Gonçalves, he seemed able to make good his boast.

Cunhal and Gonçalves could not, however, persuade the other members of the government to postpone national elections, which were held in April 1975, the first anniversary of the coup. When the votes were tallied, the Socialist party of Marío Soares—pro-Western, prodemocracy, and anti-Communist—won a resounding victory with nearly 38 percent of the vote in a multiparty field. The Communists came in third with a meager 12.5 percent.

News accounts at the time reported that important assistance had come to the Socialists from their comrades in the Socialist International, especially the West German Social Democratic party and its foundation, the Friedrich Ebert Stiftung. Fragmentary reports of covert support by the U.S. government also were probably accurate. At the same time, Moscow no doubt subsidized the Portuguese Communists.

The Communists, however, were not deterred by electoral failure, as Cunhal's boast made clear. Despite the election of a constituent assembly, most power remained in the hands of the Armed Forces

Movement, the government it had chosen, and to some extent in the streets. At a Communist rally in Lisbon on May Day, just six days after the election, Cunhal shared the platform with Premier Gonçalves and President Francisco da Costa Gomes, giving the event a semiofficial aura. Socialist leader Soares and other moderates were forcibly excluded. Later that month radical employees seized the offices of the newspaper *Republica*, the only major daily not under Communist sway,[49] and attempted to oust its pro-Socialist editor.

These two events helped touch off several months of demonstrations that catalyzed the anti-Communists in the Armed Forces Movement and tipped the scales of Portuguese politics against the far Left and toward democracy. In Lisbon and other urban areas, the Socialists staged huge rallies, proving that they could outdraw the Communists not only at the polls but also in the streets. In the more rural north a wave of anti-Communist demonstrations repeatedly spilled over into violence aimed at Communist offices and cadres. These actions constituted a kind of "rural revolt," in the words of one historian, that had "no obvious precedent in Portuguese history, excepting perhaps the Maria da Fonte uprising of the 1840s."[50] Protests were even more intense among the denizens of the Portuguese islands of the Azores and Madeira.[51]

This anti-Communist outpouring was a natural reaction against the attempt to impose by force an alien ideology supported by only one-eighth of the electorate. Popular indignation did not express itself spontaneously, however, but was mobilized and harnessed for maximum impact by organized groups. The demonstrations in the north, for example, were encouraged and sometimes organized by the Democratic Movement for the Liberation of Portugal. This group was headed by General António de Spínola, the moderate figurehead of the coup against the Caetano dictatorship; he had quickly fallen out with younger, more radical officers and had taken exile in Spain after an unsuccessful coup against them. This and other such groups, in addition to the Socialists, probably received material assistance from covert U.S. government sources.

El Salvador. A U.S. covert political intervention occurred in the presidential election in El Salvador in 1984. After years of military rule and an intensifying guerrilla insurgency, a coup in 1979 brought to power a mixed civilian-military government pledged to the cause of reform. After several shake-ups, the junta chose José Napoleón Duarte as its leader, an important step toward the restoration of civilian rule. Duarte was the leader of the Christian Democratic party and the country's preeminent civilian politician. He is widely believed to have polled the most votes in the presidential balloting of 1972 but was prevented by the military from taking office. During those events, he was arrested, tortured, and forced into exile. Some of those aligned with Duarte in the 1972 elections then went over to the Communist-led insurgency.

In 1982 democracy was begun anew, as promised by the junta, with elections to the National Assembly. These resulted in a close finish between the Christian Democrats and the rightist ARENA party. The assembly chose an interim president, setting the stage for a presidential election in 1984 pitting Duarte against ARENA's Roberto D'Aubuisson. Although he sought office by ballot, D'Aubuisson showed a devotion to democracy that was at best uncertain. Doubts arose not merely because he was associated with the landed aristocracy and military elite that had so long ruled El Salvador without benefit of democratic mandate or procedures. He was also, in the eyes of the U.S. government, deeply implicated in the activities of death squads responsible for the murders of Archbishop Arnulfo Romero, of two American labor organizers, and of thousands of other Salvadorans. D'Aubuisson, it was feared with reason, might use the power of presidency not to strengthen Salvador's nascent democracy but to strangle it and to perpetuate his own rule. In addition, the U.S. Congress might stop allocating military aid for El Salvador's counterinsurgency. That would have further polarized El Salvador, pitting far Right against far Left in a contest of ruthlessness, with innocent civilians the principal victims.

Against this background, conservative Senator Jesse Helms, a backer of D'Aubuisson, made public accusations that the CIA was secretly funneling money to the campaign of Duarte. In the next few days, newspapers reported that the U.S. government had spent $2 million "as part of a two-year effort by the Central Intelligence Agency to facilitate national elections and assist parties competing with right-wing candidate Roberto D'Aubuisson."[52] According to these accounts, the agency had secretly provided funds to Duarte's campaign and in lesser amounts to smaller parties, including a conservative party that did not support D'Aubuisson in the runoff. In addition the news accounts suggest that American funds had been passed through the German Konrad Adenauer Foundation to the Venezuelan Institute for Popular Education, which was reported to have campaigned for Duarte and lent 300 paid employees to El Salvador's official Central Elections Council to help ensure the smooth administration of the election.[53] Duarte won the election with about 55 percent of the vote in the runoff and this time was not prevented from assuming office.

Evaluation of Covert Operations

These examples give some inkling of the varieties of covert action and also the disparities in results. In Italy in 1948, in Portugal in 1975, and elsewhere in Western Europe in the years between, democracy triumphed largely because of the actions of groups secretly aided by the United States. History allows no answer to how those groups would have fared without American help.

In El Salvador, Duarte won the presidential race in 1984. In the next presidential election, the ARENA party nominated Alfredo Cristiani for president rather than D'Aubuisson, and he defeated the Christian Democrats' candidate chosen to succeed Duarte. Although they came from the same party, Cristiani showed much more attachment to democracy than D'Aubuisson had. Cristiani's civil government faced threats from extremists on the Right as well as guerrillas on the Left, just as Duarte's did, but Salvadoran democracy remained intact.

In the Philippines the CIA's operation was successful, but Magsaysay died. With him went the hopes for stable, effective, democratic government that had motivated the CIA's support for his candidacy. In Chile democracy also died; the operation had been botched.

The regional or international programs like CIDES in Latin America or the Congress for Cultural Freedom certainly gave substantive support to democrats. No one, however, has been able to measure the impact of this support or the repercussions from the embarrassment and resentment felt by those involved in these groups when the CIA's secret support was disclosed.

Whatever its successes, however, covert action is inevitably controversial. The Church committee reported that it

> gave serious consideration to proposing a total ban on *all* forms of covert action. The Committee has concluded, however, that the United States should maintain the option of reacting in the future to a grave, unforeseen threat to U.S. national security through covert means. . . . when overt means will not suffice.[54]

The Church committee's criticisms of covert action were couched in terms of its utility as an instrument of national security. Such objections would presumably apply all the more forcefully to covert action as an instrument for promoting democracy, given that national security is the paramount purpose of foreign policy and that covert action seems inherently antithetical to democratic goals.

Circumvention. One of the Church committee's main objections was that "secrecy can . . . become . . . a means of circumventing the established checks and procedures of government," that "covert action . . . offers a secret shortcut around the democratic process."[55] In the years since the committee's report, however, a rather effective system of congressional oversight of intelligence activities has been established. Such oversight does fall far short of full public scrutiny and debate. But Americans since the founding fathers have recognized that the exigencies of foreign policy in a perilous world often require a government, even a democratic one, to act with "secrecy and dispatch," as John Jay put it in *Federalist* 64. The oversight committees do ensure that any covert action must bear the scrutiny of some three dozen legislators from both parties. The committees do not wield a direct veto over executive branch actions, but when many members object, they can block an action either by persuasion or by legislation. In the Iran-contra affair, it is true, President Ronald Reagan evaded oversight by circumventing the CIA. This sorry episode constitutes not an argument against covert action but one against abuse of process. Even a total ban on covert action cannot stop presidents from abusing their authority if they are determined to do so.

Dependence. Another concern raised by the Church committee was that covert support of political forces can encourage

> a debilitating dependence on the United States. In one Western nation the covert investment was so heavy and so persistent that, according to a former CIA Station Chief in that country: "Any aspiring politician almost automatically would come to the CIA to see if we could help him get elected."[56]

Expressed in this anecdotal, almost flippant, way, this argument cannot be assessed. The committee did not say whether other U.S. officials who served in this station corroborated the description. Perhaps it was a vain boast or a recrimination or simply an exaggeration.

Even if the quoted description of the mentality of native politicians is accurate, it does not prove that U.S. influence was as pervasive as they believed. In countries that admire or are awed by the United States there are many examples of politicians striving to project an image of being closer to U.S. officials than they really are. And even if American influence was pervasive, what harm did it cause? Surely the Church committee must have asked these questions; surely if the answers buttressed its case for alarm, the committee would have said so.

Divergence of Goals. Equally unpersuasive is the warning of committee staff member Gregory Treverton that "covert support, once given, is hard to withdraw when circumstances change."[57] Treverton cited the activity of some Chilean military officers who were encouraged by the CIA to plot a coup against Allende. They continued their plotting even after the United States apparently tried to call them off. But the example shows not that the United States may be caught in its own intrigue but that the foreign nationals supported by the United States may do things we deplore or ought to deplore. This leads to two other criticisms from Treverton that are far more telling. First, foreigners with whom we work may have goals different from ours. Second, it has become difficult to keep covert actions secret.

"'Their' purposes may not be 'ours,'" says Treverton of the groups that we may secretly fund.[58] He offers the striking example of the Nicaraguan contras and the Boland Amendment. To finesse congressional opposition, the Reagan administration agreed to legislation stipulating that no public funds be used "for the purpose of overthrowing the government of Nicaragua." It was declared that support for the contras was to continue, solely to pressure Nicaragua's government into ending its support for the guerrillas in El Salvador. The painfully obvious question was whether the Nicaraguan rebels could be expected to risk their lives for the sake of El Salvador.

The conflict in this case, however, was more apparent than real. The administration's position was a subterfuge. Concerned though it may have been about El Salvador, it was no less concerned about Nicaragua itself. It certainly did intend that the contras try to overthrow the Nicaraguan government. Treverton's argument is perhaps better illustrated by the case of the Kurds in Iraq who with covert American assistance fought a guerrilla war for their independence in the early 1970s. When the shah of Iran, America's principal ally in the region and the principal backer of the Iraqi Kurds, withdrew his support from them, America followed suit. Our purposes had been to harass a hostile government in Baghdad and to assist a friendly one in Teheran. When it suited us to change course, the Kurds were left in the lurch.

The salient point about the Kurdish example is the great gulf between their objectives and ours. In any international alliance, covert or otherwise, the goals of the parties naturally differ, but if the differences are not great, the partners should be able to agree on common goals. American goals and those of the Portuguese Socialist party from 1974 to 1975 were presumably not identical, but both wanted to see the triumph of parliamentary democracy in that country, so mutually beneficial collaboration was possible. If there is little coincidence of goals, however, then the collaboration has less the quality of an alliance than an effort by one party to manipulate the other. Such stratagems are hardly unknown in international politics, but they raise difficult ethical questions and risk backfiring.

Cord Meyer, former director of the CIA's covert political operations, said, "In all the years of our cooperation in attempting to promote the democratic cause abroad, I cannot remember a single incident in which the Agency was accused of attempting to manipulate or unfairly influence the policies or activities of those with whom we dealt."[59] Similarly William Colby, the former CIA director who had earlier headed the agency's operations in Italy, said, "The program in Italy gave aid to the democratic forces to obtain *their* goals."[60] But Colby also implied that he sometimes worked to influence positions taken by the parties that received American aid:

> I would tell him [an agent working as his liaison to some party] that he had to urge them to change their position slightly, so that the government could survive and I could answer the furious cables I was receiving as to how headquarters could possibly continue giving any further aid to such a recalcitrant group.[61]

In promoting democracy, differences between American goals and those of groups we are supporting need not be a problem. If groups committed to democratic ends are fighting groups with contrary ends, it often behooves us to help them whether or not we share or even know every aspect of their program (that is, if they want our help and if we can find safe ways to give it). Efforts to control or manipulate the policies of foreign groups, however, tend to vitiate democratic processes.

Assistance to a political group or party from a foreign power distorts the democratic process. CIA aid generally has served to counterbalance aid to Communist forces furnished, usually far more lavishly, by Moscow. Dollars funneled to Christian Democrats in Italy or in Chile offset rubles funneled to Communists in those countries. At best, no outsiders would interfere, but interference by many is preferable to involvement by just one foreign power.

In the Philippines and El Salvador, the presidential candidates who received CIA support were not running against Communists. Magsaysay's opponent was corrupt and regressive. Duarte's was murderous. In both cases these adversaries were undermining democracy but were not manifest philosophical opponents of democracy in the way that Communists are. Both countries too faced a real threat of Communist takeover through insurrection, not election. The CIA judged that the man it backed stood the best chance of preventing that. The support given to Magsaysay or Duarte is defensible, but the case is more complex and contingent than a simple argument for providing a level playing field. In general, covert action of this kind can be justified if the fate of democracy in a country seems inseparable from the fate of a particular candidate. But care ought to be taken not to stretch this justification.

Which Democrat? What if more than one candidate manifests democratic mettle? Should America then underwrite all the democrats or pick one horse to ride? In Italy it appears that support was given to several parties, but the lion's share went to the Christian Democrats. Most often, it seems, U.S. officials believe that support mobilized for a single candidate has been most effective. In Chile in 1964 the effort behind Frei appears to have worked well. In 1970 an American adminstration unable to choose between the Christian Democrats and Conservatives limited itself to sponsoring propaganda against Allende. The result was failure.

From a prodemocracy standpoint, if several democratic candidates are in a field with enemies of democracy, America should support all the democrats if it supports any. U.S. officials may believe they know which of the democrats will be the most effective. To make such a choice, however, is to intervene too deeply in another nation's political life, and judgments of this type are too fallible. Supporting democracy's champions against its enemies is one thing; selecting one democrat over others is another.

Leaks. Treverton also touched an important problem when he mentioned the difficulty of keeping covert actions secret. "In the 1980s and 1990s, large secret interventions almost inevitably will spill into print," he said. This seems an exaggeration: Treverton himself reported that 900 "major or sensitive" projects were carried out in the prior three decades, but only a few dozen have leaked into print.[62]

The point, nonetheless, is a strong one. Not every operation needs to be exposed for the risk of exposure to be too great. This is especially true if the costs of exposure are high, as we may expect them often to be. One cost may be that those we intend to help are instead damaged by the association. Another may be that these beneficiaries, if they are unwitting, may become embittered. Juan Bosch wrote in 1965 that "CIDES was not administered by the Alliance for Progress, nor did it have any bureaucratic tie with the U.S. Government. In fact, it was precisely in its independent status that the organization's worth as an experiment lay."[63] Imagine his embarrassment when it was revealed two years later that CIDES was financed by the CIA. Perhaps this contributed to the strident anti-Americanism and even antidemocratism that came to characterize his politics in later years.[64] And Treverton is also correct that the exposure of such operations encourages the tendency to treat the United States and the Soviet Union as morally equivalent. A vast moral difference can be shown between the record of the CIA and that of the KGB, but revelations of political CIA chicanery obscure this.

A further problem about maintaining secrecy is that some genies cannot be put back in the bottle. After the revelations about CIA activities in the 1960s and 1970s, covert action by all accounts decreased dramatically.[65] The budget for covert action was reported rising again in the 1980s, but perhaps mostly for covert military assistance to anti-Communist guerrillas under the rubric of the Reagan Doctrine, rather than for political action. If the United States resumed widespread covert political activity, could we keep it hidden now that so much is known about past actions? If political parties or youth organizations or the like espouse platforms consonant with U.S. interests and display material resources beyond their visible means, won't people wonder whether the U.S. government is involved? And if they seek to discover the answer, can it be kept secret?

Covert to Overt? Can some CIA actions done covertly in the cause of democracy be done overtly instead? Radio Free Europe and Radio Liberty were two of the largest and most important covert projects in the agency's history. Founded respectively in 1949 and 1951 by a committee of prominent private citizens, both relied from their inception on covert CIA funding and with it a measure of administrative oversight. Because they were staffed by exiles and refugees from the target countries, the radios projected an image of representing an authentic, repressed native voice, an image that might have been weakened by admitting U.S. government support. It was public knowledge, however, that these were American-based organizations. In 1971 Senator Clifford Case revealed the agency's relationship to the radios, and at once their continuation was in doubt. After some temporizing, the Congress created the Board for International Broadcasting, which took over responsibilty for the radios, and government funding was renewed openly. This shift to acknowledged sponsorship by the U.S. government appears not to have diminished the radios' effectiveness.

In the 1980s the United States funded anti-Communist guerrilla forces in Nicaragua, Afghanistan, Angola, and Cambodia. The first two operations began as truly covert operations. The Angolan and Cambodian projects began with considerable publicity, although they too were administered by the CIA. By the mid-1980s the four together were the focus of a noisy national debate over the Reagan Doctrine, replete with numerous subsidiary arguments about exactly which weapons to supply, which factions to favor, and what codes of conduct to impose on the guerrillas. Although some operational details remained shrouded, as in any war, the basic policy was no longer covert. This micromanagement was surely detrimental to the guerrillas, but making the basic policy overt rather than covert did no apparent harm. Indeed, where congressional consensus did not disintegrate, the guerrilla groups may well have drawn strength from having visible official support from the U.S. government.

The National Endowment for Democracy gives small grants either directly or through four subsidiary agencies—sponsored respectively by the Chamber of Commerce, the AFL-CIO, and each of the two major political parties—to support democracy-building projects in the non-democratic world. (A detailed account of the NED follows in chapter 12.) It underwrites such projects as labor organization, periodical and book publishing, voter education and registration, and election monitoring. Many of these projects are similar to those sponsored in the past covertly by the CIA. But the NED has a strict prohibition on any ties to the CIA, and all its activities and records are public.

Not that the NED can do all the kinds of political work that the CIA has done. It does not directly support candidates for office; NED does, however, come close. In the 1989 Chilean plebiscite over renewing the reign of President Pinochet, the NED's Democratic party subsidiary assisted the campaign against renewal. The NED did not involve itself in the Polish elections of 1989; its labor subsidiary, however, was long a principal backer of Solidarity, which organized the opposition's campaign. In other countries voter registration work underwritten by NED may affect election outcomes.

One rationale for the CIA's covert political activities has been that deserving groups often will not openly take money from the U.S. government for fear it might becloud their legitimacy. The NED alleviates this dilemma, although it does not eliminate it, by placing several layers of insulation between the U.S. government and the recipient. Most important, the NED itself is not a government agency but a private corporation, legally responsible only to its own board. It relies on government funding but also receives private money. Its grants are ordinarily made to private American organizations active in the international field, which in turn make grants to counterpart groups abroad. Under this system, foreign beneficiaries are willing to tolerate the onus of accepting funds that are known by all to originate in the U.S. Treasury.

The experience of Radio Free Europe and Radio Liberty, the history of the Reagan Doctrine, and the activities of the National Endowment for Democracy together demonstrate that a wide range of activities once done covertly can be carried on overtly. The reasons for their being covert were good, but the costs were high. Covert funding avoids problems, but none of them may be as severe as the trouble that arises when a covert operation is exposed. The test should be not whether a given project is easier to carry out covertly or overtly but whether it can be done overtly. If the answer is yes, then it is probably better done overtly, no matter how much more difficult or expensive.

All in all, the standard urged by the Church committee, that covert action be reserved for "reacting . . . to a grave, unforeseen threat to . . . national security," seems far too restrictive. For one thing, covert action, at least the political kind, seems much more suited to foreseen threats than unforeseen ones. And although covert action troubles us, especially if democracy is our touchstone, we must recognize that some laudable results can be credited to it, at least in part. Who would renounce the accomplishment of keeping the Communists from power in Italy in 1948 or in Portugal in 1975?

As these examples suggest, covert action is easiest to justify in the context of a cold war. Undeniably, covert action cuts against the democratic grain. Democracy means self-government, and any kind of foreign interference derogates from self-government, hidden interference all the more so. But where covert action has been the alternative to the triumph of communism, it has been, from a democratic viewpoint, the lesser evil. Communism, with its totalitarian drive to control every aspect of life, is the most thorough negation of democracy. And communism, once established had never fallen until 1989 (with the trivial exception of Grenada). Communism's triumph in any country forestalled the democratic prospect indefinitely.

This last point has now changed. Several countries are in transition from communism, and more will follow. Estimates of the likely costs and benefits of future covert projects may therefore look different in terms of the expected duration of any Communist triumph. If communism continues to collapse or transmogrify in the Soviet Union itself, the calculation will be altered even further. The threat of a Communist triumph in, say, Peru will certainly count differently to North Americans if Moscow no longer presents a global challenge to the United States.

What if communism disappears altogether as an ideology competing with democracy? Will covert action still be justifiable? It seems that there have been cases, although no public record exists, where America has covertly helped democratic forces to triumph over dictatorial ones that were not Communist. The American motivation was presumably not sheer democratic idealism but the belief that the democratic forces would provide a sterner barrier against communism. In a world freed from the depredations of a global antidemocratic ideology, the United States would still have ample moral cause to lend aid of various kinds to democrats against their adversaries. But whether it should intervene covertly would require careful weighing of ends and means.

That problem still lies in the future, notwithstanding the rapid changes in world politics that began in 1989. In the meantime covert action remains an available tool both for the advancement of democracy and for the defense of American security. It is, however, a two-edged sword. America should continue wherever possible to develop overt mechanisms to do the useful things that have in the past been done covertly.

The Reagan Doctrine

One other type of American government action that may advance democracy is support for guerrilla forces fighting to overthrow Communist regimes. The Reagan Doctrine, as this came to be called, was the most dramatic and probably the most expensive form of covert action undertaken by the CIA in the 1980s.

Although this activity is linked to Reagan's name, its antecedents go back to the end of World War II, when America secretly supported resistance groups, modeled on the wartime antifascist underground, in Eastern Europe, the Baltics, and the Ukraine. In the years that followed, according to various accounts, the CIA supported anti-Communist paramilitary activity in Tibet and Indochina and intended something of the sort in Cuba, which aborted in the disastrous Bay of Pigs landing.

Nor did American support for the four anti-Communist wars of the 1980s begin with Reagan. In the case of Afghanistan, provision of military supplies to the mujahedin began during the Carter administration as a genuinely clandestine activity. When Reagan came to office, the CIA began to support resistance elements in Nicaragua as well. Support for guerrilla forces in Angola and Cambodia did not start until 1985, and in those cases the impetus came from Congress rather than the executive branch. By then all of these projects had become so overt that President Reagan himself "leaked" to reporters his decision to send arms to Angola's UNITA.[66]

Much of the administration's rhetoric in the ensuing policy debates over this aid to rebel forces was couched in terms of fighting for democracy. Oliver North, it was revealed during the Iran-contra investigations, dubbed his own irregular activities on behalf of the Nicaraguan resistance project democracy. Charles Krauthammer, the percipient essayist who had coined the term "Reagan Doctrine," described U.S. support for democratic transitions in the Philippines and Haiti in 1986 as a kind of annex to the Reagan Doctrine.[67] And in his book *The Democratic Imperative*, writer Gregory Fossedal counted military support for guerrilla movements as one of the principal means of "exporting the American revolution."[68]

Despite these views, support for anti-Communist guerrillas was less a tool for spreading democracy then for strengthening U.S. security, a quite brilliant and useful one. It righted a critical imbalance in the cold war, namely, that the Soviet side was always on the offensive, looking to expand its domain, while the American side was always on the defensive, looking to contain the Soviets. By helping to even the competition by putting some of their territory at risk too, the Reagan Doctrine yielded not only practical benefits but psychological ones. It punctured communism's mystique of representing irreversible historical forces, as if the Red Army represented some kind of deus ex machina. Insofar as democracy's fate was interwoven with America's success in the cold war, the Reagan Doctrine served democracy.

But should we believe that the mujahedin are likely to establish democracy in Afghanistan, that UNITA will do so in Angola, or that the forces of Son Sann will do so in Cambodia? These countries are in parts of the world that have yet to be swept by the tide of democracy. The Afghan fighters are divided among various groups; some do profess democracy, but others espouse a religious fundamentalism with political impulses toward authoritarianism. Son Sann, because of the weakness of his forces, works in alliance with the erratic Prince Sihanouk and the murderous Khmer Rouge. UNITA's leader, Jonas Savimbi, may be a sincere democrat, but the likelihood that UNITA could establish democracy in Angola if it wins the civil war (which has largely divided the country along tribal lines) seems modest. Of all the Reagan Doctrine beneficiaries, the Nicaraguan rebels were the most plausible democrats. They have now proved their democratic convictions by disarming, once the freely elected government of Violetta Chamorro took office.

The case of Nicaragua has shown that Mikhail Gorbachev's "new thinking" may yet give the Reagan Doctrine more efficacy in creating democracy, almost serendipitously, than first seemed likely. The other three countries where the United States has supported anti-Communist insurgencies are subject to intense diplomacy. Before the Gorbachev era, such diplomacy could hardly have been expected to result in any kind of democratic settlement; to the Communists, such a settlement would have been tantamount to surrender. They would negotiate only to see if they could induce, or trick, the other side to surrender. Now, however, the Soviets have shown themselves willing to consider genuine compromise in the interest of resolving regional disputes—and to urge the same upon their allies. One form of such a compromise is internationally supervised elections. The U.S.-supported guerrillas had little prospect of bringing democracy by their own efforts, but the stalemates they have forced may engender democratic outcomes.

The changes wrought by Gorbachev also create a new context for considering whether military aid to anti-Communist insurgencies could promote democracy in the future. At most such aid seems likely to be a limited tool. Eastern Europe is no longer Communist or is in transition from communism. In the Soviet Union itself and much of the rest of the Communist world, communism is tottering, having lost its legitimacy and self-confidence. At this moment therefore U.S. policy ought to focus on political instruments designed to encourage divisions and self-doubts among Communist rulers and to embolden oppositionists. Why resort to lethal means when peaceful ones might achieve the same result? Moreover the Reagan Doctrine is also losing its national security rationale. If the Soviet Union is discarding its empire rather than expanding it, then anti-Communist insurgency is no longer required as a countervailing force.

Although it is not easy to picture guerrilla insurgency breaking out in Cuba, North Korea, or Vietnam, principle alone would strongly commend support for such a rebellion if the rebels raised the democratic standard. A more interesting question would arise—and indeed it seems a more likely one—if civil war broke out in China between forces championing democratic reform and those opposing it. A substantial number of U.S. officials, judging by their response to the events of 1989 at Tiananmen Square, would incline toward neutrality in such a conflict. They would reason that if America aided the liberals and the conservatives nonetheless won, the ensuing Chinese government would be irreconcilably hostile to America. But they would be wrong. The Chinese government that emerged from any such showdown would necessarily be vicious toward its own people and xenophobic toward the democratic world. The effort to appease it preemptively would bring little reward, and constitute a betrayal of our values. The more principled thing to do in such a scenario—and the better risk from the point of view of self-interest—is to give whatever aid we can to the liberals.

This scenario is not only highly speculative; it has also taken us far afield from the Reagan Doctrine, which concerns support of insurgencies. Armed insurgency is not now on the agenda in China, and America should be in no rush to place it there. Tremors of change continue to rock the Communist world, and China's top leaders are now all over eighty. Despite the setback at Tiananmen Square, there is cause for hope for a democratic transition in China through far less drastic means.

As a catalyst of decommunization, the Reagan Doctrine has a far prouder history than has yet been acknowledged. But in part as a result of its success, it appears to have a limited future.

10
Crisis Diplomacy

It is hard for one government to persuade another to do something merely by the force of argument. In the 1970s and 1980s it was often said that the United States ought to rely more on diplomacy and less on more forceful instruments of policy. This dichotomy ignored the fact that the weight of a diplomatic communication depends on the power of the nondiplomatic weapons at the communicator's disposal. The ambassador from Djibouti or Vanuatu may be a veritable Socrates, but his arguments will rarely be as persuasive as those of the ambassador from the United States or the Soviet Union, though he may be a dolt. Even a superpower can rarely talk a dictatorial government into abolishing itself: therefore to employ diplomacy to create democracy is ordinarily to employ a means insufficient to the ends.

Diplomacy can serve the more modest goal of addressing specific human rights cases. This does not mean prevailing upon another government to self-destruct, or even necessarily so much as to change its practices, but to release a particular prisoner, to allow a certain individual to emigrate, or to spare a condemned man or woman. This type of human rights "social work," as Senator Moynihan once called it,[1] is more within the reach of diplomatic instruments.

In certain extraordinary situations diplomacy can have a more profound impact. At moments of crisis the entire constitutional arrangement of a country, not merely a particular policy or government, can hang in the balance. The outcome can determine whether the country will embark on a democratic or dictatorial path for the foreseeable future. Such moments offer special opportunities for diplomatic intervention, especially in countries where the United States has a history of influence. In an unstable situation a determined push from Washington can sometimes throw the balance in one direction or the other.

The Philippines

The case which cast into bold relief the potential importance of American crisis diplomacy in helping another country to establish, or reestablish, democracy is the Philippines in 1986. That country had lived under martial law at the increasingly dictatorial hand of Ferdinand Marcos for fifteen years. In one of his 1984 campaign debates with Walter Mondale (October 21 in Kansas City, Missouri), President Reagan had seemed to say that only Marcos was preventing "a large Communist movement . . . tak[ing] . . . over the Philippines." But by 1985 officials within Reagan's own administration were growing increasingly worried about the viability of Marcos's rule.

The U.S. foreign aid bill enacted during the summer reduced military assistance to the Philippines and warned of further cuts as a result of human rights violations there. As the year wore on, a sense of disintegration mounted, characterized by numerous guerrilla attacks, allegations of atrocities by government forces, antigovernment demonstrations in the cities, some ending in violence, and the tumultuous trial of Chief of Staff, General Fabian Ver, for the murder of Marcos's leading opponent, Benigno Aquino. This turmoil set the stage for President Reagan to dispatch his closest political ally, Senator Paul Laxalt, as a special envoy to Marcos in October. Marcos had long enjoyed Reagan's support, and only someone of Laxalt's celebrated intimacy with Reagan could convince Marcos that American dissatisfaction went all the way to the top.

Laxalt delivered a letter to Marcos from Reagan. In that letter and in his conversations with Marcos, Laxalt conveyed the message, he later wrote, that Reagan

> was concerned about the general political instability in the Philippines, and whether President Marcos still enjoyed the support of the people. He was concerned about the decline of the Philippine economy. . . . And he was concerned about whether the Philippine military was taking the steps necessary to deal with the growing Communist insurgency.[2]

This message, said Fred Barnes of the *New Republic*, "chastened Marcos."[3]

Plans for 1986 Presidential Election. Marcos responded with the dramatic announcement that he would ask the Philippine legislature to advance the date of the next presidential election to early 1986, only a few months away, instead of sometime in 1987. The legislature quickly complied. It is not clear whether this idea was Marcos's own or had been proposed to him by Laxalt, as Raymond Bonner suggested.[4] Laxalt has not clarified the answer and has added some tantalizing complexity by asserting that the idea "had been previously broached to [Marcos] by C.I.A. Director William Casey."[5]

Whatever its provenance, American officials strongly endorsed the idea of a new election. And although they did not take sides, they did want to make sure that the opposition was able to compete despite the short notice. "Partly in response to U.S. prodding," said Sandra Burton, "a revitalized political opposition had been set up and mechanisms designed to select a common candidate."[6] The candidate was Aquino's widow, Corazon.

Aquino rallied a normally fractious opposition behind what was in effect a one-issue campaign: Marcos, his corruption, and his abuse of power. Ammunition for her fusillades was contributed by American investigations. According to Bonner's account, Congressman Stephen Solarz, chairman of the House Subcommittee on Asian and Pacific Affairs, "kept the [corruption] issue alive by holding hearings, subpoenaing the Marcoses' agents in the United States to testify. Each day there would be new revelations: another multimillion-dollar building or apartment here; another offshore corporation that was really part of Imelda Marcos's vast financial empire."[7]

Meanwhile the Senate Foreign Relations Committee, led by its chairman, Richard Lugar, and ranking Democrat, Claiborne Pell, began to bring pressure to assure a fair election. Writing to Marcos directly, they urged him to appoint a genuinely impartial commission on elections and laid out other criteria of fairness. They also urged the independent American organization, Center for Democracy, to conduct a preelection visit to the Philippines to assess the electoral conditions. The U.S. Agency for International Development channeled a few hundred thousand in funding to the Filipino group NAMFREL (National Citizens Movement for Free Elections), which had been formed during the 1984 legislative campaign. Although composed largely of opponents of Marcos, its essential task was not partisan; it was to prevent electoral irregularities. As election day approached, President Reagan added a carrot to these sticks. He promised that

> if the will of the Filipino people is expressed in an election that Filipinos accept as credible—and if whoever is elected undertakes fundamental economic, political, and military reforms—we should consider . . . a significantly larger program of economic and military assistance to the Philippines for the next five years. . . . over and above the current levels.[8]

He simultaneously announced the appointment of an official team of election observers that had been "invited" by President Marcos.

Election Results. On election day, February 7, NAMFREL denounced a variety of irregularities, including bribery and coercion of voters, multiple voting, stolen and stuffed ballot boxes, missing voter lists, and attempts to deny NAMFREL observers access to polling places. Senator Lugar immediately described this as "a very disturbing pattern." When the Commission on Elections delayed announcing early returns, Lugar said that "obviously the count has been slowed and obviously someone is worried."[9]

Both Aquino and Marcos claimed victory. The day after the election, NAMFREL announced that its tally showed Aquino leading, and so did the official Commission on Elections, although both said that a majority of ballots had yet to be counted. A day later the official body announced that Marcos had pulled into the lead, but thirty of its employees then walked off the job and accused the commission of rigging the count.

Whatever the actual vote, Marcos seemed in a position to keep control of the situation. Under Philippine law it was up to the National Assembly to certify the winner; with two-thirds of the seats held by Marcos loyalists, little doubt existed about how the assembly would act. With cynical magnanimity Marcos announced that he would abide by the assembly's decision.

President Reagan's initial reaction to these events was cautious. His words seemed to reflect the belief that Marcos would likely succeed in holding on to power and the desire to avoid a sharp break with him. On February 11, two days after the election commission walkout had made apparent the reality of electoral fraud, the *Washington Post* published an interview with President Reagan in which he made little of this.[10] "Even in elections in our own country there are evidences of fraud," he said. That night in a televised news conference he again acknowledged "the appearance of fraud" but added that "it could have been that all of that was occurring on both sides." Despite the allegations he said, "we hope to have the same relationship with the people of the Philippines that we've had for all these historic years."

No sooner had Reagan made these comments, which engendered controversy both at home and in the Philippines, than the administration began to shift away from the implication that it was acquiescing in Marcos's machinations. The same day as the news conference the White House announced that the president had asked the venerable diplomat Philip Habib to go to the Philippines "to assess the desires and needs of the Filipino people" in the wake of the election. The day after the news conference, according to the *New York Times*, the State Department instructed the U.S. ambassador in the Philippines to tell Mrs. Aquino that Reagan had not meant to imply that he was resigned to a Marcos victory.

The next day, February 13, Senator Lugar, cochairman of the official observer team that Reagan had sent to the Philippines, commented publicly that the president "apparently was not well informed about there being fraud on both sides."[11] After he and the other cochairman, Congressman John Murtha, reported their findings to the president and Secretary of State Shultz, the White House issued a statement that fraud and violence in the Philippine election were a "disturbing fact" and concluded that it would be "inappropriate for the United States to make . . . a judgment at this time" about who had actually won.[12]

Two days later, February 15, the president's shift was completed when the White House issued a statement in his name that "the elections were marred by widespread fraud and violence perpetrated largely by the ruling party." The abuses, he now said, were "so extreme that the election's credibility has been called into question both within the Philippines and in the United States."

The following day the Philippine National Assembly announced Marcos the winner, although NAMFREL said that its still incomplete count continued to show Aquino in the lead. Marcos invited Aquino to join a new Council of Presidential Advisers, but she replied by again claiming victory in the election and summoning her followers to a campaign of nonviolent protest.

Opposition to Marcos. During the next six days, while envoy Habib held conversations with leaders of the government, the opposition, and the Roman Catholic church, the center of action shifted to the streets of Manila and the halls of Capitol Hill. Aquino told large rallies of her supporters that she would settle for nothing less than full vindication of her electoral triumph. She would neither cooperate with Marcos nor agree to a new election. In Washington the Senate voted 85 to 9 for a resolution that declared that the Philippine elections were "marked by such widespread fraud that they cannot be considered a fair reflection of the will" of the people. The House Subcommittee on Asian and Pacific Affairs voted unanimously to halt aid to the Philippines until a "legitimate government" was in office.

Then on February 22 events took a critical turn. The two highest military officials of the Philippines—Juan Ponce Enrile, defense minister, and Fidel Ramos, acting chief-of-staff of the armed forces—switched allegiance from Marcos to Aquino and said, "We want the will of the people to be respected."[13] The two, together with 300 troops, took control of the Ministry of National Defense. Almost at once the White House issued a statement offering strong implicit endorsement of Enrile's and

Ramos's actions and their charges of fraud against Marcos. "The recent Presidential elections," it said, "were marred by fraud, perpetrated overwhelmingly by the ruling party, so extreme as to undermine the credibility and legitimacy of the election and to impair the capacity of the Government of the Philippines to cope with a growing insurgency and troubled economy." Enrile and Ramos had met with Habib not long before their mutiny, but the White House said that it had no advance knowledge of their plans.

Although Enrile and Ramos commanded the support of some parts of the military, Marcos retained substantial support. As rumors spread of a pending attack by Marcos loyalists against the Ministry of National Defense, large numbers of civilians thronged to the surrounding streets to show their support for the rebels and ironically to protect them by blocking access to their bastion.

The next day the National Security Council met in Washington to hear Habib's findings. He concluded that Marcos's rule was no longer viable and that Aquino in contrast would be capable of governing. After the meeting a statement issued in President Reagan's name noted that Enrile and Ramos enjoyed "substantial popular backing." It threatened a halt in military aid if violence was used against them. Another statement a day later warned that "attempts to prolong the life of the present regime by violence are futile" and called for "a peaceful transition to a new government." In the meantime the United States pressed into service a string of intermediaries, both American and Filipino, to urge Marcos to step aside. The messages included offers of asylum in the United States if he refrained from using violence against his opponents.

But behind a defiant mask Marcos's will to resist was rapidly eroding. Late on the night of February 24, he telephoned Senator Laxalt. Marcos was clinging to hope that President Reagan was not personally behind the increasingly chilly messages coming from Washington, and he wanted to learn whether the U.S. administration would support any compromise solution. Laxalt tried to disabuse Marcos of the illusion that Reagan's representatives were misrepresenting the president's views; he reiterated, in Reagan's name, the offer of asylum in America and discouraged any notion of compromise. Marcos asked directly whether Reagan wanted him to resign, a question that Laxalt said he could not answer. Then Marcos asked for Laxalt's own advice. Laxalt recalled:

> I said, "Cut and cut cleanly. The time has come."
> There was the longest pause. It seemed to last minutes. It lasted so long I asked if he was still there. He said, "Yes." And then he said, "I am so very, very disappointed." And then he hung up the phone.[14]

That same night talks were held between the U.S. embassy and aides to Marcos on the logistics of Marcos's departure. The next day, February 25, Marcos and Aquino held rival swearing-in ceremonies, but Marcos's was all for show.[15] Later that day he left for asylum in Hawaii after failing in a last desperate attempt to secure permission to retire to his native northern Luzon rather than be exiled abroad.

The next day, speaking to the nation on television, President Reagan hailed Aquino's triumph as "a stirring demonstration of what men and women committed to democratic ideals can achieve." He was referring to the Filipinos and their nonviolent "people power" crusade. But he may also have had in mind a thought about the contribution his own administration had made. As Paul Gigot put it in the *Wall Street Journal*, "Filipinos deserve the lion's share of credit for their own amazing revolution, of course, yet the Reagan policy of active support for democracy also played a role."[16]

Haiti

It was natural enough for the president and other Americans to feel a sense of pride and satisfaction over the efficacy of U.S. diplomacy in helping to steer the crisis in the Philippines to a democratic denouement. This feeling was magnified by the fact that the drama in Manila had not occurred in isolation but was paralleled by events unfolding almost simultaneously in another third world country at the opposite side of the globe, Haiti. There too months of political turmoil culminated in exile for a despot and the promise of democratic renewal. There too American diplomacy was instrumental in persuading the old dictator that his time was up and in facilitating a transfer of power with minimal violence.

The departure of Jean-Claude "Baby Doc" Duvalier from Haiti, where he had been president for life, came just eighteen days before Marcos's departure from Manila. The two situations, newsworthy as they were in themselves, drew added attention because they cast the United States in the surprising role of encouraging the ouster of dictators whose foreign policies were pro-American. Their simultaneity created the aura of a new turn in U.S. foreign policy, and Charles Krauthammer wrote of an annex to the Reagan Doctrine consisting of diplomatic efforts to oust rightist dictators.[17] But the history of Haiti since those heady days in February 1986 and American experience in several other crisis situations reveal the difficulty of orchestrating transitions to democracy with diplomatic instruments.

Baby Doc's Presidency. Jean-Claude Duvalier acceded to the presidency in 1971, at the age of nineteen, upon the death of his father, President for Life François "Papa Doc" Duvalier. The elder Duvalier had provided one of the cruelest and most despotic regimes to a country that had almost never known any other kind. His son was a bit milder in his rule and a bit less effective. Once one of the richest colonies in the Americas, Haiti had sunk under the weight of generations of misrule to the status of the hemisphere's poorest country. Its foreign policy was pro-Western although given its small size and backwardness it cut an insignificant figure in international affairs. The stress that the United States began to place on human rights issues in the late 1970s and 1980s discomfited the Haitian government, especially as the issues became linked to U.S. foreign aid allocations. Duvalier responded with vacillation and occasional small concessions, without altering the structure of his rule.

In April 1985 Baby Doc announced a program of constitutional reforms, which were combined in a plebiscite with the question of confirming his own presidency for life. To the surprise of no one, the government announced that the measures won approval from 99.98 percent of the voters. Also to the surprise of no one, save perhaps Duvalier, these reforms neither mollified foreign critics nor assuaged domestic discontent.

Led by students and abetted by the Roman Catholic church, opposition to the regime, although perilous, grew increasingly visible. In response Duvalier vacillated between repression and conciliation. In November security forces in the town of Gonaives fired on student demonstrators and killed three or four. In December the government closed down the church-run station, Radio Soleil, and arrested opposition leader Hubert de Ronceray on charges of subversion. The same month, in the hope of appeasing opponents, Duvalier fired part of his cabinet and ordered a reduction in the prices of various goods. Then, in the first days of January, he allowed Radio Soleil to reopen. A few days later, turning tough again, he ordered the closing of all schools and universities to prevent demonstrations and to preempt boycotts. He announced that he had instructed the security forces to "rigorously put down all illegal action."[18] But then he had the charges against de Ronceray dropped and once again cut retail prices.

These alternations between concessions and repressions were in vain. Although in the capital, Port au Prince, the authorities managed to keep the lid on popular discontent, by January 1986 demonstrations were occurring in most other large towns. (Other than the capital, Haiti's largest urban areas are much smaller than 100,000 people.) By this time Baby Doc had run out of tactics save for one more futile reshuffling of his government and army. Lacking his father's ruthlessness, as *Time* magazine put it, "Jean-Claude had no stomach for an all-out campaign of repressive violence to bring the country under."[19] By the end of the month the game was up.

On January 30 the United States announced that because of Haiti's failure to meet the standards of respect for human rights embodied in American foreign aid legislation, it would withhold $7 million. The same day the American ambassador, Clayton E. McManaway, Jr., held talks with Duvalier about the possibility of his taking exile.

The remaining week of Baby Doc's tenure seems to have been devoted almost entirely to a search, with American assistance, for a place of asylum for the dictator. The governments of Greece, Switzerland, and Spain declared him unwelcome. According to varying reports, Argentina, Italy, Gabon, Morocco, and others also slammed their doors. Finally on February 7, coincidentally the same day as the Philippine election, Duvalier departed. Two specially dispatched U.S. Air Force transport planes, one for Duvalier and his entourage, another for their luggage, flew them to France, which had agreed to admit them temporarily.

Duvalier's Successors. A National Council of Government, headed by Lieutenant General Henri Namphy, took the reins of power. It consisted of four military officers and two civilians; only one—Gerard Gourge, founder of the Haitian League of Human Rights—was not associated with the old regime. General Namphy pledged that the new government would "work for . . . real and functional democracy founded on absolute respect for human rights."[20] It suspended the constitution, dissolved the National Assembly, and appointed a new cabinet. The schools were reopened, and the dissident radio stations were allowed to resume broadcasting. Most important, the council took immediate steps to eradicate the legacy of the Duvaliers. It restored the old national flag, which had been replaced by one more to Papa Doc's liking. It announced plans to recover the wealth accumulated by the Duvaliers. And it abolished the Tontons Macoutes, their dreaded praetorian guard.

After these steps the U.S. government announced the release of $25.5 million in aid that had been withheld from Haiti because of human rights violations. The announcement was made February 26, just a day after Marcos left the Philippines. Understandably the United States felt it had done a good season's work with its prodemocracy diplomacy.

For a while, Haiti continued on a slow but hopeful course toward democracy. In April General Namphy announced a schedule for the reconstruction of constitutional government, and he demonstrated his sincerity by pledging not to run for president in the coming elections. The first step of his plan was the creation of a constituent assembly, partly elected, partly appointed, charged with rewriting the constitution. These elections were held in October, and a liberal constitution was subsequently drafted. It was submitted to the populace in a referendum on March 29, 1987, and won near unanimous approval. This time the one-sided vote count was attributed to "a national consensus, not any manipulation of the result," as one U.S. official put it.[21]

In the meantime, the United States had sought to encourage Haiti's democratic progress by increasing aid. Not only were the withheld funds from the 1986 budget released, but the new budget for fiscal year 1987 provided an increase of more than a third in the amount allocated to Haiti. As one American journalist noted during a 1987 visit to that country, "The AID [Agency for International Development] mission . . . is larger than most ministries of the Haitian government."[22]

Despite American efforts and the new constitution, democratization began to falter by mid-1987. In June the Provisional Electoral Council submitted its draft electoral law to the government as scheduled under the new constitution. The governing council rejected it, however, and insisted on an electoral law of its own devising, which was designed to keep control of the electoral process in its own hands. Almost at the same moment, the authorities responded to strikes sponsored by a major labor organization by occupying its offices and arresting its leaders. These two actions catalyzed the opposition to the regime, which organized a successful general strike and a series of street demonstrations. By July these actions forced the government to back down. It rescinded its own electoral law and allowed the labor union to resume its activities, but not before the confrontation had resulted in violence. According to one journalist's account the toll of these events was more than thirty dead and two hundred injured.[23]

The summer's bloodshed proved to be a preview. The fall presidential campaign was wracked with violence; two candidates were killed. When the violence—perpetrated apparently by members of the military and the theoretically disbanded Tontons Macoutes—reached a crescendo on November 29, the scheduled election day, the governing council announced cancellation of the vote. Indifferent to U.S. opinion, the forces opposed to the election even fired upon American representatives who had come to observe the election.

After canceling the election, the governing council dissolved the Provisional Electoral Commission and rescheduled elections under its own administration for January 1988. Those elections were boycotted by most opposition groups and viewed with deep suspicion by most international observers. The government claimed a 35 percent turnout, while the opposition said the true figure was only a small fraction of that. No one knows how accurate the count was, but Leslie F. Manigat was declared the winner. Manigat was a moderate Leftist who led a party called the National Progressive Democrats. Yet the circumstances of his selection created the expectation that he would be nothing more than a figurehead for General Namphy and his allies. After four months in office, however, Manigat attempted to assert his presidential authority against Namphy. He failed. The general had the president arrested and exiled, and he abolished the constitution of 1987.

Three months later General Namphy got his just deserts when he himself was ousted in a coup by Brigadier General Prosper Avril, one of the original members of the governing council and a former aide of Duvalier's rule. Avril continued Haiti's all-too-familiar authoritarian pattern. After a rough crackdown on oppositionists in January 1990, one Western diplomat commented, "Tell me what Papa Doc would have done next and it's a fair bet that's what we'll see now from Avril."[24]

Two months later, however, Avril was compelled to flee, and American diplomacy played a big part. During the first week of March, eleven political parties and one civic group formed a coalition and called for Avril's resignation. "[It] appears to represent the first unified pro-democracy force Haiti has known," said the *Washington Post*.[25] According to the *New York Times*, "Some of the Haitian political leaders said the United States ambassador, Alvin P. Adams, had played a key role in bringing General Avril's opponents together."[26] As opposition rallied behind the Group of Twelve, as the coalition was called, Adams met with Avril and told him "that like Nixon, he had lost the confidence of key sectors of the country. . . . In a highly personal conversation, Adams also spoke to the general about the capacity for overcoming loss," reported the *Post*.[27] A few days later Adams went to Avril's home at 2 AM. He sat and talked with the general at his kitchen table until 5 and then saw him to the airport, where a U.S. military transport took him to exile in Florida.[28] The next day a justice of the Haitian supreme court, Ertha Pascal-Trouillot, was sworn in as provisional president, after being selected by the Group of Twelve. "My essential task is . . . to pass power to a democratically elected government chosen with complete liberty," she declared.[29]

Since February 1986, democracy in the Philippines has endured, although it has not achieved stability. President Aquino has fought off numerous coup attempts, one in December 1989 so serious as to require assistance from the U.S. Air Force in putting it down. In Haiti the democratic transition of 1986 proved a chimera. But despite a bitter disappointment, Haitian democrats continue their struggle, and American diplomacy continues to support them.

Alas, Haiti is a more typical example than the Philippines of the situations where America has tried to rescue democracy through crisis diplomacy. The most notable such situations were in the Dominican Republic in the 1960s, in Nicaragua and Iran in the 1970s, and in Panama and China in the 1980s.

Dominican Republic

On May 30, 1961, Rafael Trujillo, who had ruled the Dominican Republic for more than thirty years with a willful despotism—emblematically, he had renamed the capital city, Ciudad Trujillo—fell victim to an assassin's bullet. Trujillo's death did not spell the immediate fall of his government. The nominal president, Joaquin Balaguer, remained in office, and Trujillo's son, Rafael junior (known as Ramfis), took command of the armed forces. Nonetheless it was clear that this regime, which had been tottering even before it was beheaded, could not last.

Although the assassination did not take U.S. officials entirely by surprise (by some accounts CIA agents may even have furnished the weapons),[30] the United States was deeply concerned about the ensuing political transition. At this time American alarm about the influence of Castro's Cuba on the rest of the hemisphere was at its apex. Washington hoped for a transition to democracy in the Dominican Republic both as a value in itself and as a means of forestalling communism. But it also wanted to avoid any risks that might provide an opening for the Communists. Arthur Schlesinger quoted President Kennedy as saying: "There are three possibilities in descending order of preference: a decent democratic regime, a continuation of the Trujillo regime or a Castro regime. We ought to aim at the first, but we really can't renounce the second until we are sure that we can avoid the third."[31]

In the immediate wake of Trujillo's death, the United States took two steps to make its presence felt in the Dominican Republic. It sent a naval task force into the area, and it supported a decision by the Organization of American States to send a four-member committee (of which the United States was one) to the Dominican Republic to keep tabs on events. In the following months, the U.S. government's analysis focused on three factors. The first was the genuine indigenous democrats, who seemed to be weak and divided. America hoped that a forceful leader would emerge from them, but none had yet done so. The second was Ramfis Trujillo, who loomed as the most formidable obstacle to democratization. The third was President Balaguer, who, though of dubious democratic pedigree, seemed a reasonable man, amenable to American wishes. According to Schlesinger, Kennedy commented in one meeting that "Balaguer is our only tool. The anti-communist liberals aren't strong enough. We must use our influence to take Balaguer along the road to democracy."[32]

Democratic oppositionists among the Dominicans also saw Ramfis Trujillo as their main nemesis. They suggested that they would be willing to cooperate with Balaguer if Trujillo were removed. Under American pressure Trujillo agreed in November to leave the country.

But when two of his uncles suddenly returned from abroad, he cancelled his departure and fueled suspicions that a Trujillist coup was in the making. The United States responded by declaring its strong interest in the situation and dispatching a detachment of marines and warships to the area. U.S. officials also lobbied key Dominican officers against the Trujillos. General Pedro Rodriguez Echevarria of the air force declared his defiance of Ramfis Trujillo, U.S. Navy jets flew overhead, and the Trujillos fled.

With Ramfis Trujillo gone, the next step, as the U.S. administration saw it, was to encourage cooperation between Balaguer and the democratic opposition. By the end of 1961 Balaguer was persuaded to shift power to a new Council of State, in which he included members of the democratic opposition. In response the United States promised to restore diplomatic relations, which it had severed to show its disapproval of Trujillo, and to increase its purchases of Dominican sugar, which had been cut for similar reasons. It also dispatched a new aid mission to the country, and thus laid the basis for an increase in U.S. assistance.

A few weeks later the same General Rodriguez who had been instrumental in thwarting Ramfis's coup staged a coup of his own against the Council of State. Upon learning of Rodriguez's intentions, the U.S. government threatened to reverse the various steps it had announced to improve relations with the Dominican Republic. When this failed to deter the coup, U.S. officials lobbied other elements of the Dominican military. Two days after the coup Rodriguez was arrested by other officers and allowed to leave for exile in the United States. The Council of State was reinstated.[33]

Within days Balaguer too was forced to resign, with the Council of Government left as the vehicle for a transition to democracy. The United States backed the council with all the means at its disposal. It made good on its promise to increase trade and to restore formal relations, and it began to infuse substantial amounts of aid. The OAS helped to draft a new election law, which called for elections in December, and American advisers organized a mass media campaign of civic education to maximize voter participation. Wary of the absence of any tradition in which electoral losers accept defeat, the U.S. ambassador, John Bartlow Martin, called in both leading candidates for president, Juan Bosch of the Dominican Revolutionary party and Viriato A. Fiallo of the National Civic Union, for a face-to-face meeting at which he solicited from each a pledge to abide by the outcome.

Bosch won the election handily and took office in February 1963. President Kennedy, said Schlesinger, hoped that now "the Dominican Republic might become a democratic showcase in the Caribbean."[34] But the hope was in vain. Bosch's far-reaching reforms left key elements of the military and the old elites unreconciled to his rule, and his own political ineptness compounded his problems. U.S. officials alternated between dismay at Bosch's handling of his job and alarm at the menaces emanating from his opponents. In September, seven months after he took office, the long-anticipated coup against Bosch succeeded in removing him.

The United States denounced the coup, suspended its military and economic assistance, and refused to recognize the new junta. But by the end of the year, after receiving assurances from the junta that it would hold elections in 1965, Washington extended recognition and resumed foreign assistance. In April 1965 younger officers launched an insurrection aimed at restoring Bosch and his Dominican Revolutionary party. The insurrection led to civil war, in which the rebels appeared to be getting the upper hand. Although they fought under the banner of restoring the duly elected government, President Johnson feared that they were in danger of coming under Communist control and dispatched U.S. Marines, who thwarted the rebels, restored order, and installed an interim government. Under U.S. supervision elections were held in June 1966. In those elections ex-President Balaguer defeated Bosch, inaugurating an enduring period of relatively democratic governance.

This happy ending was the product of the U.S. military invasion, which itself was the product, it might be said, of the failure of America's diplomatic efforts to steer the Dominican Republic onto a democratic track. Clearly, military means were more efficacious than diplomatic ones in promoting democracy in the Dominican Republic. But in the long run the story proved more complex. In 1978, a dozen years after Balaguer's election, his party was finally defeated in a presidential election by the Dominican Revolutionary party, led by Bosch's successor, Antonio Guzman. No one knew whether the military and other powerful backers of Balaguer would countenance a peaceful transfer to the moderately leftist Guzman. On election night, as the outcome grew clearer, the military interrupted the counting of ballots. But urgent telephone calls with forceful words from high U.S. officials deterred the Dominican military from aborting the process, and the election was honored. Dominican democracy was preserved by a forceful bit of crisis dipomacy.

U.S. military action in 1965 was not an unalloyed success. At the time the United States was still able to induce the Organization of American States in effect to endorse the American invasion, but this show of force left many Latin Americans with a sense of wounded pride. Their seething resentment propelled the pendulum of Latin politics in the years that followed from docile acquiescence to automatic defiance. This accounted for the widespread condemnation by Latin leaders of the American invasion of Panama in 1990 despite the manifest delight of the people of Panama. It also hampered American efforts to forestall the rise of communism in Nicaragua in the late 1970s.

Nicaragua

Probably the most spectacular failure of American crisis diplomacy, measured in terms either of the goal of democracy or of American strategic interests, occurred in Nicaragua in the late 1970s. Some would say that the U.S. failure in Iran at almost the same time was more significant in that Iran is much larger and strategically more important. Important though Iran may be, however, the United States had little apparent influence on the events that culminated in the triumph of Ayatollah Khomeini. America's response to the Iranian crisis certainly left much to be desired, but even a far wiser policy might not have made a decisive difference. In Nicaragua, in contrast, U.S. influence was overwhelming, and a more deft U.S. performance would probably have yielded a different outcome. Indeed Nicaragua's crisis was largely created by American actions. As William Bundy, surely not an ideological or partisan critic of the Carter administration, put it in late 1979: "If Gerald Ford had been elected in 1976. . . . it seems a safe bet that Tacho Somoza would still be in charge of Managua."[35]

Anastasio Somoza Debayle had ruled Nicaragua since 1967; he succeeded his older brother, Luis, who succeeded their father, Anastasio Somoza Garcia, who had seized power in 1936. This dynasty was characterized by a level of brutality commensurate with Nicaragua's sanguinary history and a level of venality that may have surpassed any of their predecessors.

Somoza's rule was opposed by the Democratic Union of Liberation (UDEL), a prodemocracy group led by Pedro Joaquin Chamorro, the editor of the country's main newspaper, *La Prensa*, and by the Sandinista National Liberation Front (FSLN), a small but audacious guerrilla group inspired by Fidel Castro. For a long time, neither of these foes was effective.

In the 1970s, however, the regime was weakened by three factors. First, after an earthquake largely leveled Managua in 1972, a large share of the disaster relief from abroad was siphoned off by larcenous government officials, in a display of rapacity so raw as to eviscerate the regime's remaining legitimacy. Second, Somoza suffered a heart attack in July 1977. This put him out of commission for a short period and made him seem vulnerable, always a dangerous situation for a dictator. Third, the

U.S. Congress and the Carter administration took various measures, including reducing aid to Nicaragua, to censure Somoza for human rights violations. These weakened the regime not only materially but also politically, because Somoza liked to pose as the favorite of the omnipotent Yanquis.

The regime's weakening condition reached a crisis in January 1978 when Chamorro was gunned down. Although most observers now agree it is unclear who was behind the crime, which may not have been political, most Nicaraguans at the time believed that Somoza was responsible for silencing his most prominent opponent. Thousands of Nicaraguans took to the streets in antiregime protests, and a general strike ensued, led by the business sector. The murder also solidified opposition to Somoza among the leaders of three neighboring countries: Panama, Costa Rica, and especially Venezuela.

In March Venezuelan President Carlos Andres Perez appealed to President Carter for joint action to oust Somoza. Carter shared Perez's distaste for Somoza and enumerated the steps he was taking to bring pressure against him, but, as his aide Robert Pastor explained, he rejected Perez's proposal because "he did not believe that the United States should engage in a policy of changing the governments of small nations."[36] Perez found this inadequate and began to send arms to the Sandinista Front.

Sandinista Victory. In August 1978 a band of Sandinistas led by Eden Pastora seized the National Palace in Managua. They took hostages, including many government officials, and then exchanged them for a large ransom, safe passage out of the country, release from Somoza's jails of many of their comrades, and lengthy broadcasts of their manifesto over state-run media. The stunning coup suddenly made the Sandinistas, who still numbered only a few hundred, a major force in Nicaragua's unfolding drama.

They built on this momentum by launching a military offensive the next month with attacks in virtually all of Nicaragua's major cities. Somoza's National Guard defeated this offensive but only after fierce fighting. Government barrages against guerrillas barricaded in residential areas caused much collateral damage and injury, widening the alienation between the public and the regime. A rattled Somoza compounded the hostility by ordering a wave of arrests of his opposition.

By September 1978, ten months before the Sandinistas' ultimate triumph, the U.S. government concluded that it wanted Somoza replaced. On September 23, U.S. special envoy William Jorden said as much to Somoza but to no effect.[37] For the time being, Jorden's rather gentle suggestion was as far as the United States was willing to go.

162

Some in the Carter administration, notably Viron Vaky, the assistant secretary of state for Latin America, favored an all-out push to remove Somoza quickly, but President Carter heeded the counsel of those who opposed such interventionism. Instead, he tried to persuade the leaders of several Latin states, especially Costa Rica, to undertake mediation between Somoza and his opposition. When this démarche failed, the Americans proposed to the Organization of American States that it become the mediator. An OAS team, consisting of the United States, Guatemala, and the Dominican Republic, was designated, with the United States the main party.

The multinational composition of the mediation team made it unwieldy. More important, the U.S. government did not give it sufficient priority, in part because some officials seemed to doubt the efficacy of any compromise and in part because other issues overshadowed Nicaragua at the highest levels of the U.S. government.[38]

The failed mediation was probably the last chance for a peaceful or democratic outcome of the Nicaraguan crisis. Shirley Christian said that "after the collapse of the OAS mediation, the United States was left with no policy toward Nicaragua."[39] The United States did, however, impose new sanctions on Nicaragua, blaming the failure of the bargaining on President Somoza.[40] The sanctions could not have gone much further. They included termination of the military aid program (the flow of military aid had ceased earlier), rejection of any new economic assistance, withdrawal of the Peace Corps, and recall of more than half of the embassy's personnel.

Although the Nicaraguan dictator did deserve much of the blame, Pastor revealed that when he accidentally allowed Carter to see an outline of Somoza's position, the president found it not unreasonable. Pastor suggested that if other issues had not drawn the president's attention, Carter might have ordered his subordinates to try to accommodate Somoza's stance.[41]

In theory the sanctions may have been intended to wring concessions from Somoza, but in reality they were more punitive or demonstrative than instrumental. Pastor conceded as much when he wrote: "Sanctions are more effective as a threat than as a punishment. They were necessary in this instance in order to restore the Administration's credibility with the opposition and with other governments in the region." He also acknowledged that "no one expected" the sanctions to cause Somoza to "change his mind."[42]

The sanctions would have made more sense if the United States had redoubled its mediation effort, just as President Carter pressed Egypt and Israel to continue bargaining however irreconcilable their positions seemed. By ending the mediation and imposing sanctions, the

United States tore away the foundations of Somoza's rule, even while turning its back on the democratic opposition. Pastor reported that the Broad Opposition Front—the coalition of groups that stood between Somoza and the Sandinistas—grew bitter because the United States "hardly contacted them" after abandoning the negotiations.[43]

From February through May, while the Nicaraguan democrats stewed, the Sandinista Front continued to gain recruits, whom they equipped with arms from Venezuela and Cuba. The Cuban arms were channeled through Panama and Costa Rica to disguise their origin. The United States meanwhile continued its embargo on arms for Somoza's guard and pressed other governments to follow suit. Late in May the Sandinistas launched their final offensive.

In June, as the fighting intensified, the Sandinistas announced the creation of a provisional government in San José, Costa Rica. The United States leaned hard on its dependent ally, Israel—perhaps Somoza's last supplier—to renege on promised shipments for the beleaguered National Guard. And it also began to demand more directly that Somoza leave office.

As the seriousness of the crisis became clear, the U.S. government asked the Organization of American States to convene a meeting of foreign ministers. The United States offered a resolution calling for a cease-fire and Somoza's departure in favor of a government of national reconciliation. It also authorized an OAS peace-keeping force to enter Nicaragua, but this was quickly rejected by the other foreign ministers.

Instead the OAS, with American concurrence, adopted a resolution embracing most points of the American proposal without the peace force. In practice the only operative portion of the resolution was the further pressure it constituted for Somoza's departure. All its other provisions, embodying the aspiration for a democratic Nicaragua, were unenforceable without the peace force.

By late June Somoza told the U.S. ambassador, Lawrence Pezzullo, that he was ready to leave. The U.S. government then began to focus on stratagems to avert an outright Sandinista victory. The Sandinistas' provisional government in Costa Rica was headed by a junta of five members: two from the democratic opposition; one a proclaimed Sandinista; and two others—Moises Hassan and Sergio Ramirez—Sandinistas who obscured their affiliation. While this subterfuge fooled most of the American press, it did not fool the U.S. government.[44] Some U.S. officials wanted to negotiate to add more moderates, while others wanted to create an alternative body of democrats to replace Somoza and broker power with the Sandinistas. Others seemed to believe—correctly—that both of these tactics would fail but favored an equally futile alternative: to "work with" the Sandinistas to "moderate" them.[45]

All the U.S. diplomatic maneuvers during Somoza's last weeks were in vain. As Pastor put it: "Since the United States could not stop the flow of arms to the FSLN and would not send arms to the Guard, U.S. negotiators were playing poker against a stacked deck."[46] He did not labor the obvious: they had stacked the deck themselves. In the end the United States achieved the only goal on which it had worked single-mindedly: ousting Somoza. It had no positive influence on what came in his stead. What plainer admission of failure could there be than the pleading in Pastor's memoir:

> To understand U.S. policy toward Nicaragua in the month prior to Somoza's departure on July 17, it is essential to realize the extent to which President Carter and his senior advisers were absorbed with many other matters, which they viewed, with justification, as of far greater importance to the United States.[47]

1990 Election. The failures of American diplomacy contributed to the onset of a tragic decade of Communist rule in Nicaragua, but U.S. diplomacy also contributed to Nicaragua's rescue through the election of February 1990. That the Sandinistas held the free election they had avoided for ten years, and abided by its results, yielding the presidency to Violeta Chamorro, is credited above all to changes in the Kremlin. But U.S. diplomacy took skillful advantage of the opportunity provided by Mikhail Gorbachev's new thinking. At their 1989 meeting at Tesoro Beach, the Central American presidents agreed to the rapid demobilization of the Nicaraguan contras in exchange for advancing the date of the Nicaraguan election. Then, according to Secretary of State Baker, the U.S. administration convinced "our European allies that they should condition their economic aid to Nicaragua on the holding of free and fair elections."[48] Next spokesmen for the Soviet Union, presumably at American urging, announced their support for a free and fair election and respect for its results. Taken together, these pressures persuaded the Sandinistas to play by the rules, a decision that was made easier by their mistaken conviction that they would win the vote. When the Nicaraguan electorate disabused them, they had little choice but to accept the outcome.

Iran

That Carter and his chief assistants were busy with other things scarcely excuses the ineffectiveness of their handling of the Nicaraguan crisis. Ironically, while Pastor included the crisis in Iran as one of the problems that drew the attention of top officials away from Nicaragua, both Vance

165

and Brzezinski in their memoirs explained that insufficient attention was paid to Iran because of the press of other issues, notably SALT, China, and the Arab-Israel conflict. Pastor's boss, Brzezinski, even says that one reason for the neglect of Iran was that "Nicaragua was beginning to preoccupy and absorb us."[49]

Iran did take time away from Nicaragua, and Nicaragua from Iran, and other issues from them both, but Iran and Nicaragua were clearly both policy failures. The two crises have often been paired by commentators because they occurred almost simultaneously and bore certain similarities. In each case a long-established autocrat closely tied to the United States felt himself undermined by a palpable lessening of American support after the accession of President Carter with his new emphasis on human rights. Oppositionists were emboldened by the ruler's faltering confidence and by the ambivalence of his American patrons. As opposition mounted, America counseled against a repressive response, but few of the ruler's opponents were appeased. Hopes for compromise evaporated, and eventually the autocrat fled, presaging total victory by the revolutionary opposition and the rise of a new dictatorship.

Despite these parallels, the Nicaraguan and Iranian situations differed in important ways, in particular in relation to democracy. First, democracy figured less in U.S. policy toward Iran than toward Nicaragua, because the strategic stakes seemed much greater in Iran. The idea that the shah might fall distressed U.S. officials; the idea that Somoza might fall did not. Moreover Iran seemed to have far less possibility than Nicaragua of achieving democracy in 1978–1979. With hindsight, a democratic outcome can be imagined in Nicaragua, but far less so in Iran.

The Turning Point. Mohammed Reza Pahlavi, the shah of Iran, ruled firmly for some twenty-five years. He had been restored to his throne in a 1953 coup orchestrated by the CIA against Prime Minister Mohammed Mossadegh. Through a combination of cooptation and repression, the shah had little difficulty in quelling dissent until the opposition that mushroomed in the late 1970s. On January 9, 1978, police fired on a demonstration of theology students in the holy city of Qom and killed several. After the traditional Islamic forty-day mourning period, demonstrations spread to other cities, evoking more violence. This forty-day cycle then repeated itself several times with increasing intensity into the summer of 1978.

At first the U.S. government, like most observers, feared little for the shah's ability to withstand these tremors.[50] Indeed, according to author Barry Rubin, "critics within the new administration much more often expressed concern that the shah was becoming too powerful rather than that he might lose power."[51] The critics focused on human rights abuses by the shah's authoritarian regime, especially its intelligence and secret police organization, SAVAK. The human rights advocates issued admonitions and succeeded in curtailing the sale of police equipment to Iran, but they failed to persuade President Carter to impose more severe sanctions.[52] Mild though the sanctions were they seem to have made the shah feel uncertain of the support he enjoyed from the U.S. administration. This probably further weakened his spirit, which must already have been weak as a result of his illness. Throughout the crisis months of late 1978 the shah apparently knew that he was dying of cancer, a fact unknown to American intelligence or allied services. The drugs and other treatments he received to retard the cancer may have added to the depression and listlessness reported by many who met with him.

However uncertain of U.S. support the shah may have felt, Washington certainly did not wish to see him ousted. Brzezinski wrote that Vance and other top State Department officials were "preoccupied with the goal of promoting the democratization of Iran and feared actions . . . that might have the opposite effect."[53] But Vance was far from having a free hand in formulating U.S. policy. Brzezinski's account suggests, as do other reports, that his own more staunchly pro-shah views served as a strong countervailing influence within the councils of the Carter administration.[54] The shah no doubt sensed that Washington was of two minds about him and his troubles, and this ambivalance must have reinforced his own tendency to vacillate between appeasement and repression. When he yielded concessions, he was applauded by Vance; when he turned to tough tactics, he got a pat on the back from Brzezinski.

In August the shah announced that free elections would be held in 1979 to elect a new parliament. His new prime minister, Jaafar Sharif-Emami, had friendly ties to the clerical community and established a government of "national reconciliation."

> The Imperial calendar was withdrawn and the old Islamic one restored; press censorship was lifted . . . ; the debates in the Majlis were broadcast live throughout the country, giving the shah's opponents in parliament a national platform they never had before; and the shah now began consulting with his opponents on policy matters. Both Karim Sanjabi, the leader of the National Front, and the Ayatollah Shariatmadari, the chief religious figure in Iran, were invited to participate in discussions about the future of the country.[55]

The shah's opponents were unappeased, however, and in September he swung the other way. Bowing to pressure from his generals and perhaps also from his ambassador to Washington, Ardeshir Zahedi, who had been fortified by strong expressions of support from Brzezinski, the shah announced a ban on street demonstrations. The next day his soldiers opened fire on defiant marchers in the streets of Tehran and caused hundreds of casualties in the Jaleh Square massacre. Martial law was declared and a few opposition figures were arrested. President Carter placed a phone call to the shah in the aftermath of the massacre to commiserate and assure him of America's unwavering support. But the shah's opponents were no more intimidated by his repressions than they had been mollified by his concessions.

The next month, October, he tried some more concessions. Vance recalls meeting then with the new Iranian foreign minister, Amir Khosrow Afshar, who told him "that the shah was determined to press ahead with his political liberalization program in order to undercut the secular opposition and divide it from Khomeini. I assured him that we strongly supported this effort."[56] In the weeks that followed, the shah announced an amnesty for hundreds of political prisoners and the firing of thirty-four officials of SAVAK.[57] He also sent out feelers to leaders of the moderate opposition about their entering the government. But sensing that the shah's authority was waning, one after another turned him down and threw in their lot with Ayatollah Khomeini.

In the first days of November, the shah sought American advice on what to try next.[58] One direction led to formation of a coalition government by sharing power with some of the opposition, if they would agree. The opposite choice was to create a military government to crack down more sharply. Washington shrank from the responsibility of recommending either action. Instead it replied with a strong statement of support for the shah and assurance that it would back him whichever course he took. Later that week he announced the resignation of Prime Minister Sharif-Emami and the appointment of General Reza Gholam Azhari, but characteristic of the vacillation of the entire period, General Azhari's government was, as Vance recalls, "military in name only, with most ministries headed by civilians."[59]

Differences over U.S. Policy. As the crisis deepened, so did divisions within the U.S. government. Brzezinski recalled that the appointment of General Azhari left him "greatly relieved" that "the Shah had finally opted for a military government."[60] Washington publicly endorsed the new government and released a shipment of tear gas and other riot-control equipment that had been held up by the State Department's human rights bureau.[61] But two weeks later Vance "cabled [the American ambassador] that we must offer the shah our frank advice in helping him try to put together a new civilian government."[62]

According to Vance, Carter did not wish to be "so blunt with the shah" as to suggest he leave power, but by December the president had begun to hedge his support for the shah.[63] "We personally prefer that the shah maintain a major role but that is a decision for the Iranian people to make," said Carter.[64] A consensus began to grow within the U.S. administration that the shah's rule could not survive the crisis. "The president clearly recognized," said Vance, "that we had passed the point of unreservedly supporting the shah."[65] And by the end of the month Vance himself "had little hope that even an English-style monarchy was possible."[66] Even Brzezinski, until then the shah's staunchest supporter, concluded that "the issue . . . ceased being how to help the Shah save himself but became instead how to save Iran even without the Shah."[67]

Although reaching consensus that the time had come for the shah to leave, the U.S. government remained divided within itself over what should replace him. Vance favored a transfer of power to elements of the opposition while Brzezinski still looked toward creation of a military government.

Without clear American advice, the shah moved of his own initiative toward a resolution of the crisis. While several leaders of the liberal opposition National Front had rejected his probes about joining or forming a government, one of them, Shahpour Bakhtiar, now agreed to accept appointment as prime minister if the shah left the country. After some hesitation the shah acceded, perhaps with American encouragement.[68] The shah's staunchest supporters appealed to him not to leave. "For several days a behind-the-scenes battle raged over whether the shah would depart Iran," said Rubin.[69] According to Vance, he and President Carter weighed in heavily and directly urged the shah to obey Bakhtiar's terms and leave.[70]

At about the same time the U.S. government dispatched General Robert Huyser to Iran on a mission of typical ambiguity. In Vance's view Huyser's goal was to rally military support behind Bakhtiar, while to Brzezinski it seems to have been to ready the Iranian generals to impose a government of their own. Neither mission was feasible. The Iranian military at this point was being pulled in two directions, but neither corresponded with the courses favored by the divided American government. On the one hand the officer corps retained considerable loyalty to the shah. On the other hand some troops were drawn to Khomeini's fundamentalist message, and some officers were tempted opportunistically to cut individual deals with the Khomeinist juggernaut. But there was no substantial support in the military either for the liberal regime of Bakhtiar or for a military regime without the shah.

By the end of January, Bakhtiar felt he had to allow Khomeini to return from exile, and within two weeks Bakhtiar departed after the army announced it would not defend his regime. Khomeini named as prime minister Mehdi Bazargan, a member of the liberal National

Front who had thrown in with Khomeini. He believed that once the shah was gone, Khomeini and the mullahs would return to their mosques and allow him and those like him to govern the country. Within weeks Bazargan realized that his own authority was uncertain. In November 1979, nine months after taking office, Bazargan resigned after recognizing that he had been only a figurehead for the revolutionary fundamentalists.

Few deny that U.S. diplomacy in the Iranian crisis of 1978 and 1979 was unsuccessful. The victory of Khomeini and his style of radical Shiism proved a major foreign policy headache for America, but there is no agreement about the cause or nature of the failure. Two contradictory explanations mirror the divisions within the U.S. government that plagued it throughout the crisis. From Brzezinski's point of view, democracy was never a realistic possibility in Iran during this period. Therefore the concessions urged on the shah by Vance in the interests of democratization (or at least liberalization) needlessly undermined the monarch's authority. From Vance's point of view, the shah's only hope lay in democratization, and Brzezinski's encouragement of a hard-line response served only to inflame the situation and to deter the shah from making necessary concessions. Whether democratization was or should have been on the agenda during the Iran crisis remains unresolved.

Panama

In contrast to this ambiguity, ten years later the Bush administration faced two foreign crises in which the issue of democracy was clearly at the forefront—in Panama and in China. In both its diplomatic response failed but for opposite reasons. In Panama the U.S. government exerted itself to the utmost in behalf of a democratic outcome, but diplomatic methods were simply unequal to the task. Ultimately the United States did secure a victory for democracy but only by means of military invasion. In China, the U.S. government seemed to place the interests of Realpolitik ahead of democracy. Washington apparently feared the wrath of Beijing's rulers if it supported China's democracy movement and it failed. Therefore, during the height of the prodemocracy demonstrations, it offered only mild encouragement, and when the demonstrators were put down by tanks and guns, it offered feeble protests.

The crisis in Panama reached its boiling point with presidential balloting on May 7, 1989. General Manuel Noriega, Panama's military potentate, was accustomed to ruling behind a puppet president. He seems to have assumed that he could legitimate a new one in the election and control the result by ballot stuffing, miscounting, and other chicanery. But the Panamanian electorate rejected Noriega's candidate by such a huge margin that dirty tricks could not overcome it without becoming obvious. For three days after the election, the contending factions announced contradictory tallies. Independent observers, including the Catholic church, said the opposition was winning by a landslide, but the government's Electoral Tribunal put Noriega's man ahead by about two to one. Former President Jimmy Carter, leader of a team of international observers, declared on the scene: "The government has taken the election by fraud. The Panamanian people have been robbed."[71] On the night of May 10, with the count still not completed, the government announced that the election was annulled as a result of "obstruction by foreigners."

In the week before the election, President Bush had warned against the fraud, fueling expectations of a strong American response.[72] But what could America do? For a year and a half it had tried diplomatic pressure to oust Noriega amid growing publicity about his part in drug smuggling. In December 1987 Assistant Secretary of Defense Richard Armitage told Noriega that if he would resign, the United States would close down its investigations of his illicit activities. But Noriega refused, and in February 1988 he was indicted in Florida.[73]

The United States then encouraged the elected president, Eric Arturo Delvalle, to dismiss General Noriega, but Noriega instead secured a unanimous vote of the National Assembly to oust Delvalle. Washington refused to recognize this act, announced its continued support for Delvalle, and froze Panamanian government assets in American banks. During the next two months the United States imposed additional economic sanctions against the Noriega regime while sending another diplomatic mission to negotiate with the general, offering a pledge not to seek his extradition if he would go into exile. In May 1988 Washington went further and offered to quash the indictments altogether if Noriega would leave, but he would not budge.

The election fraud in May 1989 spurred Washington to new efforts. President Bush recalled the U.S. ambassador and sent an additional contingent of troops to U.S. bases there. He also was reported to have called several Latin leaders and urged them to act against Noriega.[74] The Panamanian people were incited in the same direction. "The will of the people should not be thwarted by this man and a handful of Doberman thugs. They ought to do everything they can to get Mr. Noriega out of there," Bush said.[75] Several Latin leaders did denounce Noriega, but they also warned against any U.S. intervention.

The U.S. administration did refrain from further measures of its own and turned instead to the Organization of American States. At an emergency meeting the OAS condemned the electoral fraud and created a mediating team that visited Panama three times in the next three months in the vain hope of negotiating a settlement between Noriega and the Panamanian opposition. Finally, in August, the OAS confessed failure and dissolved its mediation effort, adding some gratuitous criticism of the United States. *Newsweek* quoted one OAS official: "We have failed miserably."[76]

Washington then renewed its public exposé of Noriega's role in the international drug trade, refused to recognize a new president installed by Noriega in September, and announced that it would not approve any administrator of the Panama Canal nominated by the Noriega government. But none of these steps appreciably weakened Noriega. In October the United States cooperated in a small way in an attempted coup against Noriega but declined to take strong action when the tide turned against the rebels. In December American troops invaded Panama, toppled Noriega, and installed Guillermo Endara, the rightful winner of May's election, as president. The invasion was welcomed by Panamanians but entailed costs. Not only were lives and treasure lost, but the United States was condemned again for using force in Latin America. Whatever the ultimate accounting of the invasion, it wrote a dramatic epitaph to America's futile efforts to vindicate Panama's democratic process by means of diplomacy.

China

On April 15, 1989, the Beijing government announced the death of Hu Yaobang, who had been ousted as general secretary of the Communist party early in 1987 for favoring political liberalization. To many Chinese he symbolized a freer way of life. Posters praising Hu, in contrast with incumbent Chinese officials, appeared on campuses in Beijing and Shanghai. Demonstrations, under the banner of democracy, grew over the weeks as students were joined by workers, teachers, journalists, and even government and party bureaucrats.

In mid-May the demonstrations were fanned by the arrival of Soviet President Gorbachev for the first summit meeting between the two giant Communist states in three decades. To the demonstrators Gorbachev was a hero, a symbol of the kind of liberalization they hoped to wrest from their own rulers. To Chinese officials, however, the demonstrations were humiliating, weakening their authority in dealing with the Soviet leader and forcing them to change his itinerary. On May 17, more than a million people flocked to Tiananmen Square in Beijing, and demonstrations were reported in twenty other cities. A day later Gorbachev left, and two days after that the Chinese government declared martial law.

In response, a million people took to the streets of Beijing to support the hundreds of thousands of student demonstrators who remained in the square and to block the army's path there. The White House issued a statement that "the United States stands for freedom of speech and freedom of assembly" but did not directly criticize the martial law decree. It said that President Bush hoped that "a dialogue between the government and the students is possible."[77] The next day at a press conference, he encouraged Chinese protestors to "fight for what you believe in," but he also urged "restraint."[78] Throughout the crisis, the U.S. government expressed its underlying identification with the goals of the students without doing much to encourage them or to antagonize the Chinese government.

In China, protesters defied martial law and thwarted contingents of troops trying to push their way to Tiananmen Square without deadly force. In the square demonstrators erected a huge papier mâché replica of the Statue of Liberty, the goddess of democracy. Conflicting rumors circulated about the struggle within the government between Party Secretary Zhao Ziyang, who favored conciliation, and Premier Li Peng and others who favored repression.

On May 25 Li Peng appeared on Chinese television and signaled victory for his faction; on June 3 the repression began. Tanks rolled into Tiananmen Square while troops fired on unarmed demonstrators. Hundreds, perhaps thousands, were mowed down. President Bush issued a statement saying, "I deeply deplore the decision to use force against peaceful demonstrators and the consequent loss of life."[79] He also announced sanctions against the Chinese government, including the suspension of military sales and of meetings between Chinese and U.S. military officers. But in response to congressional appeals for sterner measures, he warned against "an emotional response" to the Chinese repression.[80]

The Chinese government followed its bloody reclamation of Tiananmen Square with thousands of arrests, a string of executions, and a ban against all independent organizations. Despite President Bush's restraint Sino-American relations deteriorated. Chinese troops fired on the U.S. diplomatic compound in Beijing. Fang Lizhi, the physicist and democrat often called the Chinese Andrei Sakharov, took refuge in the U.S. embassy, together with his wife. The Chinese government denounced Fang as a traitor and demanded that the Americans hand over the couple. The U.S. government quietly refused. Although the broadcasts into China by the Voice of America were increased, the Chinese government jammed them and expelled reporters for VOA and news organizations. When executions of dissidents evoked strong protests from West European governments, however, Washington responded cautiously. President Bush had no comment, and Secretary of State Baker said, "We deeply regret the fact that these executions have gone forward."[81]

On June 20, under pressure from Congress, the Bush administration suspended all high-level contact between the two governments and urged international financial institutions to defer Chinese loan applications. On June 27 the European Community announced similar steps, one day after the World Bank had put off action on Chinese loans. But the Beijing government continued to expel foreigners and to imprison and execute Chinese.

Congress imposed additional economic sanctions against China by a vote in the House (June 29) of 418 to 0 and in the Senate of 81 to 10. Understandably the president did not threaten or attempt to veto the legislation, but he did oppose it. "The China sanctions package does not have the Bush administration's endorsement," announced Secretary Baker.[82]

While the Congress worked to stiffen the American response to the Chinese crackdown, the Bush administration headed in the opposite direction. On July 6 the PRC rejected as "groundless" American accusations that the shooting at the American diplomatic compound the previous month by Chinese soldiers had been "premeditated."[83] The next day Washington granted a waiver to the Boeing Company to deliver jetliners to China, although they had a navigational system that was on a State Department list of militarily useful technology with export restrictions. Also in July, despite the administration's proclaimed ban on high-level contact, National Security Adviser Brent Scowcroft and Deputy Secretary of State Lawrence Eagleburger made a secret journey to Beijing to meet Chinese officials. Word of this mission reached the public months later, when a second trip by the two men raised a storm of protest. The administration then claimed that the purpose of the first mission had been to impress on Beijing Washington's objections to its repressions. But the secrecy of the trip and the contravention of the announced sanctions left many skeptical. The administration seemed more concerned with preserving ties to Beijing than with delivering protests.

This impression had grown over several months. In August Secretary Baker had publicly broken the ban on high-level contacts by meeting with the Chinese foreign minister, Qian Qichen, in Paris. In September, escaped leaders of the democracy movement and other Chinese exiles held a highly publicized conference in Paris, where the French government had made them feel more welcome than the American.[84] In October, leaders of a private organization, Human Rights Watch, charged that "the administration has apparently adopted a policy of opposing requests for political asylum from leaders of the democracy movement who have fled China."[85] As the year drew toward its close, the president yielded to Beijing's threats by vetoing legislation to extend the stay of Chinese students in the United States and sent Scowcroft and Eaglebur- ger on their second mission, where they exchanged warm toasts with officials as America began to remove economic sanctions.

The Beijing government repeated that it would not turn back from the economic liberalization Deng Xioaping called for a decade earlier, but it tightened restrictions on private enterprise. Beijing maintained its policy of repression: it tolerated no dissent; it launched vast new cam- paigns of political indoctrination; and it forced students into military training to instill obedience. China became a far more closed society now than it had been in many years.

Beyond the near term, however, the prospects for democratization in China remained bright. A far greater depth of democratic yearning was shown in the spring of 1989 than anyone had imagined, and the tyrants who repressed it were reaching the end of their days. This favorable outlook owed nothing, however, to the crisis diplomacy of the U.S. government, which minimized antagonism toward the Chinese government before the massacre and afterwards. Deng and Li Peng and the others probably would have done the same no matter how America behaved, once they had launched their savage repression. But for five or six weeks before it ordered the tanks to roll into Tiananmen Square, the Chinese government was divided about how to respond. Pressures from Washington might have helped those like Zhao Ziyang who favored conciliation. The Bush administration's low profile accomplished noth- ing for the cause of democracy.

U.S. Balance Sheet

The Bush administration's best defense of its actions on China is the example of Panama, where the most strenuous crisis diplomacy against a government far less powerful or insular than the Chinese proved fruitless. Although the Bush administration's failure in China, like the Carter administration's in Nicaragua and Iran, can easily be criticized (justifiably, in my judgment, in all three cases), the underlying problem is that crisis diplomacy is a weak instrument, probably insufficient to produce a better outcome even if wielded more ably. Far fewer criticisms have been voiced of President Kennedy's handling of the Dominican Republic or President Reagan's of Haiti, yet America's crisis diplomacy failed to rescue democracy in either case. The Philippines stands as the single strong example of successful diplomatic intervention in behalf of democracy, although it is no trivial example. Moreover, although crisis diplomacy failed in the Dominican Republic in 1963–1964, Haiti in 1986–1987, and Nicaragua in 1978–1979, subsequent diplomatic interventions helped to put all three on the democratic track. This shows that although crisis diplomacy is a weak instrument, it is not a useless one. Persistence and vigilance for new opportunities or dangers can yield important results.

Much the same can be said about quotidian diplomacy outside crisis situations. In the past decade and a half, a few dozen countries have turned or returned to the path of democracy, many of them countries closely allied with the United States. Although American urging alone did not propel them toward democracy, it did constitute one influence that led in this direction.

11

Foreign Aid

Money is a common means by which states try to influence the acts or evolution of other states: bribery, for instance, is as old as statesmanship. But the state-to-state transfers that we call foreign aid are largely a modern practice, in which the United States was the pioneer.

Rebuilding Europe and Asia

In the first months after World War II, America began to pour funds and food into Europe and Asia for helpless civilian populations. By the time the Marshall Plan began, America had already spent more than $12 billion on aid.[1] What then was new about the Marshall Plan? First, its vision was long term: it aimed at economic reconstruction, not merely alleviation of immediate misery. Second, and more important, its goals included a strong political element. In announcing the plan, Secretary of State George Marshall said that its purpose was "to permit the emergence of political and social conditions in which free institutions can exist."

The political effects of the Marshall Plan, however, were indirect: the plan did not entail any specific building of political institutions. Even its economic impact was in part indirect because the aid worked as a catalyst. Although the $12 billion was a huge sum, it still amounted to a fraction of the capital that went into European reconstruction, as Alan Milward has painstakingly demonstrated.[2] Its force then was in part psychological, just as Marshall hoped it would be, nurturing the optimism needed for fruitful economic behavior.[3]

The project succeeded handsomely. Not only was Europe put back on its feet economically, the political benefits must have exceeded even the most hopeful expectations of American officials. The historian Charles Mee summed it up:

> The Marshall Plan seriously damaged the Communist Parties
> of Western Europe—and gave prodigious support to the
> liberal and conservative political forces. . . . it is difficult to

see how, without the Marshall Plan, Europe could have been
drawn together as quickly as it was after the war. . . . Nor . . .
how . . . the United States could have been placed so firmly
at the center of Europe.[4]

Above all, the delicate scaffolding of democracy was strongly
reinforced. As described in earlier chapters, the direct political work by
U.S. occupation authorities, CIA agents, and indigenous leaders established democratic institutions in these war-torn lands, but they might
not have survived were it not for the economic recovery that lifted the
people above desperation and convinced them that democracy works.
(Although it was not included in the Marshall Plan, much the same was
accomplished in Japan, which received about $2.2 billion in U.S. aid
during the six-year occupation.)[5]

During the years between the world wars, democracy was tried in
continental Europe and seemed to fail. It collapsed outright in most of
central and southern Europe, while in France the Third Republic had left
the nation so divided and paralyzed that it fell before its direst enemy.
(Although it had not become a democracy, Japan's experience was of a
piece with these: a strong democratic current had intensified in the 1920s
only to recede before the rise of militarism.) After World War II, in
contrast the rebirth of democracy was accompanied by the rebirth of
industry and prosperity, giving democracy an aura of success.

Institutionalization of Foreign Aid

The success of the Marshall Plan led to the institutionalization of foreign
aid in U.S. foreign policy. As the European economic recovery was
completed and the front line of the cold war shifted to Asia, so did the
bulk of American foreign aid. Beginning in fiscal year 1955, U.S. aid to
Asian countries exceeded that to Europe. In the 1960s aid to Latin
America increased under the Alliance for Progress but never equaled the
amounts designated for Asia, the primary target area until the mid-
1970s. Then, with the collapse of South Vietnam and the intensification
of the Arab-Israel conflict, the Middle East in fiscal 1976 began receiving
the largest share of U.S. aid.[6]

In addition to shifts in its regional focus, the ambitions shaping U.S.
foreign aid have also changed. The focus on postwar reconstruction and
military defense gave way to the promotion of development under
President John Kennedy, who declared that "the 1960's can be—and
must be—the crucial 'decade of development.'"[7] The agency that dis-
bursed foreign aid, the International Cooperation Administration, became the Agency for International Development.

This approach to development reflected the theories of Walt W.
Rostow, a presidential assistant and counselor of the State Department.

In his widely read book *The Stages of Economic Growth,* Rostow said that societies could progress from stagnant traditional economies to a level of prosperity with "self-sustaining" economic growth by reaching a point of "take-off." One key to reaching takeoff was an adequate supply of "social overhead capital" to finance infrastructure, such as railroads, that private investors are unlikely to build. "Foreign capital flows have proved extremely important," he said.[8] The attractiveness of this theory to policy makers was the promise that a finite amount of aid for a finite duration could lift countries to the takeoff point—modest investments could achieve large results.

Yet the fatal flaw in Rostow's approach was the image it conveyed of a critical turning point in a country's development. Even if a takeoff occurs, that historical moment may last ten or twenty years and may be identifiable only in hindsight. As American voters and their representatives saw the years pass and the dollars flow with few countries reaching an observable takeoff, a sense of disillusionment set in.

Americans are willing to share with the world's neediest as a matter of simple charity, and they support military aid to allies, but they are chary of underwriting all of the poorer countries on a perpetual basis. Even President Kennedy, a champion of aid, emphasized that one of his chief objectives was "to achieve a reduction and ultimate elimination of United States assistance by enabling nations to stand on their own as rapidly as possible."[9] But the high hopes that he and others fostered to win support for development assistance proved its undoing.

Expectations were unrealistically inflated not only by the rhetoric of aid advocates but also by the experience of the Marshall Plan. The differences between reconstructing Europe and developing its former colonies ought to have been obvious. Populations that had already built modern economies and had to build them anew after war had ravaged the physical plant needed only capital and courage. Populations raised in primitive conditions, however, had somehow to absorb the skills and habits of modernity. George Kennan, one of the architects of the Marshall Plan, cited in his memoirs a 1947 paper he had helped to write in connection with it: "There was no reason to believe that the approaches here applied to Europe will find any wide application elsewhere."[10] And yet while many recognized that the third world was not like Europe, the developmental progress of third world countries could be measured against few other bench marks. The ambiguous results achieved by aid to the third world were therefore compared with the dramatic success of the Marshall Plan.

In 1973, under the rubric "New Directions," American foreign aid legislation turned away from development to the goal of fulfilling "basic human needs." Ostensibly this change was designed to ensure that the benefits of development reached those who needed them most. By concentrating on providing food and medicine to the poorest of the poor, though, we confessed the failure of our grander plans.

Americans' assessments of foreign aid can be measured in dollars. Since the end of World War II, the United States has spent between $300 billion and $400 billion in foreign aid, the equivalent of a trillion of today's dollars. But the annual outlays have been decreasing steadily. From fiscal 1946 through fiscal 1952, they averaged the equivalent of $32 billion a year (in 1989 dollars). From fiscal 1953 through 1974, that is, roughly from the end of the Marshall Plan until the end of the Vietnam War, they averaged $22 billion a year. Since then, they have averaged $16 billion, about half the average during the Marshall Plan years.[11]

When measured against the expanding U.S. economy, the decrease in aid is even more dramatic. During the Marshall Plan, America donated upward of 2 percent of its gross national product to European recovery, peaking at 3.2 percent in 1949. Then, through the Kennedy years, aid levels remained above 1 percent of GNP. Since then, they have fallen rapidly, to a mere 0.27 percent in FY1989.[12]

America's diminishing generosity has earned it many scoldings, which have only compounded the problem. In 1980 the so-called Brandt Commission issued its heralded report on North-South relations. Ominously titled *A Program for Survival*, the report concluded that without vast new concessions and transfers from the rich countries to the poor, "the world situation can only deteriorate still further, even leading to conflict and catastrophe."[13] Hearing this dire assessment some twenty years and scores of billions of dollars after President Kennedy proclaimed the development decade, Americans were more likely to wonder what use had been made of their past largesse than to increase their donations.

The censorious tone reinforced Americans' feelings that foreign aid had earned us little gratitude. Although we had provided assistance to more than a hundred countries, America found itself isolated in the United Nations and the whipping boy of governments that eagerly vied for American handouts. Israeli Prime Minister Shimon Peres quipped that he represented the one state that had accepted American generosity and did not resent America for it.

The deepest cause for disillusion, however, was not the ingratitude but the loss of confidence in our understanding of how countries raised themselves out of poverty and how we might assist them. President Kennedy emphasized, as have other American leaders, our desire to aid most "those nations most willing and able to mobilize their own resources [and to] make necessary social and economic reforms."[14] But what were the necessary reforms?

For more than thirty years after World War II, Socialist ideas dominated economic thinking in the developing countries. Even where socialism was not embraced, a heavy government role in the economy usually was. This tendency was abetted by many development specialists from the advanced countries and from UN bodies. Even Americans tended to undervalue the role of private enterprise and emphasize planning, a term freighted with statist implications in third world economics. In addition, as Robert Cassen pointed out, cold war pressures encouraged U.S. officials to pander to third world misconceptions: "The donors were more willing to finance the kinds of development the recipient wanted. They competed, for example, to supply India with public sector steel plants—something that would be unimaginable today."[15]

Some critics have suggested that aid dollars spent on statist programs may have been not only wasted but harmful. Nicholas Eberstadt suggests that aid may have made "injurious practices and destructive policies feasible for governments that could not have sustained them without this source of external finance."[16] P. T. Bauer and John O'Sullivan argue that

> aid ... necessarily increases the power, resources, and patronage of government in the society. This result is reinforced by preferential treatment of governments which try to establish state-controlled economies—a preference supported by the spurious argument that comprehensive state planning is necessary for material progress. In fact, economic controls introduced in the name of so-called development planning divorce output from consumer requirements and generally waste resources and obstruct their growth.[17]

Changes in Development Economics

Whatever the justice of these criticisms, the 1980s witnessed a dramatic turnabout in development economics. The past twenty years established a growing international consensus that a thriving private sector is the necessary engine for propelling countries out of poverty. Taiwan, South Korea, and other states of the Pacific rim have set the pace for third world economic growth through policies emphasizing private enterprise. In mainland China, economic liberalization spurred a decade of growth so rapid that the country exceeded its audacious goal of doubling GNP. But that is only the beginning of the story.

Not only is it unimaginable, to borrow Cassen's example, that the United States today would compete to finance a state-owned steel mill in India, it is nearly as unlikely that the Soviet Union would do so. As it struggles for economic reform, Moscow no longer encourages third world countries to mimic its statist economic model. The Gorbachev plan of economic reform, adopted by the Supreme Soviet in 1990, declares, "The whole world experience proved the vitality and efficiency of the market economy."[18] India too would be less and less likely to pursue such a project. A survey of forty-two less developed countries by the U.S. Agency for International Development showed that twenty-eight, including India, have "increased significantly" their "reliance on competitive markets and outward-oriented trade" from 1979 to 1987.[19]

As the Communist world struggles toward free market reforms, West European Social Democratic policies have been suggested as a middle way between Socialist and capitalist economics. But as Seymour Martin Lipset demonstrated in a recent study, the Social Democratic parties are themselves in the midst of a radical revision of doctrine toward free market policies:

> In country after country, socialist and other left parties have taken the road back to capitalism.... Most of the overseas parties of the left have explicitly reversed their traditional advocacy of state ownership and domination of the economy and openly espouse the virtues of the market economy, of tax reduction, even of monetarism and deregulation.[20]

The Reagan and Bush administrations created three new trends in U.S. foreign aid programs, each with implications for the promotion of democracy. First, they have tried to support democratic institutions directly, rather than as a product of economic development. Second, they have emphasized security issues. Third, they have shifted toward freemarket strategies for economic development.

Building Democratic Institutions

AID today describes "pluralism, including the promotion of democracy, freedom and competition in the political, economic and social institutions of a nation" as one of its "fundamental, and essentially universal goals."[21] The idea of promoting democracy with foreign aid is not novel. The early aid practitioners hoped that democracy would be an organic outgrowth of development. Lucian Pye in the 1960s pointed out an irony: U.S. strategy assumed that we could achieve the political results by engineering economic change, while the Soviets, who were nominally economic determinists, concentrated on the political realm:

> We [Americans] are quite prepared to accept the suggestion that the secondary and tertiary effects of a policy action can be readily charted through a series of chain reactions....
> The Soviets, in spite of a formal ideology that pretends to a scientific explanation of human society, act as though they

are far less confident about the possibilities of predicting the indirect consequences of policy actions. They generally take a more direct and frontal approach to the problem of directing social change.[22]

In 1966 the Foreign Assistance Act was amended to call for "maximum participation in the task of economic development on the part of the people of the developing countries, through the encouragement of democratic private and local governmental institutions." But this reprise of a famous theme of the domestic war on poverty was more a reflection of the temper of the times than a plan for action. In practice the emphasis remained on economic aid in the belief that political development would flow from that. After fifteen years this amendment (title 9) was rescinded.

What is new within the past decade is the effort to strengthen political institutions directly. In the Carter years, Congress earmarked a small fraction of the aid budget for projects to encourage respect for human rights. During the 1982 election in El Salvador, however, AID was called upon to provide technical support—materials and training for registration, voting, and vote counting—to ensure a fair election in a country that had practically never had one. The first Salvadoran election was followed by another and then by elections in other countries unaccustomed to them. The success of these important ventures led to increasing demands for technical support from AID—everything from systems of maintaining a voters' roll to indelible ink for stamping voters' hands to prevent double balloting.

Even with a freely elected government in El Salvador, the death squads, often composed of official personnel, made that country less than a true democracy. Although the identities of the perpetrators were often widely known, virtually none was ever brought to justice, in part because they were protected by the military and police, and in part because the criminal justice system was appallingly weak. AID in 1985 initiated a program to train court personnel, from judges to prosecutors to bailiffs, and to provide other support to judicial structures. In Africa too AID is funding the training of legal professionals as well as the purchase of law books and other accoutrements of legal education.

AID has also begun projects to strengthen legislatures by offering technical assistance and training for legislators and their staffs and by building research facilities and other infrastructure. It also underwrites programs of human rights education and the writing of constitutions, and in some countries it subsidizes independent human rights organizations. By 1990 AID officials estimated that they were spending $40 million to $50 million annually for projects that build democratic institutions.[23]

Security Assistance

Military aid can preserve democratic governments threatened by hostile neighbors or armed insurgencies. Of course it can preserve nondemocratic governments, as well. Our greatest exercise in military aid, Lend-Lease, helped to preserve both Churchill's England and Stalin's Russia. As with our aid to the USSR, assistance to an undemocratic ally is sometimes essential to our own security, and justifiable for that reason. Given that America is democracy's mainstay, such measures of self-defense arguably serve democracy's cause in the long run, though we should be cautious about using such an ends-justify-means argument.

Because the military forces in many countries are an impediment to democracy, the question arises whether strengthening the military in those countries is tantamount to retarding democracy. Military forces that impose their will on domestic polities rarely need U.S. aid to do so; and military aid can be a wedge for the United States to pressure those armed forces to respect civilian authority. The United States should exercise great caution, however, in extending aid to military governments or to armed forces that interfere in political life, even when security compels us to do so.

Security aid consists not only of arms but also of cash. Critics of aid sometimes sound as if it can be positively detrimental to the recipient country. Perhaps in the long run it can—if it distorts economic growth. But infusions of funds ordinarily strengthen governments under challenge, notwithstanding waste and misuse. Israel, Egypt, and El Salvador are prime recipients of American funds for security reasons. Although many people have criticized the economic policies of these governments, only those who want to see them toppled advocate cutting off American aid.

New Democracies. Just as foreign funds can boost governments under duress, they can also be used to strengthen democratic institutions where they are young and fragile. Larry Diamond pointed out that

> economic assistance can make a difference to new and struggling democracies. International assistance, especially generous U.S. support under the Alliance for Progress, helped keep the Colombian economy afloat during the difficult years of the new regime in the late 1950s and early 1960s. Economic assistance also helped Costa Rica consolidate economic growth and democracy in the decades after 1946. . . . To be sure, unending aid dependence has serious long-term costs for the recipient country, but aid that is structured specifically to nurture a country through difficult straits . . . can benefit both development and democracy.[24]

In such cases, aid programs need not repeat the error, so forcefully criticized by Bauer and O'Sullivan, of encouraging statism. In 1989, for example, Congress passed the Support for East European Democracy Act (SEED), providing aid to stimulate the private sectors in Poland and Hungary. The bill contains some funds to rebuild infrastructure, notably Poland's nearly defunct telephone system; some to train citizens in economic and technological skills; some to facilitate the sharing of know-how by American entrepreneurs; some to encourage American private investment; and the like. It also aims to help cushion the shock of a sudden transition to currency convertibility and market pricing. Although the use of government funds to build the private sector may seem contradictory, government had an active hand in erecting the successful capitalist economies in Japan, Korea, and Taiwan.

Free Market Development Strategies

Although the Reagan administration reduced development assistance, it did not eliminate it. For Reagan's eight years, development assistance levels in constant dollars averaged 7 to 8 percent lower than during the previous eight years. In both periods the level was just a fraction of what it had been during the 1960s.[25]

Despite the cuts, at the conclusion of Reagan's presidency the United States continued to maintain AID resident missions in seventy-nine countries.[26] Since the 1980s the U.S. government has emphasized the role of the private sector. This approach features "policy dialogue," an effort to use discussions about aid to encourage more liberal economic policies in developing countries. In addition AID today supports business training programs, the growth of local business associations, and technical assistance and the transfer of technology to businesses in developing countries. It underwrites marketing studies and brokers joint ventures. The agency extends credit or guarantees loans through a variety of programs aimed at stimulating private enterprise, especially "microenterprise," that is, individual craftsmen and tradesmen.

Another pillar of Reagan administration foreign aid was the fostering of local and private institutions within recipient countries to further decentralization. U.S. officials now speak more often of the importance of private American capital flows to developing countries, both philanthropic and profit-seeking.

Even if these changes make development assistance more successful, this may not make it an effective instrument for spreading democracy. The critics of aid have raised two main questions: Can aid stimulate development, and does development conduce to democratization? Even before the Reagan era changes, the second was more telling, especially if the critics meant to imply by the first that aid can never, or almost never, be useful economically.

Robert Cassen, a proponent of aid, acknowledges that "inter-country statistical analyses do not show anything conclusive—positive or negative—about the impact of aid on growth."[27] But he and others cite cases where aid seems to have boosted growth. Taiwan received U.S. aid from 1950 to 1965, averaging about 34 percent of total gross investment.[28] In 1965 Taiwan graduated from the class of aid recipients, and today it is a donor of aid, after achieving economic growth perhaps without historical parallel (with distributional equity, as well). Indeed, embarrassed by its huge trade imbalance with the United States, Taiwan began spending money to facilitate American exports to Taiwan; in a sense the United States began receiving aid from Taiwan.

South Korea is another aid graduate, after receiving $6 billion of economic assistance in the 1950s and 1960s. South Korea was then so poor that the $12 per capita received from the United States from 1953 to 1958 amounted to nearly 15 percent of its gross national product, according to some informed estimates.[29] Today its per capita gross domestic product exceeds $2,000, and according to more sophisticated measures of purchasing power, its standard of living is a great deal higher than that.[30] Its automobiles and electronic products compete effectively in U.S. markets.

Cassen cites less successful countries that have used aid effectively. India, Pakistan, Mexico, and the Philippines, for example, have increased agricultural output as a result of research and irrigation sustained by foreign aid.

Other countries have slid backward economically despite considerable aid. The United States has given more than a billion dollars to Zaire, more than two-thirds of a billion to Somalia, more than half a billion to Ghana, each of which has received billions from other donor nations as well. Yet each has suffered a net decline in per capita gross domestic product from 1950 to 1986.[31] After thirty-six years of development assistance they are poorer than when they began.

Such cases, reinforced by a numbing succession of stories about privation and disaster in third world countries, are apt to give Americans the impression that those parts of the world are stagnant. In truth the third world as a whole has made considerable economic progress. In little more than a generation, it has enjoyed a ten- to twenty-year increase in life expectancy, a reduction by half in child mortality, an increase in primary school attendance from less than half of the children to more than 80 percent, and a 75 percent increase in per capita gross national product.[32] This last figure excludes China and the major oil exporters, which would make the figures even higher.

There is no way to measure the contribution of aid to this progress, but a reasonable estimate of its effectiveness comes from the Task Force on Concessional Flows, composed of members of the Boards of Governors of the World Bank and the International Monetary Fund: "The overall aid record is comparable to that of many large domestic programs in industrialized countries."[33] The use of aid to stimulate industrialization does indeed seem more problematic than early advocates recognized, but aid can bring valuable results in such things as education, public health, and family planning. Such human investment is worth supporting on humanitarian grounds alone, but it also appears to bring economic returns as well.[34]

But does economic progress conduce to democracy? Lucian Pye cleverly pointed out long ago that if the relationship between the two were as clear as some believed, "we should welcome Soviet contributions to economic growth in the underdeveloped areas as promoting our interests."[35] Two important cases in which democracy has indeed seemed to spring from economic progress are South Korea and Taiwan. The former made a smooth transition to freely elected government in 1988; the latter seems still in transition but has already passed the milestone of legalizing opposition parties and publications. In both countries, the spectacular economic development seemed to buy a level of social peace, as the ruling group—in Korea the army, in Taiwan the Kuomintang—safely relaxed its grip on power.

The opposite relationship between economics and politics seems to hold, however, in other recent transitions to democracy. In Latin America and Eastern Europe, a sense of economic despair undermined ruling groups: in Latin America the military, in Eastern Europe the Communist parties. Conversely the two parts of the world least touched by the global trend of democratization are sub-Saharan Africa and the Arab countries. The former area is still in the vise of grinding poverty, while the latter is awash in petrodollars. What can we conclude? Where democracy is in its childhood, economic progress seems to strengthen its sinews, but where it is still struggling to be born, either economic growth or contraction may hasten its gestation.

Ironically, while at some moments we have acted from the premise that we could stimulate democracy by extending aid, at others we have acted from the premise that we could stimulate it by withholding or cutting aid to punish undemocratic governments. While in some instances such foreign aid "conditionality" has served as a lever to extract certain concessions, the general record of using aid cuts to foster political progress is poor.[36]

There are many poor and undemocratic countries to which America should give aid for purely humanitarian reasons, especially to alleviate disease, hunger, and illiteracy. We remain by far the wealthiest people on earth, and we ought not to stint in helping to feed the hungry, to clothe the naked, and to heal the sick around the world. But we should not expect that we can create democracy by fostering development. The relationship between economic and political development is too indeterminate. Aid can, however, serve the cause of democracy in other ways: by sustaining fledgling democratic governments or ones under siege and by directly underwriting elections, courts, and other institutions of democracy.

12
Overseas Broadcasting and Exchanges

The U.S. government possesses the means to communicate directly with most members of the political elites of virtually every society on earth; indeed we may have the capacity to reach the majority of the world's inhabitants. We can bring to them information about alternative political systems and present to them evidence of the virtues of democracy. Where their rulers attempt to keep them mired in lies or ignorance, we can furnish objective news about events in their own countries and the world. Even without advocacy, such reporting can weaken tyranny by preventing thought control and can plant the seeds of democratic philosophy by exemplifying the idea that lies at democracy's heart: no one has a monopoly on truth.

The principal agencies embodying that capacity are the United States Information Agency (USIA) and Radio Liberty and Radio Free Europe (RL–RFE). Three USIA subdivisions are important agencies in themselves: the Voice of America (VOA), Radio and Television Marti, and the Fulbright program for the international exchange of students and scholars. The impact of broadcasting is important for its breadth, of the exchanges, for its depth. Radio is the one means by which America can speak directly to the masses overseas. Exchanges touch only the elite but often in a powerful way. A few years' study in a foreign land has left a lasting impression on the outlook of many individuals.

Fulbright grants are given to university teachers and students. Since 1982 the exchange of pre-college-age teens has become a large-scale activity. In addition USIA gives grants to private institutions sponsoring exchanges and runs several such projects of its own.

In neither broadcasting nor exchanges does the USIA exercise a monopoly on American activities. In broadcasting, Radio Liberty and Radio Free Europe, which also are sponsored by the U.S. government but are independent of USIA, account for a substantial part of our country's total foreign broadcasting. As for scholarly exchanges, a large share of them are conducted by private organizations. And in the activity likely to have the greatest political ramifications, study in America by foreigners, USIA programs account for only about 2 or 3 percent of the total.

Broadcasting

History. The practice of overseas radio broadcasting came into its own during World War II. The ferocious propaganda of the Nazi Joseph Goebbels set the pace; Germany's Axis partners and its enemies soon joined in. By war's end, said David Abshire, "belligerents and most neutrals had virtually covered the globe, broadcasting in over 40 languages from more than 340 transmitters in 55 countries."[1]

The Voice of America began broadcasting a few months after Pearl Harbor. Its first words signaled that although the medium was the same, the nature of its message would differ from that of the Axis broadcasts: "Today America has been at war for seventy-nine days. Daily we shall speak to you at this time about America and the war. The news may be good or bad. We shall tell you the truth." In the spirit of wartime, few Americans would have scrupled about the veracity of our broadcasts if lying proved useful to our self-defense. But tactical wisdom told us that truthfulness would be to our advantage, for it would give our broadcasts credibility. Ever since, American broadcasting has been the subject of frequent debates about the degree of advocacy or polemics that is appropriate, but deliberate lying has never been advocated.

After the war, VOA went into a brief decline, together with other government information activities, until the cold war gave it a new raison d'être. The cold war spawned America's other radio broadcasting ventures. When the Soviets refused to share access to Radio Berlin, whose facilities they controlled, the American occupation authorities created Radio in the American Sector. Operating at first with makeshift equipment and aiming to reach only the American sector of Berlin, it became the most popular station reaching East Germany, with an audience estimated at three-fourths of that country's adult population.[2] Over the years the staffing and financing of RIAS shifted increasingly into West German hands, although it remained a joint program of the American and West German governments.

Radio Free Europe and Radio Liberty (initially called Radio Liberation) were started in 1949 and 1951, respectively, by privately incorporated committees of prominent American citizens, but were secretly underwritten by the CIA.[3] For staff, they drew on the pool of talented and highly motivated refugees from the newly communized states and territories. When the CIA's role was revealed in 1971, the Congress voted to replace it with overt appropriations. The Congress created the bipartisan Board for International Broadcasting, which assumed responsibility for the two stations; they were administratively consolidated during the next several years. In 1985 Radio Marti began broadcasting to Cuba, and in 1990 it began to experiment with the broadcast of television signals.

Audiences. Voice of America estimated that it had 127 million listeners in 1988, defined as those who tune in at least once a week, in more than 160 countries.[4] Radio Free Europe–Radio Liberty (RFE–RL) estimated variously that in 1988 it reached 55 or 56.5 million listeners at least once a week.[5] Radio Marti estimated an audience of 2 million in 1987.[6] Surveys showed that nearly 50 percent of the populace in the Soviet Union listened to Western broadcasts at least once a week, 28 percent to VOA, and 15 percent each to RL and to the BBC.[7] Similarly for Eastern Europe, surveys showed that 70 to 80 percent of the population listened weekly; Radio Free Europe had the biggest share, followed by VOA and the BBC.[8]

Formats. The staple of both VOA and RFE–RL is news; both systems (as well as Radio Marti) are committed to the principle of reporting the news as honestly as possible. The VOA charter and the RFE–RL code begin with almost identical language, each pledging news reports that will be "reliable," "accurate," "objective," and "comprehensive."[9]

Beyond this, however, the two main American stations differ in several ways. VOA is supposed to be what its name implies: an American voice, emphasizing the news of the world as it is seen from America and news about America. RFE and RL are surrogate stations; that is, they are supposed to represent the voice of the opposition forces from the countries to which they broadcast. The revelations of CIA financing in a sense gave the lie to this posture and showed that the hand of the U.S. government lay behind RFE–RL. But in another sense there was no lie, for although the government might have paid the bills, the refugees and exiles who wrote and read the broadcasts were indeed genuine voices of opposition from societies in which the internal opposition was silenced.

Thus the news broadcasts on RFE–RL focus on news about the target country and world news that affects it directly. The non-news hours are devoted to feature reports, cultural programs, religious broadcasts, readings of underground literature, all from or about the target country. On VOA, news broadcasts share time with offerings of American culture, including popular music, as well as features with more

191

political content. The difference in vantage points of the two services naturally entails a certain difference in style. RFE–RL is known as more political, more feisty. VOA sees itself as akin to other American news organizations.

The dissident movements in the Soviet Union and the Eastern bloc grew up in a constructive symbiosis with American overseas broadcasting. Writers of *samizdat* or participants in the various tiny groups fighting for freedom of worship or emigration or conscience learned ways to get their works or statements or news into the hands of RFE–RL and then to the ears of millions of their compatriots. Helpless though they were before the grim power of the totalitarian state, this gave them a weapon with which they could battle their tormentors for the soul of their nation. VOA also sought to nurture dissident movements by broadcasting dissident literature and offering systematic reading of Scripture when Soviet believers were largely denied access to Bibles. But VOA, an official arm of the American government, functioned in a more cautious, circumscribed way.

Both services include some programming aimed directly at promoting democratic ideas, increasingly so in recent years as optimism grew about democratic transformations. VOA broadcast a series on democracy in action, divided into segments on politics and economics. The former includes programs on *The Federalist*, New England town meetings, election campaigning, filibusters, neighborhood civic associations, and the like. The latter includes programs on such subjects as credit unions, "mom and pop" stores, and the Federal Reserve Board. Radio Liberty also broadcast a weekly feature on democracy in action and another on human rights. The latter might include readings from Andrei Sakharov or discussions of anti-Semitism; the former, programs on the difference between communism and social democracy or between presidential systems and parliamentary ones. As democratic transitions gained momentum in Eastern Europe, RFE–RL added a new feature, "The Democratic Experience," with detailed accounts of the functioning of American trade unions, electoral campaigning in West Germany, the practices of Western news organizations, and the like.

Both VOA and RFE–RL scrambled to find new ways to strengthen Eastern Europe's emergent democratic structures but would be hard pressed to match their past contribution. Solidarity's Lech Walesa said about Radio Free Europe: "Its contribution was enormous. Poland without [it] would be like a land without sunshine."[10] The Czech writer Ivan Klima told Philip Roth in an interview:

> Nor should we pass over the great part played in propagating what was called "uncensored literature" by the foreign broadcasting stations Radio Free Europe and the Voice of

America. Radio Free Europe broadcast the most important of the *samizdat* books in serial form, and its listeners numbered in the hundreds of thousands. (One of the last books I heard read on this station was Havel's remarkable *Long Distance Interrogation*, which is an account not only of his life but also of his political ideas.) I'm convinced that this "underground culture" had an important influence on the revolutionary events of the autumn of 1989.[11]

Vaclav Havel himself, visiting America for the first time as president of Czechoslovakia, paid tribute to VOA as "the most listened-to Czechoslovak radio station. You have informed us truthfully of events around the world and in our country as well and, in this way, you helped to bring about the peaceful revolution which has at long last taken place."[12]

In 1985 RFE added a new dimension to its service in Hungary, Czechoslovakia, and Bulgaria that further weakened the state's terrifying grip on its citizenry. With the advent of direct long-distance telephone dialing in those countries, RFE advertised a telephone number in Munich that any citizen could call to leave a recorded message: opinions, complaints, appeals, revelations about official misconduct, or news that had been kept out of their official media. These items were then broadcast back to their countrymen. The messages were limited to two minutes to prevent tracing, and they were read by broadcasters, rather than played in the caller's own voice, to protect anonymity. Within the first two years nearly 50,000 calls were received.[13] In this way Czechs, Hungarians, and Bulgarians could speak publicly and freely to one another for the first time in nearly forty years (except for brief moments in 1956 and 1968).

As flames of freedom were kindled in Poland and elsewhere in 1989, foreign broadcasts helped to fan them into a conflagration that engulfed the region. The *Times* (London) carried this account from Bratislava, Slovakia, the day after the first mass demonstrations in Prague:

> The apartment grew silent as the scenes [in Prague] were described by Radio Free Europe. A decision was taken to walk to the city center next day with as many friends as they could muster to light candles in protest. That in itself was a brave decision. . . . [but they] found that by next morning events had overtaken them and they were now merely part of a great movement.
>
> That same radio broadcast brought every student body out on strike and sent the city's actors and actresses into factories to pass out leaflets and ask for support of the workers. Juraj Vaculik, a student leader, said: "The Radio Free Europe broadcast was like a flame."[14]

As revolution spread over Eastern Europe, the tightly controlled media in Nicolae Ceausescu's Romania attempted to keep out all news of it. But the *Washington Post* reported that "Romania's conspicuous silence for most of the past year was not the dismal quiet of hopelessness. Rather, it was the stillness of people paying attention" to American and other foreign broadcasts on their radio bands.[15]

These anecdotes illustrate how overseas broadcasting helped to defeat the totalitarian project, which aimed at complete control over people's behavior by control over their minds, and control of their minds by control over the information they could receive. Possibly the human spirit could have triumphed over this evil design even had its practitioners carried it out in full, just as some prisoners can withstand solitary confinement. But when captors exercise complete control over their captives' environment, the captives sometimes give in—the so-called Stockholm syndrome. Could totalitarian governments have induced a Stockholm syndrome in entire populations, as George Orwell feared? Perhaps not, but broadcasting more than anything else aborted the experiment.

As Nicolae Manolescu, new chief editor of the leading Romanian intellectual journal, *Romania Literara*, put it:

> What did these radios mean to us until the events of last December? The metaphor of the reeds comes to mind. It was as if we were living under water and we needed reed pipes for air to breathe. The reeds were the radios. Without them, the entire people surely would have suffocated.
>
> Practically everyone listened to the radios. At a certain time of day, in the evening during broadcast hours, or when something especially important was being aired, such as General Pacepa's book [Pacepa was a top Romanian defector to the West], on RFE, we saw that auto traffic in Bucharest simply stopped. No one was in the streets. . . .
>
> And the next day, on streetcars and buses and in offices everyone talked about nothing other than what they had heard the night before.[16]

The era of *glasnost* has brought changes to the functioning of the overseas stations. VOA now broadcasts radio bridges with panelists in the Soviet Union, and Radio Liberty uses several free-lance Soviet citizens to report news from their homeland, scurrying to scoop their own media. Perhaps the most interesting testimonial to the American broadcasts came in an article that appeared late in 1989 in *Sobesednik*, the weekly supplement to *Izvestia*: "The popularity of RL broadcasts can be explained not only by the station's achievements, but by our own shortcomings. . . . 'So that's what he wants, some readers might think, a radio station like Radio Liberty in the Soviet Union. . . .' And why not?"[17] Indeed, in the hopes of aiding the growth of Western-style independent journalism in Eastern Europe, VOA launched a program in early 1990 for training East European journalists.

Has foreign broadcasting succeeded to the point of making itself superfluous? It was born in the cold war; as the cold war recedes, should VOA and RFE–RL go with it? Some members of Congress seem to think so; most of these were never enthusiastic about the radios and viewed them as an obstacle to improving relations with the Communist governments.[18] In my view, VOA will have a role far into the future. Most of the world has yet to become democratic, and even in a world of democracies America has every reason to speak in its own authorized voice. The purpose of Radio Free Europe and Radio Liberty will have been accomplished when all countries to which they broadcast are fully functioning democracies with independent presses of their own. That day seems nearer at hand than ever before, but it has not arrived. For the time being, it behooves us to augment rather than to diminish the efforts of RFE–RL to help ensure the completion of this transition.

In the longer term, VOA may turn more to television broadcasting. Under the direction of Charles Wick, USIA built up Worldnet, a television broadcast capability that is used mainly for transmitting lectures, interviews, or press conferences to U.S. facilities abroad, where selected audiences may be invited to view them. Some efforts were made to reach a television audience directly through cable hookups in some European hotels, but Congress concluded that the results did not equal expenses. Technological evolution, however, may make satellite dishes as commonplace as shortwave receivers are today and allow television images to be broadcast directly into the living rooms of millions around the world. Even today Television Marti is experimenting with direct-to-home broadcasting, although it has yet to solve the problem of Fidel Castro's jamming. In the twenty-first century, however, this new capability is destined to make life all the more difficult for the world's remaining dictators.

Educational Exchanges

In the academic year 1988–1989 more than 366,000 foreign students studied at accredited American colleges and universities, an increase of more than tenfold from the 34,000 who studied here in 1954–1955. The United States has by far the largest number of foreign students of any country, three times as many as France, with the second largest number, and six times as many as the Soviet Union, according to the best available figures.[19]

The United States hosts more students from the third world than all the European countries combined. Seventy-nine percent of Indians studying abroad study in the United States, 68 percent of South Koreans, 62 percent of Nigerians, 49 percent of Malaysians, and 76 percent of Chinese.[20] Even Iran sends more of its students to the "Great Satan" than anywhere else. Of all third world countries, virtually the only ones that do not send the greatest share of their overseas students to the United States are several of the former French colonies of Africa and the Levant, which send most to France.

Most of these foreign students do not come to study politics, but in a year or more here they absorb a good deal about American ways, including the democratic ethos woven throughout the fabric of American life. Its presence is strong in our universities with their faculty senates, student councils, rigorous guarantees of free speech, audacious student newspapers, tenure for faculty, and codes of student rights. This ethos reaches into the classroom and the style of American education. A few years before the emergence of China's democracy movement, *Newsweek* reported on PRC students here: "In China, notes Columbia's Yang Jun, grades are awarded for memorizing, not thinking, and 'it's only once students graduate that they realize what they learned was useless.'"[21]

A minority do study politics and related fields. According to the most recent survey, 7.7 percent of foreign students are specializing in the social sciences, 3.8 percent in the humanities, and 3.1 percent in education. Another 18.9 percent are in the field of business and management, where, if they are not directly studying the workings of a free polity, they are at least studying the cognate ones of a free economy.

With American institutions accounting for such a large share of third world students who go abroad to study, it follows that these students account for a significant number of the college graduates in their countries, especially of those receiving advanced degrees. Fred Strebeigh has compiled some interesting figures for the People's Republic of China:

> China today has approximately 120,000 graduate students within its borders, whereas it has some 20,000 enrolled here. Moreover, through national exams and institutional selection, China directs official support for overseas study to the cream of its intelligentsia—to an extent unprecedented among other nations. The selection process brings to America not just the Chinese scholarly elite but also the power elite. Douglas Murray, until recently the president of the China Institute of America, says, "Every Chinese leader seems to have a son or daughter in the United States."[22]

China may be an extreme case, but it is far from unique. Those who come to study in the United States constitute an important segment of the emerging elite of many third world countries, including many who will rise to pivotal positions. There are already numerous examples. The most important democrat in Central America during the traumatic 1970s and 1980s was El Salvador's José Napoleón Duarte, who studied at the University of Notre Dame. The woman who led the Philippines back to democracy, President Corazon Aquino, studied at Mount Saint Vincent College in New York. Mexican President Carlos Salinas de Gortari attended Harvard University, as did Jamaican Prime Minister Edward Seaga. Swedish Prime Minister Ingvar Carlsson studied here (at Northwestern University) through the Fulbright program, as have dozens of other present and former cabinet ministers, parliamentarians, and supreme court justices.

Study in America does not automatically produce democrats. King Birendra of Nepal studied here as did President for Life Hastings Kamuzu Banda of Malawi; so have some leaders of nondemocratic revolutionary movements. Two leaders of the Iranian revolution, Abdul Hasan Bani Sadr and Sadegh Gotbzadeh, did so, as did two top Nicaraguan Sandinistas, Luis Carrion Cruz and Moises Hassan.

Even some of these revolutionists eventually showed signs of wavering in their commitment to antidemocratic causes. Bani Sadr, who lost a power struggle with Shiite fundamentalists, is today a leading figure of the Left opposition in exile. Whether he leans more toward dictatorial leftism or democratic leftism remains an open question. Nicaragua's Moises Hassan, although he has not made a clean break with the Sandinistas, has deviated more by way of open dissent and criticism than any other top Sandinista. Bani Sadr and Hassan struggled to prevent democracy in their homelands, yet either or both could end up in the democratic camp. The experience of living in a democracy might not have been entirely lost on them even though they at first rejected it.

Students from China. The largest blocs of third world students in America are from the two Chinas, which until the Tiananmen massacre each had about 30,000 students here at any one time. In both cases these students have probably had a considerable impact on their respective polities. The Republic of China is undertaking a rapid, peaceful transition from dictatorial to democratic rule, with the Kuomintang converting itself from a democratic-centralist, vanguard party to a Western-style open party that competes in free elections. This transition was spurred by younger, reform-minded leaders, many educated in the United States. The Thirteenth Party Congress of the Kuomintang in 1989 chose a central committee of 180 members. No fewer than 39 of them held doctorates from foreign universities and another 25 held foreign master's degrees. Of the 31 members of the central committee's inner standing committee, 7 held foreign doctorates and 4, foreign master's degrees.[23] Almost all of these foreign degrees were probably American.

The People's Republic of China nearly made a spectacular leap to democracy in the spring of 1989 under the impetus of one of the most enormous protest movements in history. Generations of Marxists have fantasized about the kind of spontaneous mass movement that took over Beijing for those few weeks. There is no sure way to measure the impact of those who had studied in America, but the movement's choice of the Statue of Liberty as its symbol speaks volumes about the influence of America.

Communist China began to allow its students to come to America in the late 1970s. The government's aim was to spur modernization; most students pursued engineering, mathematics, and the hard sciences. But a survey conducted in the early 1980s revealed that a significant fraction were in softer fields. In the 1981–1982 school year 13 percent of undergraduates and 15 percent of graduate students were majoring in the humanities and 11 percent of undergraduates and 6 percent of graduate students were in the social sciences.[24] And in 1987 *Newsweek* reported that 200 students from the PRC were enrolled in American law schools.[25] The implications are suggested anecdotally by Strebeigh:

> [Chinese] students and scholars are discovering new scholarly methods and directions for their study of Chinese culture. A graduate student at the University of Wisconsin is working with types of sociological surveys and psychological experiments that are unknown in China. A law student at Yale is doing a comparative study of freedom of speech—"a somewhat sensitive topic," he supposes.... [A]t Stanford University, Fu Zhengyuan, a professor from the Chinese Academy of Social Sciences, recently began a study of the determinants of political behavior in Britain, the United States, China, and the Soviet Union, including determinants that orthodox Marxist analysis overlooks.[26]

Early in 1987, 1,000 Chinese students in America signed a public letter to Chinese authorities protesting the removal of Hu Yaobang as general secretary of the Communist party and the expulsion of reform-minded intellectuals from the party as "not conducive to building a system of democracy."[27] From this time, the Chinese students in America constituted an important arm of the nascent democracy movement. When the movement flowered in the spring of 1989, some of the students in the United States rushed back to China to take part, while others assembled a telephone and fax network linking them with 30,000 terminals in China.[28] After the bloody crackdown, the network tried to circumvent the government's efforts to control the flow of information. The survivors used it to send their stories to the West and even to communicate with different parts of China through Western links, when direct lines of communication were severed.

Most participants in the Tiananmen Square Spring had not studied abroad, and virtually none of the leaders had done so. Most were young undergraduates. But several of the adult intellectuals who emerged as the main advisers to the students had been to America on fellowships or exchanges, including Fang Lizhi and his wife Li Shuxian, the literary critic Liu Xiaobo, the political scientist Yan Jiaqi, the journalist Liu Binyan, and Su Shaozhi, social scientist. These were formidable intellectuals whose views had many roots and whose dissents, often couched within a Marxist framework, antedated their visits to America. But their first-hand observation of American democracy probably helped them to visualize more the alternative they were seeking. Fang Lizhi—the Chinese Sakharov—described his own experience in a speech at Shanghai's Tongji University in 1986:

> The newspaper often refers to National People's Congress (NPC) representatives coming for an "inspection" tour.... At one time I thought that it was perfectly natural for big officials from the NPC to come "inspect" us. But during the first half of this year I was at Princeton's Institute for Advanced Studies in New Jersey, doing research in cosmology. While I was there I received a mailing from our local member of the United States Congress, explaining what Congress had been up to lately and what he had been doing during the session. He wrote quite a bit about his voting record, explaining what he had voted for and against. He spoke about his achievements in office, how he had gone on the record for this or that, and why he had done so. In short, he was "reporting" to us. Although I was only a temporary resident, he had sent me this material, showing respect for anyone living in his district. He wanted us to know where he stood on the issues and to see if we agreed with him; if not, we could raise our concerns and he could turn around and express them in Congress. Despite representing a "false democracy," this man was clearly accounting for his actions. Now what about our "true democracy"? I have never known what my representative supported or opposed, or what his accomplishments in office were. And the next time I have to go cast my vote for this person, I will still be totally in the dark. Our "true democracy" had better get on the ball so that it can do better than their "false democracy"! I lived in China a long time without being aware of these problems. But when I went

abroad and was finally able to see for myself, the contrast was glaringly obvious.[29]

Although the young leaders of the democracy movement had not been to America, the intellectual climate on Chinese campuses has been influenced by students and scholars who have returned from the United States and by visiting American teachers. The returnees, reported the *Washington Post*'s correspondent in Beijing, provided "information and insights [to] fill the gaps in the VOA broadcasts, and they create a mystique of American life and language that influences thought and behavior here."[30] The Fulbright program has also funded a small number of Chinese scholars pursuing American studies in the United States and American scholars to teach this subject in China. According to the *Washington Post*, "one of the first official agencies [in China] to endorse the [Tiananmen Square] protests was the American Studies Institute of the Academy of Sciences," which was headed by the son of a cabinet member.[31]

The PRC government signaled its belief that exchanges were a source of trouble by its actions in the wake of the Tiananmen massacre. Although it blustered against Western sanctions that curtailed intercourse with China, Beijing itself cut back on scholarly exchanges by restricting the outward flow of its students and by subjecting them to far more rigorous screening. It suspended the Fulbright exchanges entirely.[32]

U.S. Support. America's emergence as the world's preeminent center of international scholarship and study clearly conveys large secondary benefits for this country and the democratic cause. Still, the government's role in supporting this is questioned. Given that upward of 97 percent of foreign students in the United States are supported by their own governments, out of their own pockets, or by the host universities, why, it is asked, should the U.S. taxpayer underwrite more? Even a staunch advocate for USIA like Fitzhugh Green asked: "Why must USIA or any other federal agency pay more people to come to America? . . . [the] rationale is persuasive for providing a few selected grants each year. It does not support the cries of zealots . . . who would expand the present level of grants by many multiples."[33]

Green may be right that such programs do not warrant large expansions, but the government-sponsored exchanges and scholarships fill several important gaps. If study in America by foreigners is left primarily to those who can pay their own freight or can gain the sponsorship of their governments, such study risks being limited to the wealthy and the obedient. To encourage the spread of democratic thinking, America should ensure that the flow of foreign students passing through our universities includes a significant representation from families not wealthy enough to send them. Those from humble backgrounds who achieve the academic credentials to study here are often among the brightest students and the most likely to play important political roles later. Many undemocratic governments use rewards such as scholarships for foreign study as "carrots" to elicit docility. By providing scholarships we can weaken that control. The exchange of postdoctoral scholars for research or teaching can also be important to spreading democratic ideas—as in the examples of Fang and the American teachers who were turned away by Beijing. There are far fewer alternative sources of support for this key component of the Fulbright program than for the students.

Former Congressman Jim Courter argued that we fail to take advantage of our role as host to foreign students "by being afraid to teach them anything about American political principles." He said, "If we are going to bring men and women here to live among us at public expense for four or five years, we should ask them to learn something of the fundamental principles of American life." He stopped short, however, of proposing that this be compulsory: "Scholarship students at undergraduate institutions should be strongly advised to complete a college course introducing them to the classics of American political thought."[34]

It would be valuable to furnish these students with a grounding in the political philosophy that undergirds the American experiment: they should not imagine that this nation's success is the product of mere luck or geography or of the abuse of others. But Courter's proposal raises several problems. First, anything that is compulsory or smacks of indoctrination is likely to make them resentful. Second, history, philosophy, and political science departments are filled with instructors who deplore American political theory: Will Courter's purposes be served if foreign students are introduced to American political thought by teachers who hold it in contempt? Third, foreign students may not be much more ignorant of American political theory than American students. As Sidney Hook argued in his 1984 Jefferson Lecture, we have neglected to teach it to our own students for fear of engaging in indoctrination.[35]

Nonetheless Courter's idea points to a larger issue. With the collapse of communism, liberal democracy now stands alone on the battlefield of ideas, having triumphed mostly on its merits not least its success at providing the good life. This philosophy originated with French and British thinkers but was developed and brought to life by Americans. Yet American political theory receives less attention in our academia than such failed alternatives as Marxism, and certainly less than is warranted by its success. Correcting this neglect would be a service to

American and foreign students alike, but correcting it is a task for the schools themselves, not for government.

Telling Democracy's Story

There is a broader analogy to the question that Courter raised. It affects the entire mission of USIA. Courter did not deny that study in America per se spreads the democratic idea, but he asked whether it could not do so more effectively if we made a more deliberate effort. Similarly, merely by telling America's story, USIA is inevitably spreading ideas about democracy. America is the world's first and foremost democratic model. Accurate portrayals of American life may constitute the most effective way to convey certain ideas about democracy to the masses of nonintellectuals who are no more likely to read *The Federalist Papers* than are most Americans who have not attended college.

In a society like the Soviet Union, whose populace has for generations been force-fed a diet of lies about America, the transition to democracy might be hastened by the use of literature and mass media to give a truer image of American life. We should seek agreements to give them American books and even movies and television series: not primarily documentaries and educational programs but entertainment that is likely to draw a wide audience. "Hill Street Blues," "L.A. Law," and "St. Elsewhere," which give fairly true images of life in an American police precinct, law office, and hospital, would be eye-opening to Soviet audiences.

Yet telling America's story is not the beginning and end of promoting democracy. In the 1980s, spurred by the more ideological approach to foreign policy of President Reagan and those who filled policy posts in his administration, USIA began to pay more attention to promoting democracy as distinct from promoting America, but still in an inchoate way. Michael Schneider, USIA's acting associate director for programs, said about the agency's role in encouraging democracy, "It permeates our work, but we haven't thought it through."[36] Democracy building is not yet a part of the agency's formal mission. Thus USIA's book program does not include the works of Adam Smith and John Locke because they were not Americans.

But it is less important to make other countries like America than to make them *be* like America—in the sense of being democratic. Here something can be learned from the Communists even though their position has collapsed. They recognized long ago that in addition to the rather narrow band of foreigners who could be brought to admire the Soviet Union, a far wider spectrum could be won to Soviet purposes. In all but a few countries, the official Communist parties and Soviet friendship societies are much weaker than an array of other movements, groups, and journals that, from a nationalist or Socialist or independent Marxist perspective, propound themes of anti-Americanism and advocate policies that correspond to Kremlin goals. Often they are all the more effective for not being outright supporters of the USSR.

By analogy the proliferation of democracies or democratic movements is bound to be beneficial for America, even if not all of these movements or governments are unambiguously pro-American. We have our arguments from time to time with virtually all the world's other democracies—Costa Rica one week, France another, Israel another—but they never reach sword's point and rarely do they even damage our interests. We need have no hesitancy about propounding America's virtues—we have so much to be proud of—to recognize that some people will be more receptive to a pitch for democracy than a pitch for America. Such people can serve our long-term interests merely by being good democrats. Ironically the one part of the U.S. government that appreciated this decades ago was the CIA, which often furnished clandestine support to democratic left-of-center groups that were adversaries of communism even though they were ambivalent or worse toward America. The USIA could well learn from this example.

13

The National Endowment for Democracy

In 1984 the American government for the first time spawned an agency expressly to promote democracy abroad. The National Endowment for Democracy, however, is not an arm of the government. Instead, like the National Endowment for the Arts and the National Endowment for the Humanities, it is privately incorporated and governed by its own board—a careful balance of Democrats and Republicans, of businessmen and labor leaders, of scholars, and of politicians. The agency does receive annual appropriations from the U.S. Congress, which account for the bulk of its budget and make it subject to congressional review.

Occasionally congressional critics have objected to giving the taxpayers' money to a body that is free from direct government supervision. But there is good reason why the NED was so created, rather than as a bureau of the State Department. NED's main goal is to assist democrats, especially in undemocratic countries. Naturally these democrats are often at odds with their governments. If the United States has diplomatic relations with those governments, as it does with most, it can hardly give material support directly to opponents of the government. At the same time, many democrats we want to aid would feel compromised by accepting funds directly from the U.S. government. Funds that originate in the U.S. Treasury but are distributed by an independent private agency not tied to any particular U.S. administration are more acceptable.

NED's Operation

The NED's method of operation ordinarily creates a second layer of insulation between the recipients and the U.S. government. The NED is not an action agency but an endowment. Its role is to provide grants to private organizations that are promoting democracy or more limited ends that contribute to democratization, such as combating human rights abuses or publishing an independent newspaper. Although such work is carried out abroad, the NED rarely gives funds directly to foreign groups. More often it makes grants to American groups that work in cooperation with foreign counterparts, such as to American labor unions that assist unions in other countries. Thus a union of agricultural workers in the Philippines may receive assistance from the Free Trade Union Institute, an offshoot of the AFL-CIO created for overseas activities, in publishing its newspaper or training its organizers. FTUI in turn receives grants from the NED.

This is quite different from a Filipino union receiving a direct subsidy from the U.S. Treasury. That union might well be in competition with a Communist union, which would make much of such direct U.S. backing, as might the employer whose workers the union is attempting to organize. These adversaries in any event may denounce the union's American connection, but it is much harder to make the charges stick given the indirect route of the help. Although the NED's methods are not secretive—its programs and financial books are open to public scrutiny—the recipient is placed at some remove from the U.S. government.

Assisting private organizations in this manner to serve public purposes confers other benefits. It frees the government from the responsibility of choosing among various democratic or apparently democratic groups in a given country. Private American organizations that work in the field are well equipped to make such choices, which whether right or wrong are freighted with fewer implications if not made by the U.S. government. For any given country, more than one American organization may receive NED grants, and each of these may work in turn with several indigenous groups. Thus working through the private sector breeds an element of pluralism into the process of endowing democracy, one of the basic goals in the target countries.

In addition, the private intermediaries have crucial talents and experiences to contribute. The hypothetical Filipino farmers' union can surely benefit from material aid, but it can benefit all the more if that aid is provided by American unionists who are themselves veterans of similar campaigns. They can teach about running strikes and conducting negotiations. They can convey something of the spirit and ethos that are often essential to unions in their fledgling stage. One could scarcely expect to use State Department foreign service officers to perform this function. And the intermediaries help administer and oversee the grants so that the NED need not create a bureaucracy of its own.

When the idea for the NED was in its early stages, Secretary of State George Shultz commented that such a program "was so clearly in our interest that I asked, 'Why hasn't this been done before?'"[1] Something

205

of the sort had been done but covertly (see chapter 9). From the late 1940s until the mid-1960s the CIA had channeled funds to political groups, publications, and labor unions of democratic bent. It had done so covertly for the same reasons that the NED was organized as a private foundation: to spare the recipients the taint of U.S. government support and to spare Washington the embarrassment of supporting groups that opposed governments with which it had relations.

Beginnings of NED

The costs of working in a clandestine manner, however, are high, and the deception inherent in it is itself corrosive of the democratic ethic. More important, once the cover was blown by a leftish staffer for the National Student Association who revealed his group's ties to the CIA, many of these operations were hopelessly compromised. Accepting U.S. funds might in itself be embarrassing, but accepting them through the channels of an intelligence agency was tantamount to self-incrimination. If there is nothing wrong about American assistance, why do so secretly?

In the aftermath of the CIA revelations, a committee chaired by Under Secretary of State Nicholas Katzenbach was appointed by President Lyndon Johnson to respond to the crisis. It recommended that some overt means replace the CIA in funneling American dollars to democratic forces. Another committee, chaired by Secretary of State Dean Rusk, was appointed to come up with such a mechanism, but its deliberations proved fruitless.[2] This failure no doubt reflected the temper of the times. America was growing disillusioned with the war in Vietnam and accordingly wary of foreign involvements. Little spirit was brought to the task of creating a mechanism for political action overseas. During the following decade proposals were occasionally floated in Congress— by Senator Hubert Humphrey and Congressmen Dante Fascell and Don Fraser—to create entities to promote international democracy or human rights, but they all withered on the vine.

By the 1980s, however, the isolationist winds had passed, and America was ready to reassert itself, led by a most assertive president. President Ronald Reagan wanted America to "stand tall," and toward that end he secured large increases in spending for arms and intelligence. In a June 8, 1982, speech to the British Parliament, Reagan laid out the political component of America's renewal. He forecast that the final arbiter of the global conflict "will not be bombs and rockets, but a test of wills and ideas" and he proclaimed the goal of spreading the democratic creed.

Some months later the president signed a national security decision document creating Project Democracy, a constellation of interagency programs to be coordinated by USIA, for which the administration sought an initial $65 million budget authorization. But the Congress balked. Many members, especially Democrats, were uneasy with the strong ideological content of Reagan's foreign policy. They feared that a program of democratic advocacy abroad could devolve into a program of advocacy for Reagan administration policies. These fears were compounded by the description of one of the four planned interagency groups, Public Affairs/Nuclear, the apparent purpose of which was to counteract the influence of the nuclear freeze movement.

The entire initiative might have sunk with hardly a trace were it not for a study that had been conducted simultaneously by the private American Political Foundation under the confusingly similar rubric: "The Democracy Program." This study set forth the outlines for the National Endowment for Democracy as a publicly funded but privately operated foundation. The proposal was embraced by the Reagan administration and approved by Congress late in 1983 even as the other elements of the administration's Project Democracy were rejected.

The NED thus was born in early 1984 with an appropriation of $18 million for the remainder of that fiscal year. The bulk of these funds was earmarked for two of NED's four companion or subsidiary institutes, with a modest share left over for NED's own discretionary grant making. These four institutes are the Center for International Private Enterprise, affiliated with the U.S. Chamber of Commerce; the National Democratic Institute for International Affairs, affiliated with the Democratic National Committee; an analogous body for the Republicans, National Republican Institute for International Affairs; and labor's Free Trade Union Institute. FTUI existed before the NED; it conducted overseas projects with labor's own funds and grants from AID. The other three were created at the same time as the NED, as recommended by the Democracy Program. FTUI has received the lion's share of the earmarked funds, presumably because with a large program already under way it was best equipped to use the funds efficiently.

Several reasons underlie the multiple structures. First, political parties, businesses, and labor unions are the bedrock of democratic societies. Second, this structure would ensure the multipartisan character essential to the NED's mission. A third reason may have been narrowly political: the structure vested a variety of constituencies with an interest in the NED.

In practice, however, the multiple institutes have proved as much a liability to NED as an asset in its relations with Congress. The legislators have been especially chary of the institutes affiliated with the political parties. They fear that their constituents might consider funding these bodies as somehow giving money to the legislators themselves. Many legislators suspect, from substantial experience, that such agencies concerned with international affairs may turn into slush funds for junkets. In addition the NED is naturally held responsible for the uses of all of its funds, but it exercises only limited control over disbursements made by the subsidiary institutes.

Support for Elections

Throughout its first half-decade, NED's support in Congress was shaky. The 1983 vote to create the endowment was backed by only a nineteen-vote margin in the House of Representatives. The next year the House voted 226 to 173 to abolish the endowment. This vote expressed congressional anger at discovering that NED funds earmarked for FTUI had been passed to a Panamanian labor union that used them in behalf of a candidate in Panama's presidential elections. The congressmen had reservations about the candidate the union backed and graver reservations in principle about the use of U.S. funds in foreign elections. That year the Senate saved the NED from the House's wrath (although it could not save the party institutes, which were barred from receiving funds until a year later, when Congress reversed itself). The endowment quickly adopted guidelines to prevent such use of its funds.

Elections nonetheless remain a key focus of NED-supported activity. NED funds have underwritten international observer teams that have sought to protect the integrity of elections in the Philippines, Pakistan, Taiwan, Chile, Nicaragua, Namibia, Eastern Europe, and elsewhere. Some less neutral forms of activity have also been supported, for example, voter registration and get-out-the-vote drives. The party-affiliated institutes also subsidize educational and research projects carried out by foreign parties with which they sympathize or more often by think tanks affiliated with those parties. But the critical boundary around all of this activity is the prohibited use of NED funds for any direct support of candidates.

Even nonpartisan activities can, however, determine the outcome of a foreign election, just as they sometimes do in America: for example, in the elections held in Grenada in 1986 after the American invasion. No one knew what to expect in the way of voter turnout. Grenada had been independent for only ten years, and in that time it had known only the elected but erratic rule of Eric Gairy and the *opéra bouffe* Stalinism of the New Jewel Movement. Some observers worried that this experience would make Grenadans cynical about politics and would keep them from the polls. Ironically that reaction could have worked to the benefit of Gairy and the NJM, both competing in the election, each with a dedicated band of hard-core followers. Into this picture stepped two NED affiliates, the Republican and the labor institutes. Working with local groups, they helped to organize a noisy get-out-the-vote drive.

They distributed T-shirts, bumper stickers, and ball point pens and provided free transportation to the polls. They did not support any candidates, but the large turnout of Grenada's silent majority resulted in a landslide victory for the centrist New Patriotic party. Gairy and the NJM were both routed.

NED programs strain the boundaries of nonpartisanship most when a foreign election is contested not between ordinary political forces—liberal versus conservative or labor versus business—but between one force convincingly dedicated to democracy and the other not. In such circumstances the outcome of one election may determine not merely who will take office but whether there will be another election. This was the case with the 1988 plebiscite in Chile on continuing the presidency of Augusto Pinochet for another eight years.

The plebiscite was intrinsically unfair—the voters could say only yes or no to Pinochet, with no choice of candidates. In addition Pinochet's government dominated the airwaves. But the democratic opposition decided to seize what chance it had and coalesced Left and Right in the "campaign for the no." This unity was facilitated by a dialogue among its disparate elements that had been under way for a few years, with some of the meetings underwritten by the NED and its Democratic party affiliate, NDI.

However unfair the terms of the plebiscite, it lent itself to the one resource that U.S. political parties could offer in abundance to the no coalition: campaign technique. In this realm of competition Pinochet and his military confreres, for all their power, were out of their depth. Under NDI auspices Democratic political professionals traveled to Chile to teach voter registration methods. Using sophisticated polling techniques, the Americans were able to offer guidance on the most effective themes for the no campaign. They also helped to shape the television spots for the fifteen minutes of nightly air time allotted to the no coalition during the last weeks of the campaign. The media experts of the no campaign even commissioned a campaign jingle that by some accounts became the most popular tune in Chile at the time. According to the NDI's report a poll by a Chilean opinion research organization

> showed that the effectiveness of the "no" media campaign far eclipsed that of the "yes." Chileans rated the "no" campaign highest in every category tested in the survey, including being "credible," "optimistic," "clearly understood," "dynamic," "motivating," and the "better choice," and in communicating its "capability in governing the country."[3]

The day of the vote, the opposition used computerized sampling and counting systems, with which the NDI had assisted, to monitor the results. This had important consequences. After the polls closed, the government announced that early returns showed the yes in the lead, but its leaders must have known better. Hours passed without official agencies releasing any further returns. At midnight the ruling junta suddenly convened. It may well have been discussing whether to prevent an honest count from being completed, much as Ferdinand Marcos had done in the Philippines in 1986 or Manuel Noriega was to do in Panama in 1989. During all this time, however, the opposition was releasing results from its sampling showing that no had won. At 2:30 in the morning, the junta adjourned its meeting and the government confirmed the victory of no. The presence of international observers, combined with the opposition's accurate and publicized measure of the outcome, must have diminished any temptation for the junta to abort the plebiscite.

The Nicaraguan election of 1990 was another case where the endowment role strained the bounds of nonpartisanship. Again democracy itself seemed to hang in the balance. The Sandinista National Liberation Front (FSLN) had governed since 1979 without allowing a free election or free speech. Although Nicaragua's rule was less than totalitarian, its rulers were dedicated Leninists who aimed to replicate familiar Communist models but were inhibited by armed opposition within and fear of further angering the U.S. public.[4] A matrix of diplomatic pressures—from Central America, the Soviet Union, and the West European Left—impelled the Sandinistas to put their rule to the electoral test. Had they received the legitimation they expected, they might have taken it as license to tighten their vise on Nicaraguan society. Electoral triumph for the opposition held the promise of putting Nicaragua at long last on a democratic path.

The Bush administration at first proposed to send funds through the NED to subsidize the campaign of the United Nicaraguan Opposition. UNO is a Left-to-Right coalition of opposition groups, similar to the Chilean no campaign, aligned behind the presidential candidacy of Violeta Chamorro. Critics argued that American funds would compromise UNO, but UNO itself was desperate for the help, as the Sandinistas were receiving assistance from their outside allies and freely using for electoral purposes the full resources of the state they controlled.

Congress, however, was reluctant to make an exception to the rules restraining NED's electoral activities, and so was the endowment's own board. As a compromise Congress voted a special appropriation to the NED for the Nicaraguan election. Some funds were sent directly to UNO, but they were earmarked for infrastructure—vehicles, office equipment, and the like—rather than immediate campaign expenditures. Other funds were allocated to the Institute for Electoral Training and Promotion, a UNO affiliate devoted to ensuring the election's integrity. The institute checked voter registration rolls, recruited and trained poll watchers, and distributed educational materials to familiarize voters with the election procedures. On election day a large voter turnout ousted the stunned Sandinistas from office.

Target Countries

Countries in Transition. Grenada, Chile, and Nicaragua all are what NED calls countries in transition. These are countries in which dictatorial rule has broken down—in Grenada because of the U.S. invasion, in Chile because of internal opposition and external isolation, in Nicaragua because of economic collapse, civil war, and the tremors in the Soviet bloc. In such transitions a path to democratic rule seems available if only the polity can be nudged in the right direction.

Less Open Countries. The endowment is active as well in many countries that have yet to reach a stage of transition, countries where dictatorial regimes still seem secure. These include the majority of the world's governments, and they can be arrayed along a continuum according to the degree of freedom they allow or the intensity of state control. In the most closed societies—hard-line Communist states like Cuba, North Korea, Albania, or Romania before the fall of Nicolae Ceausescu—there is virtually no way for the endowment to support democratizing elements inside the society, for no known organized groups exist. It is therefore limited to helping exiles. The endowment, for example, supported the efforts of Cuban poet and former political prisoner Armando Valladares to document Cuban human rights abuses to American and European audiences. This led to unprecedented criticism of Cuba by the United Nations Human Rights Commission and the first glimmerings of human rights activism within Cuba.

The endowment is supporting two Vietnamese periodicals, *Vietnam Moi?* published in Washington and *Que Me* published in France, both circulated clandestinely within Vietnam. Perhaps their ability to do so is one sign of the slight liberalizing trend that has been reported there.

In other Communist countries that are not so tightly closed, the NED seeks out projects that take advantage of any opening to pry the soceties open still further. The two most dramatic examples have been Poland and the People's Republic of China. In Poland Solidarity appeared to have been crushed by martial law in 1981, but although the gains it won were rolled back, it was far from eradicated. Indeed the fissures it dug in Poland's once totalitarian edifice were so deep and numerous that the entire structure was undermined. Leszek Kolakowski explained in 1987:

The heritage of Solidarity has affected Polish society so strongly that it can never be the same again. . . . [It] survives not only in the clandestine network of the union, which has been operating over all these years and frustrating many government assaults on the workers' rights. Its heritage survives as well in a number of bodies that, although they emerged under the umbrella of Solidarity, eventually became more or less independent from its network. Above all, the educational, cultural, and editorial activity in spite of continuing repression, functions on a scale that seems inconceivable by the standards of a communist state. Some forms of this activity are entirely clandestine, some semi-clandestine or grudgingly tolerated, especially if carried out under the Church's protection. Several hundred books come out in secret every year and several hundred independent journals appear continuously—from local bulletins to serious literary, philosophical, and political periodicals. Within this "second circulation," as it is called, freedom of expression is total and all sorts of political, theoretical, and artistic trends are voiced. . . . The police try to find and to confiscate printing machinery and sometimes, unfortunately, they succeed; they arrest printers and distributors; recently, they have begun to impose ruinous fines rather than jail penalties. The activity is going on nevertheless. The help that the National Endowment for Democracy gives those people is invaluable.[5]

The help Kolakowski referred to took the form of printing equipment and supplies and direct subsidies smuggled into Poland by support committees and labor organizations in the West and underwritten by the endowment. In addition to this widespread publishing, the opposition within Poland took up the strategy of constructing institutions of what they call civil society, outside official channels. They tried to render the authorities irrelevant to as much of the lives of as many people as possible. Beyond the network of underground publishing described by Kolakowski, these alternative institutions included an underground economy, "flying" universities to teach proscribed subjects, rudimentary programs of social welfare and medical care, and even an insurance fund to reimburse fines or punitive expropriations (such as of automobiles) levied by the state against those caught distributing underground literature or engaging in similar illicit activity.

The construction of these alternative institutions was supported in part by NED. Ultimately the strength and resilience of civil society proved so great that Poland's Communist rulers gave up their eight-year quest to restore the status quo ante Solidarity. In round-table talks at the beginning of 1989, they agreed to recognize Solidarity and to hold carefully circumscribed but free elections, which led to the end of their rule.

In China the openings for action were fewer than in Poland when the NED began. No independent groups could function in the People's Republic, but thousands of Chinese students had been sent to study in the West as part of the government's drive for modernization. Liang Heng, a Chinese exile who wrote a much celebrated account of his boyhood during the cultural revolution, proposed an intellectual magazine aimed at these overseas students.[6] With endowment support, he began to publish the *Chinese Intellectual*, a journal of culture and ideas. Though including criticism of Marxism-Leninism and Maoism and articles by such staunch anti-Communists as Sidney Hook and Seymour Martin Lipset, the *Chinese Intellectual* avoided a sharply political or polemical profile.

Perhaps because of this, the journal caught the reform winds that were blowing in China in the mid- to late-1980s, and these carried it further than either Liang Heng or the NED could have imagined. In 1985 Liang secured permission to mail copies into China. At least one issue was blocked by Chinese postal authorities for touching a nerve, but most editions went through, first to hundreds of addressees and later to thousands. Liang was allowed extended visits to China, where he enlisted the editor of an official publication as the Beijing representative of his magazine and got other mainland residents to agree to contribute to it. Eventually, backed by some liberal officials associated with Zhao Ziyang, Liang published the *Chinese Intellectual* inside China. In addition he secured permission, even government assistance, to open some teahouses in Beijing and other major cities as intellectual salons, centers for the discussion of political and economic ideas. Thus he nourished the growth of democratic ideas that reached its flower in Tiananmen Square in the spring of 1989.

When the regime's bloody crackdown came, Liang's patrons in the government were arrested or fled, his teahouses were closed, and he was forced to move his publishing operation back to the United States. He had to direct his work once again to the audience of overseas students, now larger and more restive than ever.

Communist regimes are not the only kinds of dictatorships in which the NED labors to expand the space for independent activity. In Paraguay the endowment subsidized Radio Nanduti, the main voice of opposition to the Alfredo Stroessner dictatorship. The station is a private business, but government pressure against its advertisers and other forms of harassment jeopardized its solvency and led it to the NED for help. In Guyana *Stabroek News*, a paper independent of the government, was successfully launched with backing from the endowment. In

Uganda a grant to the Uganda Human Rights Activists, an indigenous organization, enabled it to purchase a van and office equipment to facilitate its monitoring of rights abuses and to publish indigenous-language versions of the Universal Declaration of Human Rights. In Haiti a grant from the NED enabled the International Institute for Research and Development to bring together a forum of twenty-eight civic and political associations for a dialogue with the military government; this collaboration is a step toward the kind of democratic united front that proved so effective in Chile and Nicaragua.

Tenuous Democracies. Other endowment programs target countries where, despite transition to democratic rule, democracy has shallow roots. Elected government has never been as widespread in Latin America as it is today, but democratic rule has ebbed and flowed in the region throughout its 160-odd years of independence. To strengthen the new, fragile democracies of Latin America, NED supports a string of women's civic education associations. The first, Conciencia, was formed by twenty-two women in Argentina during the Falklands (Malvinas) war. It now claims some 8,000 members in twenty-nine chapters across Argentina; similar groups have sprung up, some with Conciencia's direct assistance, in Ecuador, Peru, Brazil, Colombia, Uruguay, Paraguay, and the Dominican Republic.

Both in Latin America and more recently in Eastern Europe, the NED has underwritten training programs for legislators and their staffs. The death knell of many democratic governments has been failure to provide effective government. America's trove of legislative experience can spare others time and pains.

Types of Programs

Programs such as these and election monitoring fall under the rubric "democratic governance and political process," one of three categories into which the NED divides its programs. The second, "education, culture and communications," includes support for Radio Nanduti, Poland's underground publishing, and the like.

A similar program aims to propagate democratic thought in Central America. It is the publishing house Libro Libre. Its director, Xavier Zavala, explained his motivation:

> At the end of the 1950s, university studies were reformed. . . . [to] give young people a complete, balanced, humanist foundation, something similar to a liberal arts college education in the United States. . . . before beginning their strictly professional studies.
> But . . . . [t]he new, obligatory courses in philosophy, his-

tory, culture, national reality, and so forth, provided the perfect opportunity to indoctrinate the young university students against democracy and in favor of Soviet totalitarianism. Let me give you an example. . . . There is, still today, in truly democratic Costa Rica, a national university that officially establishes as an objective of some general studies courses that the student should "become conscious of economic and cultural dependency . . . and endorse the Cuban revolution as an option for the overcoming of underdevelopment and dependency."

. . . . Publishing companies have been set up to produce and supply the necessary books. . . . [L]et us examine the texts on sale at Panama's National University bookstore. Just this past April, more than 80 percent of the titles for sale in the political science section were published by pro-Soviet publishing houses; for history, more than 50 percent; and for economics, 39 percent. It is interesting to observe that these specially created publishing houses do not seem to be interested in presenting other versions of Marxism, for example contemporary Euro-communism.[7]

With the virtual phasing out of USIA's book programs in the 1960s, the leftist publishers that Zavala describes have operated virtually uncontested. Little wonder that the war of ideas among the youth of Central America seemed in recent decades so one-sided. Zavala aims to lessen this imbalance by publishing contemporary works by prodemocratic Central Americans as well as Spanish translations of classics of democratic thought: John Locke, Alexis de Tocqueville, *The Federalist*, and the like.

The NED labels its third category of programs "pluralism." Strong and numerous private, voluntary associations conduce to democracy: they disperse power throughout society and give the individual citizen a strong and attainable structure that can get the attention of government. Building up such mediating institutions can help fortify fledgling democracies. Even in dictatorships, if they are not totalitarian, such institutions can dilute centralized power. A classic mediating institution is the labor union, and the largest NED program for building pluralism is assistance to labor organizing sponsored by FTUI.

The NED also encourages pluralism on the other side. The Center for International Private Enterprise encourages the growth of private enterprise in countries where it has been discouraged or suppressed. It may not be true that, as some conservatives argue, enlarging the public sector necessarily vitiates freedom, at least not in a country with firm democratic traditions like Sweden or England. But enlarging the private sector necessarily vitiates dictatorship. Some dictatorships have free market economies, but dispersing economic power is an effective way of dispersing power.

CIPE's most famous work has been its patronage of Hernando de Soto, author of *El Otro Sendero* (*The Other Path*), one of the most read and talked about books in recent Latin American history. De Soto has become the publicist and champion of the informal sector of the economy, which he claimed produces as much as 38 percent of the gross domestic product in his native Peru. This sector consists of those who "although pursuing legal ends, such as building a house or operating a business, have not met all of the legal requirements to do so."[8]

Contrary to the premise of most political debate over whether Latin America's problems can be solved by moving from capitalism to socialism, de Soto argued that Latin America has yet to reach capitalism. It languishes instead, he said, in a kind of precapitalist mercantilism in which a thicket of state regulation strangles private enterprise. His Institute for Liberty and Democracy found that in Peru "it took 289 days—working eight hours a day—to register legally a small business with two sewing machines. The same experiment in Tampa, Florida took three and a half hours."[9] As a result much enterprise is pushed outside the law. That is why there is the huge informal sector.

From a political standpoint it is unhealthy for laws to be so widely disregarded, but does this situation matter from an economic standpoint? Doesn't de Soto's own evidence of the vast size of the informal sector show that private enterprise is proceeding satisfactorily outside the law? Not at all, argues de Soto. The informal sector operates under many dire constraints, such as the absence of credit at less than usurious terms and the unavailability of insurance. The same initiative and energy in businesses functioning within a normal free market would produce vastly bigger enterprises, more jobs, more profits, and more economic growth.

Aid to Democrats

Overarching these three categories of NED work is the most important: succoring democrats. Democracy comes about through a series of voluntary decisions by individuals who decide they want democracy. Democracies are rich and are poor, democracies are large and are small, democracies are homogeneous and are heterogeneous, democracies are Western and Eastern. Various sociological factors conduce to democracy, but only one ingredient is essential: democrats. Whether Zavala with his books or Liang with his magazine or Humberto Rubin with his Radio Nanduti; the underground civil society of Solidarity or the women of Conciencia; the campaign for the "no" or the campaign of UNO: the activity or tactics matter less than the simple fact that democrats are fighting for democracy. The essence of the endowment's work is to find democrats and support them.

One of NED's most striking accomplishments is its creation of an informal democrats' international, the counterpart of the Socialist or Communist International. In part it has done this through specific projects. The National Democratic Institute's delegation of twenty-five to monitor the October 5, 1988, elections in Chile included only nine Americans. The others were from fourteen countries including Haiti, Hungary, Poland, South Africa, the Philippines, El Salvador, and Nicaragua. The democratic winds that have blown over Latin America, East Asia, and Eastern Europe are just beginning to reach the shores of Africa, whose societies have grown exhausted with years of one-party misrule. With support from the NED the Senegal-based Centre d'Etudes et de Recherche sur la Democratie Pluraliste dans le Tiers Monde convened a conference of African democrats in late 1990 in Dakar, a first step toward a continental mutual support network. The endowment also supports Exchange, a program run by Freedom House that links some four hundred democrats in fifty countries. Documents concerning the political struggles of exchange members are mailed to the membership and create a sense of international solidarity.

Building up this kind of international is a conscious goal of the NED's president, Carl Gershman, who said: "Ultimately, the effectiveness of the Endowment derives from the existence abroad of people who are passionately and courageously devoted to democracy. These people, with whom the Endowment has established bonds of solidarity and cooperation, are part of a world wide democratic movement whose impact is already being felt."[10] In 1987 and in 1989 the endowment sponsored well-publicized conferences in Washington attended by leading democratic figures from all over the world. And in 1990 it launched (with private money) a scholarly quarterly, the *Journal of Democracy*, casting the subject of democratization in global perspective.

Support for NED

In 1989, as in each previous year of NED's existence, voices in Congress were raised against the NED. But the voices have been muted, the negative arguments have become qualified, and the grounds of debate have shifted. For FY1990 the issue was not whether to abolish the NED but whether Congress should increase its authorization to $25 million from the $15 million requested by the Bush administration. Even opponents of the increase argued little more than that the House should wait until it received an evaluation of the NED's effectiveness from the General Accounting Office.[11]

But the work of the NED necessarily defies the measuring instruments of the GAO. The best evidence of the effects of the activities supported by the endowment comes from the beneficiaries. During his visit to Washington Lech Walesa spoke of the importance to Solidarity of the support from American labor, a good part of it sustained by NED funds. Senator Fritz Hollings, the chairman of the subcommittee that oversees appropriations for the NED, was long the endowment's most powerful critic. But in 1989 he joined the move to increase the NED's funding after hearing from Ivan Havel, the brother of Czechoslovakia's president, of the difference that the NED made to the democracy movement in his country.

Would Solidarity have triumphed in Poland without outside assistance? Would the no campaign in Chile? The leaders of those movements have testified that NED support was important to them. Conversely would some tragic historical situations have ended differently had support been available to the democratic side? The NED did not exist in 1979, when the Sandinistas triumphed in Nicaragua. Throughout Anastasio Somoza's reign his democratically oriented opponents were more numerous than the small band of Sandinistas, but the democrats were disorganized and feckless. Had there been a force to strengthen those democrats, Nicaragua might have been spared its terrible Sandinista interlude. The Sandinista's triumph was a close call. The same might be said about the triumph of Lenin and even Hitler. How might history have been different if assistance had been available to the Constitutional Democrats, Mensheviks, and Right Socialist Revolutionaries in and around 1917 or to the democratic parties of the Weimar Republic?

Despite the uncertainties and the remaining doubters, the majority of Congress seems convinced of the usefulness of the NED, as evidenced by the 1990 decision to raise its budget. And some observers, like the *New Republic*'s Morton Kondracke, have suggested that this increase from $15 million to $25 million ought to be followed by another increase to $100 million.[12]

Involvement of the Private Sector

Another potential source for expanding the work of the endowment is the private sector. The endowment works through private sector groups but with public money. The small human rights and exile groups that constitute the majority of NED grantees could not carry out these programs with their own funds. But NED President Gershman would like to see public funds matched or even surpassed by the private sector. The endowment could serve as a clearinghouse, helping to link struggling democrats abroad with potential patrons in the United States.

Labor does put some of its own funds into overseas work, and a few businessmen, many of them emigrants to America, have donated their own money to political development projects, often in their countries of origin. The most promising source of private support is the charitable or nonprofit sector. Three kinds of organizations are most important, one for what it is already doing and two for what they could do. Human rights organizations already make an enormous contribution to the development of democracy. Freedom House, Amnesty International, the International League for Human Rights, and a host of smaller groups have succored persecuted democrats, pressured abusive governments, compiled timely information about human rights and freedom, and kept these issues high on the public agenda. Unfortunately some groups with antidemocratic agendas, including several whose main interest seems to be supporting Communist movements in Latin America, have masqueraded as human rights organizations, but the harm they have done is hard to measure.

Churches and charitable foundations could make an even larger contribution to spreading democracy. Both of these sectors spend millions of dollars a year on overseas programs. Much supports good works far removed from politics: health, nutrition, and, for the churches, missionary activity. But much too supports programs that are political at least in a broad sense. For 1990–1991 the Ford Foundation budgeted $43 million for international affairs programs devoted to "international economics and development," "peace, security, and arms control," "international refugees and migration," "international organizatons and law," and "U.S. foreign policy."[13] Another $63 million was budgeted for "human rights and social justice," with a large proportion for international work. The Carnegie Corporation spent more than $10 million in 1989 on international programming, with about 85 percent of it programs "to encourage recognition that the threat of nuclear war requires transformations in the way humanity handles international conflict" and most of the rest for "public understanding of development."[14] Little was used to encourage democracy. Some—such as large Ford Foundation grants to the Sandinista-advocacy group, the Washington Office on Latin America—actually helped buttress democracy's enemies.

The situation with the churches is yet more disappointing. Unlike the foundations, they are not required to make full financial disclosures, and they have proved remarkably reluctant to lay out their financial records. Clearly, however, tens of millions are spent on overseas programs, and clearly too a large share of this has been going to support liberation theology and similar leftist antidemocratic causes. The churches even more than the foundations seem to have difficulties shedding the leftist fashions of the 1960s, but surely that is overdue. Most of this pro-Communist foolishness has been motivated by humanitarian impulses. Perhaps the events of 1989 will prove powerful enough to bring home to the churches and foundations the reality that the one revolution of modern times that has not betrayed its humanitarian impulses is the democratic revolution. They have much mischief to atone for, but they can atone for much by directing their resources to helping spread that revolution in the 1990s.

14
Conclusion

In the first chapter I stated a case for the promotion of democracy as the centerpiece of American foreign policy. The spread of democracy is good for America, and promoting it brings benefits of its own. In the next four chapters I attempted to place this argument in the context of U.S. diplomatic experience, to criticize some contrary approaches to foreign policy, and to refute some objections to my proposal, such as the argument that America must adapt itself to inevitable decline. In chapter 6 I tried to prove that democracy can take hold over large parts of the globe, notwithstanding great variations in history, culture, and prosperity. I went on to show that American efforts can help to make this happen. I demonstrated, in chapters 7 through 13, that America has already contributed in numerous ways to the phenomenal growth of democracy. When modern democracy was born on these shores in 1776, it encompassed a million or so citizens, one- or two-tenths of 1 percent of the world's population. Today 2 billion people live under democratic government, about 40 percent of mankind. America has been the engine of much of this transformation.

A Continuation

To export democracy, we need only continue doing what we have done since World War II. To make democracy the centerpiece of our policy, we need to do some things more and better. To begin with, we must guard against a relapse of isolationism. Only the cold war brought America to sustained engagement with the world. The end of the cold war has already given rise to voices beckoning us to turn inward again. Such counsel prevailed at the end of World War I, and America's rapid return to isolation helped bring about World War II. Such counsel prevailed again at the end of that war, at least to the extent of demobilizing our forces without assessing the new configuration of international politics; that helped to bring about the cold war including the hot episode in Korea. We should learn from these mistakes.

We should learn too from our successes. We have won a magnificent victory in the cold war. And we have won it at a low price. This is not to belittle the sacrifice of the thousands of Americans who gave their lives in the cold war—in Korea, in Vietnam, or elsewhere. But still the price was low measured against the sacrifice required to defeat fascism or against the fearsomeness of our nuclear armed foe. Moreover this victory has come not on the battlefield but in the hearts and minds of Poles and Hungarians, Czechs and Germans, Lithuanians and Russians—and ultimately even Communists. It has come from the triumph of democracy over communism in the war of ideas.

With the cold war over, our lives will be far less dangerous. But we cannot foresee the exact form of the new global politics or new problems in other directions. Rather than withdraw into ourselves, we ought to press ahead with what has brought us this success—the advancement of the democratic idea. Although promoting democracy is not easy, we have done it with success, and it will be easier now. In 1917, just as the United States—the prime bearer of the democratic idea—made its full entry onto the international stage, a competitive idea was born. It was a great source of obfuscation because, misshapen as it was, communism traced its roots to the same Enlightenment soil that spawned democracy. And communism's claim to fulfill the same purpose as democracy—the liberation of the human individual—but better or more completely, sapped democracy's appeal. With communism dead, democracy will not find itself unchallenged. It may be challenged, for example, by some forms of religious fanaticism, but it is not likely to face soon a competitor that appeals to democracy's own sources of legitimacy.

Two basic truths should inform our foreign policy. First, America is a great force for good in the world. Neither a natural impulse to modesty nor the unnatural national self-hatred espoused by the Left ought to deafen us to the eloquent words of appreciation from Lech Walesa and Vaclav Havel and from ordinary students and workers who have spoken warmly of America's contribution to their liberation. It is important for us to recognize the great difference our efforts can make.

Second, what is good for democracy is good for America. There may be occasional short-term exceptions. One particular autocracy might be more responsive to an interest of ours than one democracy. But we ought never to forget the general rule that the more democratic the world becomes, the more likely it is to be both peaceful and friendly to America.

A Choice of Methods

The end of the cold war will influence the methods used in our continuing quest to spread democracy. Military occupation and covert action have been highly effective means of spreading democracy, but they are byproducts of war and cold war. A world without cold war, and presumably with little actual war, offers less occasion for these methods. Moreover, as communism disappears and the world grows more democratic, there will be principled reasons to forgo such methods. The heretofore utopian goal of a world of law may draw within reach. As long as America was locked in mortal combat with totalitarian foes that in principle heeded no law, we could not safely bind ourselves to constraints that did not bind our adversaries. International law under those circumstances was a snare.

International law could take told, however, in a world increasingly dominated by democracies. America surely wants to encourage this possibility. A regime of international law presents fewer opportunities to spread democracy by the sword. It would be hard to justify our recent invasion of Panama, although it was a blessing for the Panamanians. International law does allow self-defense. If we are victims of aggression, we can use the occasion not only to defeat but also to democratize our attacker, as we did with Japan. Such occasions, however, are likely to be rare.

Covert action is a valuable capability that we cannot afford to abandon as long as threats to our security persist, even more modest ones than Soviet communism once posed. But as threats of that nature diminish, covert action would be hard to justify solely for spreading democracy. Such action has contributed to the growth of democracy—in postwar Italy, for example—but secretiveness and manipulation suit poorly to democratic ends. Funneling aid to democratic forces is better done openly through the National Endowment for Democracy and the private sector.

While sheathing the more forceful instruments of democratization, we ought to strengthen the peaceful ones. Recent changes in international politics offer better opportunities for promoting democracy through diplomacy. Namibia and Nicaragua are dramatic examples. Our diplomats should tirelessly advocate free elections to resolve regional and internecine disputes. Past efforts were largely futile because Communists refused to recognize the legitimacy of free elections or insisted disingenuously on defining them differently. We thought that Joseph Stalin had agreed at Yalta to free elections in Eastern Europe, but instead crude mock-elections confirmed Communist dictatorships.

In the era of Mikhail Gorbachev the Communists have agreed that elections are the logical means of expressing popular will and that real elections require multiple candidates, free speech, and an honest count. Not only have the Soviets begun to hold some such elections, they apparently urged the same on their clients in Namibia and Nicaragua.

223

American diplomacy should strive to reinforce this emerging international consensus about the meaning and value of free elections. We should apply this to the conflicts in Afghanistan, Cambodia, Angola, and Mozambique. The conflicts in El Salvador, in South Africa, and between the Arabs and Israel, have unique complications, but elections should figure as a key part of a settlement in these situations too.

Our foreign aid budget, as a portion of our gross national product, is at an all-time low. In general, foreign aid has no natural political constituency. As Poland and Hungary began the transition from communism in 1989, the Bush administration proposed minuscule aid; Congress stepped in and increased the appropriation several-fold. When Panama and Nicaragua were liberated and the administration proposed to facilitate their democratic transition, Congress balked. Apparently trying to prove to voters that it could be as frugal as the president, it proved only that it could be as short-sighted.

The current $5–6 billion in economic assistance should be increased several billion, with the additional funds earmarked for democratic transition and reinforcement. Some funds should support the components of democratic government: the technology required for fair elections, the training and facilities for organizing judicial systems and legislatures. Others should aid the economy of fledgling democracies. Poland, for example, is attempting an immediate and painful switch to a market economy. It has a plethora of would-be entrepreneurs. But it has no banking system: aspiring Horatio Algers carry bundles of cash for each business transaction. We might help start a real bank, among other things. The change to a market economy, whether in Communist countries or in third world countries that have had state-dominated economies, involves painful, short-term losses for at least part of the population. These conditions may threaten the survival of fledgling democratic governments. We ought to be ready with aid to ease this process. In some third world countries young democratic governments are threatened by the burden of foreign debt, often accumulated by their dictatorial predecessors. Here too we should be ready with some form of relief.

The budget for the United States Information Agency is just less than $1 billion: it ought to be increased by a few hundred million. We also ought to put USIA back in the book business. The classics of democratic thought ought to be in print in as many languages as are the bankrupt classics of Marxism-Leninism, and they ought to be available in every university in the world. In the early 1980s Congress approved an overdue plan for modernizing the transmitting facilities of the Voice of America. As Gramm-Rudman legislation and unfavorable fluctuations in exchange rates squeezed VOA's budget, the Congress and administration have repeatedly shifted funds from capital improvements to operating expenses. As a result, VOA's signal does not reach all its intended audiences and is too easily jammed. The modernization program should be restored. A research and development account to refine the technology for the broadcast and reception of television signals via satellite ought to be funded. The goal should be satellite dishes so small and cheap that they are easy to afford and easy to conceal—advancing the day when VOA can be superseded by TVOA.

The appropriation for the National Endowment for Democracy was increased for FY1991 from $17 to 25 million. This 50 percent increase proves that after six years of operation the NED has convinced Congress of its effectiveness. But this increased budget does not equal NED's budget in its first year in constant dollars. A series of further increases is needed in yearly increments so they can be effectively absorbed. Because of congressional and administration penury the NED has been able to fund only a fraction of even its most successful programs and has been forced to reject most new proposals virtually out of hand. In the wake of the momentous spring of 1989, the endowment is able to allocate a grand total of a few hundred thousand dollars to sustain China's democracy movement. Its programs barely touch Africa (other than South Africa) and the rest of Asia.

All told, the investment of a few billion dollars in annual budget increases for foreign aid, USIA, and the NED can sustain the momentum of the democratic revolution and can bring political and security returns of incalculable value. Even if we are not wise enough to do this, the American example continues as a force for democratization. As technology brings the world closer and closer together, the impact of American popular culture continues to grow. MacDonald's opens on Red Square, and President Havel hosts Frank Zappa. There is something of the democratic ethic in the world's most popular garment, blue jeans, that even designer labels have not been able to destroy.

The force of America's example requires little conscious effort on our part except vigilance to refine and safeguard our own democratic ways. The civil rights movement was the most important refinement to our democracy this century, and its stirring example has inspired protest movements in distant places. On the first anniversary of the massacre in Tiananmen Square, 100,000 Chinese marched in Hong Kong singing "China Shall Be Free" to the tune of "We Shall Overcome."[1]

Although the force of our example works on its own, it can be augmented by what the United States says directly to the world. Theodore Roosevelt said the presidency was a bully pulpit, and with the growth of communications technology the pews now extend into every continent. President Ronald Reagan was a peerless articulator of the democratic creed. But an American president need not have his forensic talent to make a huge impact. The uncharismatic Jimmy Carter did much to launch the global wave of democratization through his advocacy of human rights, although his delivery was rarely inspiring. As a rhetorician, President George Bush is more in Carter's league than Reagan's. But more important the president should see himself not merely as custodian of the country, but as the leader of the democratic movement.

The American president also has an important message to deliver to the domestic private sector about the democratic revolution abroad. Private institutions can assume a much bigger part. The for-profit sector should be aggressive in investing and assisting in the economic development of countries that are changing over to democracy and market economies. The nonprofit sector, especially foundations and churches, should be contributing more to building the infrastructure of democracy and free speech.

Our Priority

The special priority for all of these efforts, public and private, in the immediate future must be the Soviet Union and China. Democracy is within reach in both of those huge countries. Much to the confoundment of conventional wisdom, both have shown that millions of their citizens yearn for democracy and are willing to fight for it. Our minimum effort must include providing VOA with the resources to overcome Beijing's jamming and to extend its service into China's other dialects besides Mandarin and a few weekly hours in Cantonese; it must underwrite through the NED the democracy movement of overseas and exile Chinese and provide them with the technical resources to maintain their linkages with their fellows inside China; and it must increase diplomatic and economic pressures on the Chinese government.

We should offer the Soviet Union moral and diplomatic encouragement for Gorbachev's reforms and gentle pressures to keep them moving forward, including succor for more radical forces symbolized by Boris Yeltsin. And we should give material support, through the NED, to all manner of independent prodemocracy political groups, publications, labor unions, and the like. Through USIA we ought to expand exchanges with the Soviet Union, especially large-scale student exchanges, and offer training programs for legislators, journalists, and lawyers whose professions are changing radically under the impetus of democratization. We ought also to press the Soviets to proceed with shifting to a market economy, including offering material inducements, and we ought to encourage investment in the nascent Soviet private sector.

The triumph of democracy in China and the Soviet Union would mean that democracy would become the global norm and eventually triumph almost everywhere. The specter of nuclear war that has over-shadowed the world since World War II would be mitigated. Democracy in China and the USSR may not be easy to achieve, but it is not much more far-fetched than the idea of democracy in India or Japan had been at one time. In both China and the Soviet Union the old structures are crumbling, and democracy is a possible outcome. For our nation, this is the opportunity of a lifetime. Our failure to exert every possible effort to secure this outcome would be unforgivable.

If we succeed, we will have forged a Pax Americana unlike any previous peace, one of harmony, not of conquest. Then the twenty-first century will be the American century by virtue of the triumph of the humane idea born in the American experiment: all men are created equal and endowed with unalienable rights. Ironically America's relative power in such a world—measured in the old-fashioned coin of guns and dollars—would diminish as other nations imitated the secrets of our success. Yet we would stand triumphant for achieving by our model and our influence the visionary goal stamped by the founding fathers on the seal of the United States: *novus ordo seclorum*, a new order of the ages.

Notes

CHAPTER 1: THE STRENGTH OF DEMOCRATIC IDEALS

1. In a talk given at the Heritage Foundation, Washington, D.C., July 16, 1990.

2. Mikhail Gorbachev, *Perestroika: New Thinking for Our Country and the World* (New York: Harper & Row, 1987), pp. 26, 32.

3. For a fuller account of my views, see my "Gorbachev, the True Communist," *American Enterprise*, vol. 1, no. 2 (March/April 1990), pp. 38–45; also reprinted as "Gorbachev's Intellectual Odyssey," *New Republic*, March 5, 1990, pp. 20–25.

4. Sarah Lubman, "The Myth of Tianamen Square: The Students Talked Democracy, but They Didn't Practice It," *Washington Post*, July 30, 1989, p. C5; Daniel Benjamin, "State of Siege: With Tianamen Square the Epicenter, a Political Quake Convulses China," *Time*, vol. 133, no. 22, p. 44; and Charles Paul Freund, "Rise of the Noble Crowd: The Legacy of Tianamen Square," *Washington Post*, June 4, 1989, p. B4.

5. See, for example, R. J. Rummel, "The Freedom Factor," *Reason*, no. 15 (July 1983), pp. 32–38; Michael W. Doyle, "Liberalism and World Politics," *American Political Science Review*, vol. 80, no. 4, pp. 1151–1169; and Bruce Russett, "The Politics of an Alternative Security System: Toward a More Democratic and Therefore More Peaceful World," in Burns Weston, ed., *Alternatives to Nuclear Deterrence* (Boulder, Colo.: Westview Press, forthcoming).

6. Paul Gottfried, "At Sea with the Global Democrats," *Wall Street Journal*, January 19, 1989; Patrick J. Buchanan, "America First—and Second, and Third," *National Interest*, no. 19 (Spring 1990), p. 81.

7. See Howard M. Sachar, *A History of Israel: From the Rise of Zionism to Our Time* (New York: Alfred A. Knopf, 1982), pp. 315–18.

8. Immanuel Kant, *Kant's Political Writings*, ed. Hans Reiss, trans. H. B. Nisbet (Cambridge: Cambridge University Press, 1970), p. 100, cited in Doyle, "Liberalism," p. 1160.

CHAPTER 2: CURRENTS IN AMERICAN FOREIGN POLICY

1. Robert Endicott Osgood, *Ideals and Self-Interest in America's Foreign Relations* (Chicago: University of Chicago Press, 1953), p. 264.

2. Ibid., p. 364.

3. See Walter Laqueur, *New Isolationism and the World of the Seventies*, The Washington Papers, no. 5 (New York: Library Press, 1972), and Norman Podhoretz, "The Present Danger," *Commentary*, vol. 69, no. 3 (March 1980), p. 27.

4. Jerald A. Combs, *American Diplomatic History: Two Centuries of Changing Interpretations* (Berkeley: University of California Press, 1983), p. 114.

5. See Robert H. Ferrell, *Peace in Their Time* (New Haven: Yale University Press, 1952), p. 260.

6. Absolute pacifists, never more than a small band, appear to have suffered a further thinning of ranks recently as Quaker activists under the banner of the American Friends Service Committee have come to embrace revolutionary violence. See Guenter Lewy, *Peace and Revolution: The Moral Crisis of American Pacifism* (Grand Rapids, Mich.: W. B. Eerdman's Pub. Co., 1988).

7. U.S., Congress, House Committee on House Administration, *The Presidential Campaign 1976* vol. 1, pt. 2, *Jimmy Carter* (Washington, D.C.: U.S. Government Printing Office, 1978), p. 272.

CHAPTER 3: THE FOLLY OF REALISM

1. John Quincy Adams, Fourth of July Address, 1821.

2. Quoted in Robert Endicott Osgood, *Ideals and Self-Interest in America's Foreign Relations* (Chicago: University of Chicago Press, 1953), p. 273.

3. Reinhold Niebuhr, *The Structure of Nations and Empires* (New York: Charles Scribner's Sons, 1959), p. 29.

4. Walter Lippmann, *U.S. Foreign Policy: Shield of the Republic* (New York: Pocket Books, 1943), p. 27.

5. Ibid., pp. 26, 24.

6. Ibid., p. 17.

7. George F. Kennan, *American Diplomacy, 1900–1950* (Chicago: University of Chicago Press, 1951), pp. 65–66.

8. Ibid., p. 95.

9. Hans J. Morgenthau, *In Defense of the National Interest* (New York: Knopf, 1951), p. 7.

10. Ibid., p. 13ff.

11. Kennan, *American Diplomacy*, p. 100.

12. Hamilton cited in Morgenthau, *The National Interest*, pp. 15–16.

13. Arthur M. Schlesinger, Jr., *The Cycles of American History* (Boston: Houghton Mifflin, 1986), p. 71.

14. Ibid., p. 73.

15. Kennan, *American Diplomacy*, pp. 53, 102–103.

16. Morgenthau, *The National Interest*, pp. 35, 36.

17. Clinton Rossiter, ed., *The Federalist Papers* (New York: Mentor Books, 1961), p. 59.

18. Reinhold Niebuhr, *The Children of Light and the Children of Darkness* (1944 reprint, New York: Charles Scribner's Sons, 1960), p. ix.

19. Kennan, *American Diplomacy*, p. 53.

20. Niebuhr, *Children of Light*, p. 11.

21. Osgood, *Ideals and Self-Interest*, p. 13.

22. Hans J. Morgenthau, *Politics among Nations: The Struggle for Power and Peace*, sixth ed., revised by Kenneth W. Thompson (New York: Alfred A. Knopf, 1985), p. 13.

23. Schlesinger, *Cycles*, p. 77.

24. Morgenthau, *Politics among Nations*, p. 4.

25. Ibid., p. 10.

26. Ibid., p. 5.

27. Schlesinger, *Cycles*, p. 76.

28. Morgenthau, *Politics among Nations*, p. 5.

29. See Joshua Muravchik, "Is Israel Good for America?" *National Review*, vol. 38, no. 5 (March 28, 1986), pp. 36–43.

30. Graham T. Allison, *Essence of Decision* (Boston: Little, Brown, 1971); Morton Halperin, *Bureaucratic Politics and Foreign Policy* (Washington, D.C.: Brookings Institution, 1974). Allison's book was organized around a case study of the Cuban missile crisis. His key concept—"where you stand is where you sit"—was refuted by his own study. The conflicting recommendations that he reported were voiced within the inner circle of President Kennedy's advisers bore little relation to the institutional positions occupied by the protagonists and much more to their varying outlooks and dispositions.

31. Arnold Wolfers, *Discord and Collaboration* (Baltimore: Johns Hopkins University Press, 1962), p. 73.

32. Morgenthau, *The National Interest*, p. 6.

33. The United Nations constitutes an insignificant exception insofar as the UN Charter

proclaims goals in the realm of human rights as well as peace and can be said therefore to embody democratic idealism as well as pacifist idealism. Nonetheless the UN system rests on the premise of the equal legitimacy of each sovereign member, the vast majority of which from the time of the UN's founding to this day are not democracies. Although the UN pays homage to human rights, its prime purpose is as a peacemaking institution.

34. Lippmann, *U.S. Foreign Policy*, pp. 33–38; Osgood, *Ideals and Self-Interest*, pp. 115–17.

35. Kennan, *American Diplomacy*, pp. 65–66, 87–88.

36. Morgenthau, *The National Interest*, p. 5.

37. Schlesinger, *Cycles*, pp. 84–85.

38. One admirable exception, with regard to Nicaragua, is Christopher Layne. See his "The Real Conservative Agenda," *Foreign Policy*, no. 61 (Winter 1985–1986), p. 92.

39. Morgenthau, *The National Interest*, p. 132.

40. Schlesinger, *Cycles*, p. 77.

41. Ibid., p. 78.

42. Aleksandr Solzhenitsyn, *Warning to the West* (New York: Farrar, Straus and Giroux, 1976), p. 48.

43. Francis Fukuyama, "The End of History?" *National Interest*, no. 16 (Summer 1989), pp. 3–18.

44. See Joshua Muravchik, *The Uncertain Crusade: Jimmy Carter and the Dilemmas of Human Rights Policy* (Lanham, Md.: Hamilton Press, 1986), chap. 6.

CHAPTER 4: NEOREALISM

1. Stanley Hoffmann, "Realism and Its Discontents," *Atlantic*, November 1985, p. 131.

2. See Kenneth N. Waltz, *Theory of International Politics* (Reading, Mass.: Addison-Wesley, 1979), and Robert O. Keohane, ed., *Neorealism and its Critics* (New York: Columbia University Press, 1986).

3. See J. David Singer, "The Level of Analysis Problem in International Relations," in Claus Knorr and Sydney Verba, eds., *The International System: Theoretical Essays* (Princeton, N.J.: Princeton University Press, 1961).

4. Tom J. Farer, "Searching for Defeat," *Foreign Policy*, no. 40 (Fall 1980), p. 171.

5. Leon Wieseltier, "What Went Wrong? An Appraisal of Reagan's Foreign Policy," *New York Times Magazine*, December 7, 1986, p. 137.

6. Ibid., p. 43.

7. Ibid., p. 137.

8. Ibid.

9. Arthur M. Schlesinger, Jr., "A Democrat Looks at Foreign Policy," *Foreign Affairs*, vol. 66, no. 2 (Winter 1987–1988), p. 283.

10. Arthur M. Schlesinger, Jr., "The Imperial Temptation," *New Republic*, March 16, 1987, p. 18.

11. Schlesinger, "A Democrat Looks," pp. 278–79.

12. Arthur M. Schlesinger, Jr., *The Cycles of American History* (Boston: Houghton Mifflin, 1986), pp. 81–82.

13. Schlesinger, "A Democrat Looks," p. 278.

14. Schlesinger, *Cycles*, p. 81.

15. Alan Tonelson, "The Real National Interest," *Foreign Policy*, no. 61 (Winter 1985–1986), p. 51.

16. Christopher Layne, "The Real Conservative Agenda," *Foreign Policy*, no. 61 (Winter 1985–1986), p. 75.

17. Ibid.

18. Tonelson, "National Interest," p. 49.

19. Ibid., p. 50.

20. Ibid., p. 71.

21. Layne, "The Real Conservative Agenda," p. 84.

22. Ibid., p. 87.

23. Ibid.

24. Ibid., pp. 92, 91.

25. Ibid., p. 92.

26. Tonelson, "National Interest," p. 70.

27. Robert W. Tucker, "Isolation and Intervention," *National Interest*, no. 1 (Fall 1985), p. 23.

28. Irving Kristol, "Foreign Policy in an Age of Ideology," *National Interest*, no. 1 (Fall 1985), p. 8.

29. Ibid., pp. 14–15.

30. Irving Kristol, "'Human Rights': The Hidden Agenda," *National Interest*, no. 6 (Winter 1986–1987), p. 9.

31. Ibid., p. 11.

32. Quote from Owen Harries et al., *The Reagan Doctrine and Beyond* (Washington, D.C.: American Enterprise Institute, 1987), pp. 24–25.

33. Charles Krauthammer, "Isolationism, Left and Right," *New Republic*, March 4, 1985, p. 21.

34. Patrick J. Buchanan, "America First—and Second, and Third," *National Interest*, no. 19 (Spring 1990), p. 80.

35. Mihajlo Mihajlov, "Prospects for the Post-Tito Era," *New America*, vol. 17 (January 1980), p. 7, quoted in Samuel P. Huntington, *The Dilemma of American Ideals and Institutions in Foreign Policy* (Washington, D.C.: American Enterprise Institute, 1981), p. 15.

Chapter 5: Is America in Decline?

1. Samuel P. Huntington, "The U.S.—Decline or Renewal?" *Foreign Affairs*, vol. 67, no. 2 (Winter 1988–1989), pp. 76–97.

2. Peter Schmeisser, "Taking Stock: Is America in Decline?" *New York Times Magazine*, April 17, 1988, pp. 24–26.

3. Owen Harries, "The Rise of American Decline," *Commentary*, vol. 85, no. 5 (May 1988), p. 32.

4. Mancur Olson, *The Rise and Decline of Nations* (New Haven: Yale University Press, 1981), p. 236.

5. Paul Kennedy, *The Rise and Fall of Great Powers* (New York: Random House, 1987), p. xxii.

6. Ibid., pp. 514–15.

7. David P. Calleo, *Beyond American Hegemony* (New York: Basic Books, 1987), p. 9.

8. Ibid., p. 125.

9. Ibid.

10. Walter Russell Mead, *Mortal Splendor: The American Empire in Transition* (Boston: Houghton Mifflin, 1987), p. 274.

11. Ibid., p. 301.

12. Ibid., p. 247.

13. Ibid., p. 264.

14. Ibid., p. 339.

15. Ibid., pp. 338, 313, 341.

16. Kennedy, *Rise and Fall*, p. 17.

17. Raymond Aron, *Main Currents in Sociological Thought*, vol. 1, trans., Richard Howard and Helen Weaver (New York: Basic Books, 1965), p. 158.

18. Ibid., pp. 17–19, 11, 15, 55.

19. Ibid., p. 197.

20. Ibid., p. 30.

21. Mead, *Mortal Splendor*, pp. 213, 54.

22. Ibid., p. 198.

23. Paul Seabury, "The Solvency Boys," *National Interest*, no. 13 (Fall 1988), p. 104.

24. Kennedy, *Rise and Fall*, p. 22.

25. Ibid., p. 77.

26. Ibid., p. 368.

27. Owen Harries, "The Rise of American Decline," p. 35.

28. Huntington, "The U.S.—Decline or Renewal?" p. 81.

29. Kennedy, *Rise and Fall*, p. 389.

30. Huntington, "Decline or Renewal?" p. 83.

31. Herbert Stein, "America Is Rich Enough To Be Strong," *AEI Economist*, February 1988, p. 3.

32. Ibid., p. 4.

33. Mead, *Mortal Splendor*, p. 3.

34. Ibid., pp. 6, 18–19.

35. Schmeisser, "Taking Stock," p. 66.

36. Mead, *Mortal Splendor*, p. 29.

37. Ibid., p. 94.

38. Ibid., p. 256.

CHAPTER 6: CAN DEMOCRACY FLOURISH AROUND THE WORLD?

1. Robert A. Dahl, "The Democratic Mystique," *New Republic*, April 2, 1984, p. 17.

2. Howard J. Wiarda, "Can Democracy Be Exported? The Quest for Democracy in United States Latin Policy" (Paper prepared for the Inter-American Dialogue on United States-Latin American Relations in the 1980s, sponsored by the Latin America Program of the Woodrow Wilson International Center for Scholars, Washington, D.C., March 1983), p. 1.

3. Owen Harries et al., *The Reagan Doctrine and Beyond* (Washington, D.C.: American Enterprise Institute, 1987), pp. 24–25.

4. Robert A. Packenham, *Liberal America and the Third World* (Princeton: Princeton University Press, 1973), p. 189.

5. Harries et al., *The Reagan Doctrine*, p. 24.

6. Packenham, *Liberal America*, p. 141.

7. Ibid., p. 339.

8. Reinhold Niebuhr and Paul E. Sigmund, *The Democratic Experience* (New York: Praeger, 1969), p. 95.

9. Nobutake Ike, *Japanese Politics: Patron-Client Democracy*, 2nd ed. (New York: Alfred A. Knopf, 1972), p. 81ff.

10. Howard J. Wiarda, "Project Democracy in Latin America: Reservations and Suggestions" (Paper prepared for a conference on Project Democracy, U.S. Information Agency, Washington, D.C., May 9, 1983), p. 2.

11. Raymond D. Gastil, "The Comparative Survey of Freedom: 1989," *Freedom at Issue*, no. 106 (January–February 1989), p. 47. The proportion of the world's populace living in countries judged not free has concomitantly decreased. When the survey was initiated in 1973, 32 percent lived in free countries and 47 percent in not-free ones. The trend lines

crossed for the first time in the annual survey released in January 1988, when the proportion in free countries exceeded that in not-free ones. The survey released in 1989 appeared to show a reversal in this trend, with the number of people living in not-free countries rising at the expense of the number living in partly free ones. This reversal, however, was illusory. For its own institutional reasons, Freedom House changed the threshold in 1989, separating partly free from not-free countries in its classification. The statistical increase in the not-free was entirely a product of this change. Had the threshold remained constant, the 1989 survey would have shown a further significant decrease in the not-free, accompanied by increases in both the free and partly free.

12. Jim Hoagland, "A Real Voice from China," *Washington Post*, April 17, 1990, p. A25.

13. Youssef M. Ibrahim, "An Affluent Kuwait Joins an Arab Trend toward Democracy," *New York Times*, March 11, 1990, p. 18.

14. Marianne Yen, "Tibet's Spirit of Change," *Washington Post*, July 22, 1989, p. C1.

15. Joseph C. Grew, memorandum of conversation, May 28, 1945, in U.S. Department of State, *Foreign Relations of the United States*, vol. 6, p. 545. Cited in Theodore Cohen, *Remaking Japan* (New York: Macmillan, 1987), p. 14.

16. Heinz Eulau, "Germany: 'A-Political' Ally," *New Republic*, June 9, 1952, pp. 15–16.

17. Hiroo Mukai, "Sovereign Japan—One Japanese Speaks," *New Republic*, May 12, 1952, p. 14.

18. David Thomson, "The Zone of Hunger," *Nation*, January 10, 1959, p. 31.

19. Waldo Frank, "Our Island Hemisphere," *Foreign Affairs*, vol. 21, no. 3 (April 1943), p. 519.

20. Arnold J. Toynbee, "Things Not Foreseen at Paris," *Foreign Affairs*, vol. 12, no. 3 (April 1934), pp. 477–78.

21. Strom Thurmond, "Constitutional Government," *Vital Speeches*, January 15, 1958, p. 212.

22. "Freedom in the World—1990," *Freedom at Issue*, no. 112 (January–February 1990), p. 7.

23. Jonathan Hartlyn, "Colombia: The Politics of Violence and Accommodation," in Larry Diamond, Juan J. Linz, and Seymour Martin Lipset, eds., *Democracy in Developing Countries*, vol. 4, *Latin America* (Boulder, Colo.: Lynne Rienner, 1989), p. 291.

24. "Freedom in the World—1990," pp. 7, 31.

CHAPTER 7: EXPORT OF DEMOCRACY AND THE FORCE OF EXAMPLE

1. "Congress Reactions," *Facts on File*, vol. 43, no. 2241 (October 28, 1983), p. 813.

2. Exceptions might be cases in which ruthless governments perpetuate a holocaust against civilians under their control, for example, Pol Pot against the Khmer Rouge or Hitler against the Jews. Arguably international law would countenance humanitarian intervention to stop such a government, and public opinion might concur. But the goal of such an intervention would not be democracy per se but the arrest of a bloodbath.

3. Adolph A. Berle, "Democracy in Its Relationship to Foreign Affairs," *Vital Speeches*, March 6, 1939, p. 381.

4. On Germany see David P. Conradt, "Changing German Political Culture," in Gabriel A. Almond and Sidney Verba, eds., *The Civic Culture Revisited* (Boston: Little, Brown and Company, 1980), pp. 212–72. On Japan see Takeshi Ishida and Ellis S. Krauss, eds., *Democracy in Japan* (Pittsburgh: University of Pittsburgh Press, 1989).

5. R. R. Palmer, *Age of the Democratic Revolution: A Political History of Europe and America, 1760–1800*. Vol. I, *The Challenge* (Princeton: Princeton University Press, 1959) pp. 239–40.

6. Cited in ibid. and in John Simpson Penman, *The Irresistible Movement of Democracy* (New York: Macmillan, 1923), p. 189.

7. Ibid., pp. 188–89. The quotes used here by Penman are all from Lafayette's memoirs.

8. Simon Schama, *Citizens* (New York: Knopf, 1989), p. 43.

9. Merrill D. Peterson, *Thomas Jefferson and the New Nation* (London: Oxford University Press, 1970), pp. 380–81.

10. R. R. Palmer, preface to Georges Lefebvre, *The Coming of the French Revolution*, trans. R. R. Palmer (New York: Vintage Books: n.d.) (original English edition published by Princeton University Press, 1947), p. vi.

11. Lefebvre, *The Coming of the French Revolution*, p. 19.

12. Schama, *Citizens*, pp. 24, 47–48.

13. Alexander Hamilton (Americanus), article appearing originally in the *American Daily Advertiser*, February 8, 1794, reprinted in Henry Cabot Lodge, ed., *The Works of Alexander Hamilton*, vol. 5 (New York: G.P. Putnam's, 1904), pp. 89, 93.

14. Penman, *Irresistible Movement*, p. 506.

15. Quoted in Henry Fairlie, "The Shot Heard Round the World," *New Republic*, July 18 and 25, 1988, p. 25.

16. George Macaulay Trevelyan, *British History in the Nineteenth Century and After (1782–1919)*, new ed. (New York: David McKay, 1947), p. 64.

17. Ibid., p. 186.

18. Quoted in Goldwin Smith, *A History of England*, 3rd ed. (New York: Charles Scribner's, 1966), p. 555.

19. Trevelyan, *British History in the Nineteenth Century*, p. 340.

20. Palmer, *Age of the Democratic Revolution*, p. 265.

21. Quoted in Arthur A. Ekirch, Jr., *Ideas, Ideals and American Diplomacy* (New York: Appleton-Century-Crofts, 1966), p. 34, and in Halvdan Koht, *The American Spirit in Europe* (Philadelphia: University of Pennsylvania Press, 1949), p. 24.

22. Koht, *The American Spirit*, p. 22.

23. Max Huber, *Rückblick und Ausblick: Gesammelte Aufsätze und Ansprachen* (Zürich: Atlantic Verlag, 1957), vol. 4, p. 236. This passage has been translated by Jeffrey Gedmin.

24. Herbert J. Muller, *Freedom in the Modern World* (New York: Harper and Row, 1966) pp. 121, 163.

25. Monsieur Guizot, *Democracy in France* (New York: Howard Fertig, 1974). See especially pp. 12–14.

26. Carl J. Friedrich, *The Impact of American Constitutionalism Abroad* (Boston: Boston University Press, 1967), pp. 52–53.

27. Wiarda, "Can Democracy Be Exported? The Quest for Democracy in United States Latin Policy" (Paper prepared for the Inter-American Dialogue on United States-Latin American Relations in the 1980s, sponsored by the Latin America Program of the Woodrow Wilson International Center for Scholars, Washington, D.C., March 1983), p. 7.

28. See Albert P. Blaustein, *The Influence of the United States Constitution Abroad* (Washington, D.C.: Washington Institute for Values in Public Policy, 1986), pp. 5, 19.

29. Enrique Krauze, "England, the United States, and the Export of Democracy," *Washington Quarterly*, vol. 12, no. 2 (Spring 1989), pp. 190–91.

30. Thomas A. Bailey, *A Diplomatic History of the American People*, 3rd ed. (New York: Appleton-Century-Crofts, 1946), p. 651.

31. Tushar Kanti Ghosh in *Parliamentary Democracy: Report of the First All-India Seminar* (New Delhi: Indian Bureau of Parliamentary Studies, 1956), p. 120.

32. P. V. Tripathi, "Perspectives on the American Constitutional Influence on the Constitution of India," in Lawrence Ward Beer, ed., *Constitutionalism in Asia: Asian Views of the American Influence* (Berkeley: University of California Press, 1979), p. 80; cited in Albert P. Blaustein, *The Influence of the United States Constitution Abroad* (Washington, D.C.: Washington Institute for Values in Public Policy, 1986), p. 11.

33. Karl Loewenstein, "Reflections on the Value of Constitutions in Our Revolutionary Age," in Arnold J. Zurcher, ed., *Constitutions and Constitutional Trends since World War II* (New York: New York University, 1951), pp. 191–92.

34. Friedrich, *The Impact of American Constitutionalism Abroad*, p. 11.

35. Fox Butterfield, "Beijing Protesters Said to Flee to a Now Uneasy Hong Kong," *New York Times*, June 30, 1989, p. A6.

36. Esther B. Fein, "Unshackled Czech Workers Declare Their Independence," *New York Times*, November 28, 1989, p. A1.

37. Blaine Harden, "Ceausescu, Wife Reported Executed after Trial: Army Defeating Secret Police in Bucharest," *Washington Post*, December 26, 1989, pp. A1, A26.

38. Helen Dewar, "Capitol Hill's Seminar on Democracy," *Washington Post*, April 10, 1990, pp. A1, A10.

CHAPTER 8: IMPOSING DEMOCRACY
THROUGH MILITARY OCCUPATION

1. Douglas MacArthur, "Address to Members of the Allied Council for Japan, April 5, 1946," in *A Soldier Speaks: Public Papers and Speeches of General of the Army Douglas MacArthur*, ed. Major Vorin E. Whan, Jr. (New York: Praeger, 1965), p. 166.

2. Robert A. Scalapino, *Democracy and the Party Movement in Prewar Japan* (Berkeley: University of California Press, 1975), p. 46.

3. Ibid., p. 1.

4. Robert E. Ward, "Conclusion," in Robert E. Ward and Sakamoto Yoshikazu, eds., *Democratizing Japan: The Allied Occupation* (Honolulu: University of Hawaii Press, 1987), pp. 392–93.

5. Ruth Benedict, *The Chrysanthemum and the Sword* (Boston: Houghton Mifflin, 1946), p. 314.

6. John M. Maki, *Government and Politics in Japan: The Road to Democracy* (New York: Praeger), p. 71.

7. Edwin O. Reischauer, *Japan: The Story of a Nation*, 3rd ed. (New York: Knopf, 1970), p. 221.

8. "Basic Initial Post-Surrender Directive to Supreme Commander for the Allied Powers for the Occupation and Control of Japan," part I, point 3a, in *Political Reorientation of Japan, September 1945 to September 1948* (Washington, D.C.: U.S. Government Printing Office, n.d.).

9. Quoted in Ambassador William J. Sebald, with Russell Brines, *With MacArthur in Japan: A Personal History of the Occupation* (New York: W. W. Norton, 1965), p. 244.

10. Supreme Commander for the Allied Powers, Government Section, *Political Reorientation of Japan, September 1945 to September 1948* (Washington, D.C.: U.S. Government Printing Office, n.d.).

11. Robert E. Ward, "Presurrender Planning: The Treatment of the Emperor and Constitutional Changes," in Robert E. Ward and Sakamoto Yoshikazu, eds., *Democratizing Japan: The Allied Occupation* (Honolulu: University of Hawaii Press, 1987), p. 38.

12. Scalapino, *Democracy and the Party Movement*, p. 1.

13. Robert E. Ward, *Japan's Political System* (Englewood Cliffs, N.J.: Prentice Hall, 1967), p. 12.

14. Reischauer, *Japan*, p. 170.

15. Robert E. Ward, "Reflections on the Allied Occupation and Planned Political Change in Japan," in Robert E. Ward, ed., *Political Development in Modern Japan* (Princeton: Princeton University Press, 1968), p. 517.

16. Scalapino, *Democracy and the Party Movement*, pp. 41–49, 87–91.

17. Ibid., pp. 347, 388.

18. Ward, *Japan's Political System*, p. 15.

19. MacArthur, "Address to the Allied Council for Japan," p. 168.

20. "Message to the War Department in Support of Congressional Appropriations for the Occupation of Japan, February 20, 1947," in *A Soldier Speaks: Public Papers and Speeches*

of General of the Army Douglas MacArthur, ed. Major Vorin E. Whan, Jr. (New York: Praeger, 1965), p. 182.

21. Theodore Cohen, *Remaking Japan: The American Occupation As New Deal*, ed. Herbert Passin (New York: Free Press, 1987), p. 9.

22. Shigeru Yoshida, *The Yoshida Memoirs: The Story of Japan in Crisis*, trans. Kenichi Yoshida (Boston: Houghton Mifflin, 1962), p. 148.

23. Supreme Command for the Allied Powers, *Political Reorientation of Japan*, p. 75.

24. Ibid., p. 34.

25. Ibid., p. 45.

26. Justin Williams, Sr., *Japan's Political Revolution under MacArthur: A Participant's Account* (Athens: University of Georgia Press, 1979), p. 39.

27. Douglas MacArthur, *Reminiscences* (New York: McGraw-Hill, 1964), p. 298.

28. Yoshida, *Memoirs*, p. 159.

29. Sebald with Brines, *With MacArthur in Japan*, p. 246.

30. Yoshida, *Memoirs*, p. 159.

31. MacArthur, *Reminiscences*, p. 302.

32. Williams, *Japan's Political Revolution*, p. 141.

33. Supreme Commander for the Allied Powers, *Political Reorientation of Japan*, p. 106.

34. Yoshida, *Memoirs*, pp. 135, 137.

35. Ibid., p. 136.

36. Quoted in Major General Courtney Whitney, *MacArthur: His Rendez Vous with History* (New York: Knopf, 1956), p. 253.

37. Kazuo Kawai, *Japan's American Interlude* (Chicago: University of Chicago Press, 1960), p. 57.

38. See Williams, *Japan's Political Revolution*, p. 122, and, by implication, Whitney, *MacArthur*, pp. 253, 263, and Cohen, *Remaking Japan*, p. 12.

39. Cohen, *Remaking Japan*, p. 357.

40. Ibid., p. 358.

41. Ibid., p. 197.

42. Maki, *Government and Politics*, p. 134.

43. MacArthur, "Address to the Allied Council for Japan," p. 167.

44. Tanaka Hideo, "The Conflict between Two Legal Traditions in Making the Constitution of Japan," in Robert E. Ward and Sakamoto Yoshikazu, eds., *Democratizing Japan: The Allied Occupation* (Honolulu: University of Hawaii Press, 1987), p. 126.

45. Kawai, *Japan's American Interlude*, p. 25.

46. Robert E. Ward, "Conclusion," p. 428.

47. Ibid., p. 397.

48. MacArthur, *Reminiscences*, p. 310.

49. Cohen, *Remaking Japan*, pp. 121, 137, 135.

50. Benedict, *The Chrysanthemum and the Sword*, pp.57–58.

51. Williams, *Japan's Political Revolution*, p. 98.

52. A light touch vis-à-vis the Japanese, that is. Toward meddling allies (including the USSR) the supreme commander showed far less indulgence.

53. See Cohen, *Remaking Japan*, pp. 146–53.

54. Quoted in Robert E. Ward, "Presurrender Planning: Treatment of the Emperor and Constitutional Changes," p. 16.

55. MacArthur, *Reminiscences*, p. 288.

56. Seymour Martin Lipset, *Political Man* (Garden City, N.J.: Anchor Books, 1963), p. 65.

57. Yoshida, *Memoirs*, p. 51.

58. Ward, "Reflections," pp. 517–18.

59. Nobutaka Ike, *The Beginnings of Political Democracy in Japan* (Baltimore: Johns Hopkins University Press, 1950), p. xiii.

60. Ward, "Conclusion," p. 399.

61. Ward, "Reflections," p. 518.

62. Reischauer, *Japan*, p. 253.

63. For this controversial judgment, I take the word of Theodore Cohen, because his own anti-Communist convictions are clear, his evaluation of MacArthur's performance is balanced, and his background as a non-Communist Marxist student activist in the lush political jungles of City College of New York in the 1930s left him better equipped to distinguish Communists from other leftist varieties than were most other occupation officials, including MacArthur. See Cohen, *Remaking Japan*, pp. 449–52.

64. Scalapino, *Democracy and the Party Movement*, p. 132.

65. Ike, *Japanese Politics*, p. viii.

66. Supreme Commander for the Allied Powers, *Political Reorientation of Japan*, p. 92.

67. Peter Gay, *Weimar Culture* (New York: Harper & Row, 1968), p. 25.

68. Peter H. Merkl, "The Impact of the U.S. Occupation on the Domestic Development of Western Germany" (Paper prepared for the Conference on Patterns of U.S. Occupation Policies, sponsored by the Hoover Institution and Stanford University, May 14–17, 1986), p. 8.

69. Ibid., p. 14.

70. Peter H. Merkl, *The Origins of the West German Republic* (New York: Oxford University Press, 1963), p. 9.

71. Carl J. Friedrich, "The Legacies of the Occupation of Germany," *Public Policy*, vol. 17 (1968), pp. 14–15.

72. Ibid., p. 13.

73. Peter H. Merkl, "Allied Strategies of Effecting Political Change and Their Reception in Occupied Germany," *Public Policy*, vol. 17 (1968), p. 102.

74. See Milton Colvin, "Principal Issues in the U.S. Occupation of Austria, 1945–1948," in Hans A. Schmitt, ed., *U.S. Occupation in Europe after World War II* (Lawrence, Kans.: Regents of Kansas Press, 1978), p. 111.

75. Oliver Rathkolb, "National Security Decision Making of the Eisenhower Administration and the Austrian Question 1953–1955–1960" (Paper prepared for the Conference on Patterns of U.S. Occupation Policies, sponsored by the Hoover Institution and Stanford University, May 14–17, 1986).

76. Frederick C. Engelmann, "How Austria Has Coped with Two Dictatorial Legacies," in John H. Herz, ed., *From Dictatorship to Democracy: Coping with the Legacies of Authoritarianism and Totalitarianism* (Westport, Conn.: Greenwood Press, 1982), p. 144.

77. See Colvin, "Principal Issues," pp. 116–17.

78. Claude A. Buss, *The United States and the Philippines* (Washington, D.C.: American Enterprise Institute, 1977), p. 5. I have relied on Buss's monograph for several other points in this historical review of the Philippines.

79. Ibid., p. 6.

CHAPTER 9: COVERT ACTION

1. U.S. Congress, Senate, Select Committee to Study Governmental Operations with Respect to Intelligence Activities (hereinafter Church committee), *Covert Action in Chile 1963–1973*, Staff report, 94th Congress, 1st session, December 18, 1975, p. 28.

2. U.S. Congress, Senate, Church committee, *Final Report*, bk. 1, *Foreign and Military Intelligence*, 94th Congress, 2nd session, 1976, p. 22.

3. Ibid., bk. 4, *Supplementary Detailed Staff Reports on Foreign and Military Intelligence*, p. 31.

4. Norman Kogan, *A Political History of Italy: The Postwar Years* (New York: Praeger, 1983), p. 39.

5. The figure purports to come from a CIA document. Cited in the unauthorized publication of the report of the congressional investigating committee chaired by Representative Otis Pike, it appeared in the *Village Voice*, February 16, 1976. Cited in Morton H. Halperin et al., *The Lawless State: The Crimes of the U.S. Intelligence Agencies* (New York: Penguin Books, 1976), p. 38.

6. Senate, Church committee, *Final Report*, bk. 4, p. 36.

7. William Colby and Peter Forbath, *Honorable Men: My Life in the CIA* (New York: Simon & Schuster, 1978), p. 116.

8. Ibid., p. 138.

9. Figure from the Pike committee report as published in the *Village Voice*, February 16, 1976, reprinted in Judith F. Buncher, ed., *The CIA and the Security Debate: 1975–1976* (New York: Facts on File, 1977), p. 88.

10. Colby and Forbath, *Honorable Men*, pp. 110–11.

11. John Ranelagh, *The Agency: The Rise and Decline of the CIA* (New York: Simon & Schuster, 1986), p. 131.

12. Halperin et al., *Lawless State*, p. 37.

13. Senate, Church committee, *Final Report*, bk. 4, p. 49.

14. Ibid., p. 36.

15. Harry Rositzke, *The CIA's Secret Operations* (New York: Reader's Digest Press, 1977), p. 158.

16. See, for example, Ronald Radosh, *American Labor and United States Foreign Policy* (New York: Random House, 1969), pp. 325–37, and Roy Godson, *American Labor and European Politics* (New York: Crane, Russak, 1976), p. 129ff.

17. Joseph R. Starobin, *American Communism in Crisis 1943–1957* (Cambridge: Harvard University Press, 1972), p. 91. A former party leader, Starobin said that in 1945, 10,000 members were "on leave" for military service.

18. Godson, *American Labor*, pp. 46–53.

19. Senate, Church committee, *Final Report*, bk. 4, pp. 49–50.

20. Peter Coleman, *The Liberal Conspiracy: The Congress for Cultural Freedom and the Struggle for the Mind of Postwar Europe* (New York: Free Press, 1989).

21. Irving Kristol, "The Way We Were," *National Interest*, vol. 17 (Fall 1989), p. 74.

22. Coleman, *Liberal Conspiracy*, p. 9.

23. Ibid.

24. Ibid., p. 247.

25. Senate, Church committee, *Final Report*, bk. 1, p. 145.

26. Ibid., p. 107.

27. Ibid., bk. 4, p. 58.

28. Ibid., bk. 1, p. 107.

29. Ibid., p. 147.

30. Gregory F. Treverton, *Covert Action: The Limits of Intervention in the Postwar World* (New York: Basic Books, 1987), p. 12.

31. Edward Geary Lansdale, *In the Midst of Wars* (New York: Harper & Row, 1972), pp. 1, 12–15, but see also, for example, Joseph Burkholder Smith, *Portrait of a Cold Warrior* (New York: G. P. Putnam's Sons, 1976), p. 103, or Thomas B. Buell, *The Quiet Warrior: A Biography of Admiral Raymond A. Spruance* (Boston: Little, Brown, 1974), p. 407.

32. Lansdale, *Midst of Wars*, pp. 24–30, 28.

33. Smith, *Cold Warrior*, p. 108.

34. Ibid., p. 112.

35. U.S., Central Intelligence Agency, "Trends and Developments in Soviet Active Measures," in U.S., Congress, House, Permanent Select Committee on Intelligence, *Soviet Active Measures*, 97th Congress, 2nd session, July 13, 14, 1982, p. 57.

36. For more details on Allende's background and ideological leanings, see Cord Meyer: *Facing Reality: From World Federalism to the CIA* (New York: Harper & Row, 1980; Lanham, Md.: University Press of America, 1982), pp. 174–76.

37. Senate, Church committee, *Covert Action in Chile*, p. 14.

38. Ibid., p. 9.

39. Ibid., p. 16.

40. Ibid., p. 15.

41. Ibid., p. 17.

42. Meyer, *Facing Reality*, pp. 175–76.

43. Steven V. Roberts, "Thomas Upholds C.I.A.-Aided Work," *New York Times*, February 22, 1967, p. A17.

44. Juan Bosch, *The Unfinished Experiment: Democracy in the Dominican Republic* (New York: Praeger, 1964), p. 171.

45. Howard J. Wiarda, "The Dominican Republic: Mirror Legacies of Democracy and Authoritarianism," in Larry Diamond, Juan J. Linz, and Seymour Martin Lipset, eds., *Democracy in Developing Countries*, vol. 4, *Latin America* (Boulder, Colo.: Lynne Rienner, 1989), pp. 433–34.

46. Bosch, *Unfinished Experiment*, p. 173.

47. Ibid., pp. 174–76.

48. Ibid., p. 172.

49. Tom Gallagher, *Portugal: A Twentieth-Century Interpretation* (Manchester, Eng.: Manchester University Press, 1983), p. 217.

50. Ibid., p. 220.

51. Ibid., p. 219.

52. David Rogers, "White House Approved Secret CIA Effort to Affect Outcome of El Salvador Voting," *Wall Street Journal*, May 10, 1984, p. A2.

53. Robert J. McCartney, "U.S. Seen Assisting Duarte in Sunday's Salvadoran Vote," *Washington Post*, May 4, 1984, p. A1.

54. Senate, Church committee, *Final Report*, bk. 1, pp. 159–60.

55. Ibid., pp. 156, 16.

56. Ibid., p. 155.

57. Treverton, *Covert Action*, p. 124.

58. Ibid., p. 118.

59. Meyer, *Facing Reality*, p. 109.

60. Colby and Forbath, *Honorable Men*, p. 115.

61. Ibid. p. 122.

62. Treverton, *Covert Action*, pp. 186, 12.

63. Bosch, *Unfinished Experiment*, p. 172.

64. See, for illustration, Juan Bosch, *Pentagonism: A Substitute for Imperialism*, trans. Helen R. Lane (New York: Grove Press, 1968).

65. See, for example, Senate, Church committee, *Final Report*, bk. 1, p. 28.

66. Constantine C. Menges, *Inside the National Security Council* (New York: Simon & Schuster, 1988), p. 249.

67. Charles Krauthammer, "Against Authoritarian Regimes, Too," *Washington Post*, February 28, 1986, p. A19.

68. Gregory A. Fossedal, *The Democratic Imperative: Exporting the American Revolution* (New York: Basic Books, 1989), ch. 7.

CHAPTER 10: CRISIS DIPLOMACY

1. Daniel P. Moynihan, "The Politics of Human Rights," *Commentary*, vol. 64, no. 2 (August 1977), p. 23.

2. Paul Laxalt, "My Conversations with Ferdinand Marcos," *Policy Review*, no. 37 (Summer 1986), p. 2.

3. Fred Barnes, "The Shaking of a President," *New Republic*, February 10, 1986, p. 17.

4. Raymond Bonner, *Waltzing with a Dictator: The Marcoses and the Making of American Policy* (New York: Times Books, 1987), p. 385.

5. Laxalt, "Conversations," p. 4.

6. Sandra Burton, "Aquino's Philippines: The Center Holds," *Foreign Affairs, America and the World 1986*, vol. 65, no. 3 (1987), p. 526.

7. Bonner, *Waltzing*, pp. 399–400.

8. "Election Developments in the Philippines," *Department of State Bulletin*, vol. 86, no. 2109 (April 1986), p. 67.

9. Bonner, *Waltzing*, p. 414.

10. Lou Cannon and David Hoffman, "An Interview with President Reagan," *Washington Post*, February 11, 1986, p. A8.

11. Don Oberdorfer and Lou Cannon, "Declaration in Favor of Marcos Seen Near: Senators Pressuring Reagan to Alter View," *Washington Post*, February 14, 1986, p. A38.

12. "Election Developments in the Philippines," President's Statement, February 11, 1986, in *Department of State Bulletin*, April 1986, p. 67.

13. "Election Developments in the Philippines," p. 68.

14. Laxalt, "Conversations," pp. 4–5.

15. Perhaps it is erroneous to say that Marcos's swearing-in was for show. According to Laxalt Marcos regarded his capitulation not as an acknowledgment of Aquino's legitimacy but as a patriotic sacrifice. "He still maintains that he is the duly elected president, and he is firmly convinced that the Aquino people cannot hold that country together and that one day he is going to return," said Laxalt. In the years between his exile and his death, periodic reports reached the press of efforts by Marcos to undermine Aquino from his home in Hawaii. The swearing-in may have been intended to further a juridical basis for his intended return. His exile machinations lend justification to Aquino's apparently heartless decision, reportedly urged by the canny General Ramos, to deny Marcos the right to remain within the country.

16. Paul A. Gigot, "Credit Reagan Some for Philippine Democracy," *Wall Street Journal*, March 3, 1986, p. 19.

17. Charles Krauthammer, "Bringing a Third Force to Bear," *Time*, March 10, 1986, p. 84.

18. Joseph B. Treaster, "Haitian Demonstrators Challenge Duvalier Again," *New York Times*, January 9, 1986, p. A9.

19. "End of the Duvalier Era," *Time*, February 17, 1986, p. 41.

20. Edward Cody, "Haitian Council Chief Vows Moves toward Democracy," *Washington Post*, February 11, 1986, p. A1.

21. Richard N. Holwill, "Promoting Democracy in Haiti," *Department of State Bulletin*, vol. 87, no. 2127 (October 1987), p. 60.

22. Michael Massing, "Haiti: The New Violence," *New York Review of Books*, vol. 34, no. 19 (December 3, 1987), p. 50.

23. Ibid., p. 48.

24. Lee Hockstader, "Haitian Ruler Seen Isolated after Baffling Crackdown," *Washington Post*, January 29, 1990, p. A18.

25. Lee Hockstader, "Embattled Ruler Quits in Haiti," *Washington Post*, March 11, 1990, p. A30.

26. Joseph B. Treaster, "Military Leader Resigns in Haiti; Election Promised," *New York Times*, March 11, 1990, p. 18.

27. Lee Hockstader, "U.S. Envoy Spoke with Avril of Nixon's Final Days before Haitian Resigned," *Washington Post*, March 12, 1990, p. A8.

28. Lee Hockstader, "Avril Leaves Haiti; Opposition Chooses Woman Judge as Interim President," *Washington Post*, March 13, 1990, p. A14; "Haiti Swears in Civilian Woman President," *Washington Post*, March 14, 1990, p. A19.

29. Hockstader, "Haiti Swears," p. A19.

30. See, for example, Jerald A. Combs, *A History of American Foreign Policy* (New York: Knopf, 1986), p. 383. Also Abraham F. Lowenthal, *The Dominican Intervention* (Cambridge: Harvard University Press, 1972), p. 10.

31. Arthur M. Schlesinger, Jr., *A Thousand Days: John F. Kennedy in the White House* (Boston: Houghton Mifflin, 1965), p. 769.

32. Ibid., p. 770.

33. I rely for my account of this episode on Lowenthal, *Dominican Intervention*, pp. 12–13.

34. Schlesinger, *A Thousand Days*, p. 773.

35. William P. Bundy, "Who Lost Patagonia? Foreign Policy in the 1980 Campaign," *Foreign Affairs*, vol. 58, no. 1 (Fall 1979), pp. 8–9.

36. Robert A. Pastor, *Condemned to Repetition: The United States and Nicaragua* (Princeton: Princeton University Press, 1987), p. 65.

37. Ibid., p. 91.

38. Ibid., pp. 118–19.

39. Christian, *Nicaragua*, p. 87.

40. *Department of State Bulletin*, vol. 79, no. 2026 (May 1979), p. 66.

41. Pastor, *Condemned to Repetition*, pp. 118–19.

42. Ibid., p. 122.

43. Ibid., p. 154.

44. See my *News Coverage of the Sandinista Revolution* (Washington, D.C.: American Enterprise Institute, 1988), pp. 36–46.

45. Pastor, *Condemned to Repetition*, p. 157.

46. Ibid., p. 169.

47. Ibid., p. 137.

48. James A. Baker, III, "Democracy and American Diplomacy," address to the World Affairs Council of Dallas, March 30, 1990, p. 4.

49. Cyrus Vance, *Hard Choices* (New York: Simon & Schuster, 1983), pp. 325–26, and Zbigniew Brzezinski, *Power and Principle* (New York: Farrar, Straus, Giroux, 1983), p. 358.

50. Michael Ledeen and William Lewis say, however, that the French and Israeli intelligence services were much less sanguine about the shah's prospects as early as the spring of 1978. See Ledeen and Lewis, *Debacle: The American Failure in Iran* (New York: Alfred A. Knopf, 1981), pp. 118, 125–26.

51. Barry Rubin, *Paved with Good Intentions: The American Experience and Iran* (New York: Oxford University Press, 1980), p. 191.

52. See my *The Uncertain Crusade: Jimmy Carter and the Dilemmas of Human Rights Policy* (Lanham, Md.: Hamilton Press, 1986), pp. 209–11.

53. Brzezinski, *Power and Principle*, p. 355.

54. Ibid., p. 356.

55. Ledeen and Lewis, *Debacle*, p. 137.

56. Vance, *Hard Choices*, pp. 326–27.

57. Rubin, *Good Intentions*, p. 366.

58. Vance and Brzezinski provide conflicting accounts of the sequence of communications at this point. Brzezinski tells of a call he made to the shah on November 3, the day after a high-level meeting of American officials to determine a response to the shah's request. Vance says that the shah called the White House on the third and precipitated the meeting that Brzezinski had placed on the previous day. The substance of the communications, however, is essentially the same in both accounts. See Brzezinski, *Power and Principle*, pp. 362–65, and Vance, *Hard Choices*, pp. 328–29.

59. Vance, *Hard Choices*, p. 329.

60. Brzezinski, *Power and Principle*, p. 366.

61. Rubin, *Good Intentions*, pp. 224–25.

62. Vance, *Hard Choices*, p. 330.

63. Ibid., p. 331.

64. Cited in Rubin, *Good Intentions*, p. 230.

65. Vance, *Hard Choices*, p. 331.

66. Ibid.

67. Brzezinski, *Power and Principle*, p. 371.

68. Rubin, *Good Intentions*, p. 238.

69. Ibid., p. 239.

70. Vance, *Hard Choices*, p. 335.

71. William Branigan, "Carter Says Noriega Is Stealing Election," *Washington Post*, May 9, 1989, p. A1.

72. The president's warning was delivered in a speech to the Council of the Americas meeting at the State Department on May 2, 1989. It is reprinted in "Commitment to Democracy and Economic Progress in Latin America," *Department of State Bulletin*, June 1989, pp. 1–3.

73. This summary of events leading up to May 1989 draws largely on Linda Robinson, "Dwindling Options in Panama," *Foreign Affairs*, vol. 68, no. 2 (Winter 1989–1990), pp. 192–95.

74. "Panama Election Voided amid Charges of Government Fraud, Foreign Intervention," *Facts on File*, vol. 49, no. 2529 (May 12, 1989), p. 330.

75. "Lead-Pipe Politics," *Time*, May 22, 1989, p. 41.

76. "On Noriega, 'We Have Failed Miserably,'" *Newsweek*, September 4, 1989, p. 33.

77. "Demonstrations in China," *Department of State Bulletin*, August 1989, p. 75.

78. "Chinese Leaders Impose Martial Law in Beijing; Massive Protests Continue; Army Fails to Move," *Facts on File*, vol. 49, no. 2531 (May 26, 1989), pp. 370–71.

79. "Demonstrations in China," p. 75.

80. "Chinese Army Troops Crush Prodemocracy Protests; Hundreds of Demonstrators Reported Killed," *Facts on File*, vol. 49, no. 2533 (June 9, 1989), p. 411.

81. "China Reports New Arrests of Protesters," *Facts on File*, vol. 49, no. 2535 (June 23, 1989), p. 449.

82. Martin Tolchin, "House Breaking with Bush, Votes China Sanctions," *New York Times*, June 30, 1989, p. A7.

83. "Shooting Incident Protested," *Facts on File*, vol. 49, no. 2538 (July 14, 1989), p. 511.

84. Jim Hoagland, "We Should Be Listening to China's Exiles," *Washington Post*, September 26, 1989, p. A27.

85. Holly Burkhalter and Robin Munro, "Repression in China," *Washington Post*, October 20, 1989, p. A23.

CHAPTER 11: FOREIGN AID

1. U.S., Agency for International Development, Office of Planning and Budgeting, Bureau for Program and Policy Coordination. *U.S. Overseas Loans and Grants, July 1, 1945–September 30, 1982* (Washington, D.C.: AID), table, p. 4.

2. Alan S. Milward, *The Reconstruction of Western Europe 1945–51* (Berkeley: University of California Press, 1984).

3. In his famous Harvard University commencement address on June 4, 1947, proposing the plan, Marshall said, "The remedy lies in … restoring the confidence of the European people in the economic future of their own countries."

4. Charles L. Mee, Jr., *The Marshall Plan: The Launching of the Pax Americana* (New York: Simon & Schuster, 1984), pp. 262–63.

5. U.S., AID, *U.S. Overseas Loans and Grants,* p. 72.

6. For details see Stanley J. Heginbotham, *An Overview of U.S. Foreign Aid Programs,* CRS Report for Congress 88–283 F (Washington, D.C.: Congressional Research Service, 1988), updated and revised by Larry Q. Nowels, March 30, 1988, U.S., Library of Congress, Congressional Research Service, p. 17.The initial report was presented to the Foreign Operations Subcommittee of the House Committee on Appropriations on March 9, 1988.

7. John F. Kennedy, "Message of the President to the Congress, on the Subject of Foreign Aid, March 22, 1961," in Robert A. Goldwin, ed., *Why Foreign Aid?* (Chicago: Rand McNally, 1962), p. 4.

8. W. W. Rostow, *The Stages of Economic Growth: A Non-Communist Manifesto* (London: Cambridge University Press, 1960), p. 50.

9. John F. Kennedy, "Message of the President to the Congress, on the Subject of Foreign Aid, April 2, 1961," reprinted in Robert A. Goldwin, ed., *Why Foreign Aid?* (Chicago: Rand McNally, 1962), p. 136.

10. George Kennan, *Memoirs 1925–1950* (Boston: Little, Brown, 1967), p. 352.

11. I have derived these averages from the data in Heginbotham, *Overview,* p. 17.

12. These figures are drawn or extrapolated from Heginbotham, *Overview,* pp. 17, 19.

13. Independent Commission on International Development Issues, *North-South: A Programme for Survival* (Cambridge: MIT Press, 1980), p. 282.

14. Kennedy, "Message on Foreign Aid, 1961," p. 6.

15. Robert Cassen and Associates, *Does Aid Work? Report to an Intergovernmental Task Force* (Oxford: Clarendon Press, 1986), p. 255.

16. Nicholas Eberstadt, *Foreign Aid and American Purpose* (Washington, D.C.: American Enterprise Institute, 1988), p. 10.

17. P. T. Bauer and John O'Sullivan, "Foreign Aid for What?" *Commentary,* vol. 66, no. 6 (December 1978), p. 46.

18. "Excerpts from Gorbachev's Economic Program," *New York Times,* October 17, 1990, p. A8..

19. Alan Woods, *Development and the National Interest: U.S. Economic Assistance into the 21st Century,* A Report by the Administrator, Agency for International Development (Washington, D.C.: U.S. AID, 1989), p. 116.

20. Seymour Martin Lipset, *Political Renewal on the Left: A Comparative Perspective* (Washington, D.C.: Progressive Policy Institute, 1990), p. 1.

21. U.S., Agency for International Development, *Congressional Presentation Fiscal Year 1991,* main vol. (Washington, D.C.: AID, 1990), p. 6.

22. Lucian W. Pye, "Soviet and American Styles in Foreign Aid," *Orbis,* vol. 4, no. 2 (1960), p. 166.

23. The AID budget is not broken down in such a way as to isolate the allocations for the various democracy-building programs. This cumulative figure was furnished to me by Richard Bissell, deputy director of AID in an interview April 4, 1990.

24. Larry Diamond, "Beyond Authoritarianism and Totalitarianism: Strategies for Democratization," *Washington Quarterly*, vol. 12, no. 1 (Winter 1989), p. 154.

25. These calculations are derived from figures given in Heginbotham, *Overview*, p. 17.

26. Woods, *Development and the National Interest*, p. 114.

27. Cassen, *Does Aid Work?* p. 33.

28. See K. T. Li, *The Experience of Dynamic Economic Growth on Taiwan* (New York: Mei Ya Publications, 1976).

29. David C. Cole and Princeton N. Lyman, *Korean Development: The Interplay of Politics and Economics* (Cambridge: Harvard University Press, 1971), p. 165.

30. See Freedom House Survey Team, *Freedom in the World: Political Rights and Civil Liberties 1989–1990* (New York: Freedom House, 1990), pp. 316–17.

31. The data may be found in Woods, *Development and the National Interest*, pp. 132–33, 148–49.

32. Alan Woods, "FY1989 Request for Foreign Assistance Programs," *Department of State Bulletin*, July 1988, p. 54.

33. Cited in U.S., Agency for International Development, *Development Issues*, 1987 annual report of the chairman of the Development Coordination Committee (Washington, D.C.: AID, 1987), pp. 5–6.

34. U.S., AID, *Congressional Presentation FY1991*, p. 60.

35. Pye, *Styles in Foreign Aid*, p. 160.

36. See my *The Uncertain Crusade: Jimmy Carter and the Dilemmas of Human Rights Policy* (Lanham, Md.: Hamilton Press, 1986), chap. 6.

CHAPTER 12: OVERSEAS BROADCASTING AND EXCHANGES

1. David M. Abshire, *International Broadcasting: A New Dimension of Western Diplomacy*, Washington Papers, vol. 4, no. 35 (Beverly Hills, Calif.: Sage, 1976), p. 21.

2. Ibid., p. 29.

3. See Cord Meyer, *Facing Reality: From World Federalism to the CIA* (Lanham, Md.: University Press of America, 1980), ch. 6.

4. U.S., United States Information Agency, *U.S. Information Agency Fact Sheet* (Washington, D.C.: USIA, October 1989), p. 4.

5. U.S., Board for International Broadcasting, *1989 Annual Report on Radio Free Europe/Radio Liberty, Inc.* (Washington, D.C.: BIB, January 31, 1989). The figure 55 million appears on p. 17, while the figure 56.5 million appears on the inside front cover.

6. *Report of the President's Advisory Board for Radio Broadcasting to Cuba* (Washington, D.C.: Government Printing Office, 1987), p. 2.

7. U.S., BIB, *1989 Annual Report*, p. 46. These data are for 1988. Note that the numbers include some who listen to more than one station.

8. Ibid., p. 42. The radios, especially RFE–RL, have devoted considerable effort to developing survey techniques from which these figures are derived. They rely on interviews with travelers from the target countries, not refugees, obviously an unrepresentative sample, but visitors planning to return. With the advent of *glasnost* RFE–RL has done direct sampling behind the former iron curtain and reported a high correlation between these results and those derived by its earlier sampling methods. See ibid., pp. 41–52; Susan Roehm and Soviet Area Audience and Opinion Research, "Soviet Youth and Radio Liberty: A Focus Group Analysis," March 1990.

9. For RFE–RL, see ibid., p. 76. For VOA, see Public Law 94-350.

10. Quoted in Cord Meyer, "A Success Story That Deserves to Continue," *Washington Times*, March 9, 1990, p. F1

11. Philip Roth, "A Conversation in Prague," New York Review of Books, April 12, 1990, p. 16.

12. Remarks by Vaclav Havel to the Czechoslovak service of Voice of America, February

20, 1990, Washington, D.C.

13. Richard Reeves, "Voices from Behind the Iron Curtain," *Reader's Digest*, July 1987, p. 103.

14. Cited in Gene Pell, "Radio Free Europe's 'Triumph for Truth' in Eastern Europe," *Human Events*, February 24, 1990, p. 10.

15. Blaine Harden, "Shortwave Radio Shaped the Revolution," *Washington Post*, December 29, 1989, p. A1.

16. Dorin Tudoran, interview with Nicolae Manolescu, aired on VOA, April 7, 1990.

17. "The Stations We Listen to ...," *Sobesednik*, no. 41 (October 1989).

18. See, for example, the editorial, "News for Uzbeks," *Wall Street Journal*, June 20, 1989, p. A18.

19. These data and all the figures in this paragraph and the next are taken from Marianthi Zikopoulos, ed., *Open Doors 1988/89: Report on International Educational Exchange* (New York: Institute of International Education, 1989), pp. 1–32.

20. The last figure is subject to two caveats, however. Its source is UNESCO, which conflates the numbers for the People's Republic of China and the Republic of China. Probably the true figure for the PRC is about 70 percent and for Taiwan about 85. These figures predate the Tiananmen Square Massacre of June 1989 and the consequent diminution of the flow of students from the PRC. Ibid.

21. Jerry Adler with Dorothy Wang, "Even Communists Like Capitalist Justice," *Newsweek*, October 19, 1987, p. 74.

22. Fred Strebeigh, "Training China's New Elite," *Atlantic Monthly*, April 1989, p. 74.

23. These statistics are contained in the appendix to an unpublished paper by Chong-Pin Lin titled "Taiwan's 1989 Election: Milestone of ROC's Democratization." He is Sun Yat-Sen Professor of China Studies, Georgetown University School of Foreign Service.

24. Thomas Fingar and Linda A. Reed, *Survey Summary: Students and Scholars from the People's Republic of China in the United States, August 1981* (Washington, D.C.: Committee on Scholarly Exchange with the People's Republic of China and National Association for Foreign Student Affairs, 1981), pp. 12–13.

25. Adler and Wang, "Even Communists," p. 74.

26. Strebeigh, "Training China's New Elite," p. 76.

27. "Thinking about Home," *Time*, February 2, 1987, p. 45.

28. This figure was given to me in an April 19, 1990, interview with Gordon Schultz, executive director of the Walker Center for Ecumenical Change in Boston, a major sponsor of the fax network.

29. Fang Lizhi, "Peering over the Great Wall," *Journal of Democracy*, vol. 1, no. 1 (Winter 1990), pp. 37–38.

30. Jay Matthews, "Movement Taps American Influences: Student Protesters Borrow Slogans, Skepticism from U.S. Campuses," *Washington Post*, May 25, 1989, p. A33.

31. Ibid.

32. U.S., Advisory Commission on Public Diplomacy, *United States Public Diplomacy in China* (Washington, D.C.: U.S. ACPD, December 1989).

33. Green, *American Propaganda*, p. 108.

34. Jim Courter, "Winning Hearts and Minds: Foreign Scholarships and Foreign Policy," *Policy Review*, no. 33 (Summer 1985), p. 76.

35. The lecture was published as "Education in Defense of a Free Society," *Commentary*, vol. 78, no. 1 (July 1984), pp. 17–22.

36. Interview with Michael Schneider, Washington, D.C., April 11, 1990.

CHAPTER 13: THE NATIONAL ENDOWMENT FOR DEMOCRACY

1. George Shultz, *Project Democracy*, Current Policy No. 456, U.S. Department of State,

Bureau of Public Affairs, Washington, D.C., February 23, 1983, p. 1.

2. Cord Meyer, *Facing Reality: From World Federalism to the CIA* (Lanham, Md.: University Press of America, 1980), p. 105.

3. National Democratic Institute for International Affairs, *Chile's Transition to Democracy: The 1988 Presidential Plebiscite* (Washington, D.C.: NDIIA, 1988), p. 42.

4. A national election was held in Nicaragua in 1984; various groups sympathetic to the Sandinistas approved its fairness. The election, however, was boycotted by the main opposition groups on the grounds that the Sandinistas had refused to come to terms on ground rules that would assure fairness. Hence it was not a meaningful contest. For a good account see Robert S. Leiken, "The Sandinistas' Tangled Elections," *New York Review of Books*, December 5, 1985. On the nature of Sandinista rule see my "The Slow Road to Communism," *This World*, no. 13 (Winter 1986), pp. 27–46. Both articles are reprinted in Mark Falcoff and Robert Royal, eds., *The Continuing Crisis: U.S. Policy in Central America and the Caribbean* (Washington, D.C.: Ethics and Public Policy Center, 1987).

5. *The Challenge of Democracy*, Proceedings of a conference on efforts to advance the cause of democracy throughout the world, sponsored by the National Endowment for Democracy, May 18–19, 1987, Washington, D.C., pp. 20–21.

6. Liang Heng and Judith Shapiro, *Son of the Revolution* (New York: Alfred A. Knopf, 1983).

7. *The Challenge of Democracy*, pp. 78–79.

8. Ibid., p. 68.

9. Ibid.

10. National Endowment for Democracy, *Annual Report 1988* (Washington, D.C.: NED, 1989), p. 4.

11. *Congressional Record*, House, April 12, 1989, p. H1073.

12. Morton M. Kondracke, "Endowment Drive," *New Republic*, May 29, 1989, pp. 10, 11.

13. Ford Foundation, *Current Interests of the Ford Foundation: 1990 and 1991* (New York: Ford Foundation, February 1990), pp. 5, 30–34.

14. Carnegie Corporation of New York, *General Information* (New York: Carnegie Corporation, n.d.), p. 3. Carnegie Corporation of New York, *Grants and Appropriations 1989* (New York: Carnegie Corporation, n.d.), pp. 51–56, 58–72.

CHAPTER 14: CONCLUSION

1. Barbara Basler, "Hong Kong Honors Beijing's Victims," *New York Times*, June 4, 1990, p. A6.

Index

About the Author

JOSHUA MURAVCHIK is a resident scholar at the American Enterprise Institute. His articles appear frequently in *Commentary*, the *New Republic*, the *American Spectator*, the *New York Times*, and the *Wall Street Journal*, and he has contributed to *Foreign Affairs*, the *New York Times Magazine*, and numerous other magazines and newspapers. Mr. Muravchik's 1988 *News Coverage of the Sandinista Revolution* was called "a magnificent volume on how the media attempt to manipulate public opinion in the United States" (*Journalism Quarterly*). His 1986 book, *The Uncertain Crusade*, was praised in the *New Republic* as "certainly one of the most important neoconservative foreign policy statements that have appeared to date."

Mr. Muravchik received his Ph.D. in international relations from Georgetown University. In 1986 the *Wall Street Journal* wrote that "Joshua Muravchik may be the most cogent and careful of the neoconservative writers on foreign policy."

A NOTE ON THE BOOK

This book was edited by Ann Petty of the
publications staff of the American Enterprise Institute.
The index was prepared by Julia Petrakis.
The text was set in Palatino, a typeface designed by
the twentieth-century Swiss designer Hermann Zapf.
Publication Technology Corporation, of Fairfax, Virginia,
set the type, and Edwards Brothers Incorporated,
of Ann Arbor, Michigan, printed and bound the book,
using permanent acid-free paper.

The AEI PRESS is the publisher for the American Enterprise Institute for Public
Policy Research, 1150 17th Street, N.W., Washington, D.C. 20036: *Christopher C.
DeMuth,* publisher; *Edward Styles,* director; *Dana Lane,* editor; *Ann Petty,* editor;
Cheryl Weissman, editor; *Susan Moran,* editorial assistant (rights and
permissions). Books published by the AEI PRESS are distributed by arrangement
with the University Press of America, 4720 Boston Way, Lanham, Md. 20706.